Wordsworth's Poets

WILLIAM WORDSWORTH (1770-1850) was born at Cockermouth, Cumbria, and educated at Hawkshead Grammar School and St John's College Cambridge. He travelled widely in France and Italy but settled in Cumbria from 1799. He was one of the most gifted poets of his generation and his best-known poems include *The Prelude* (1805, 1815, 1850), 'Lines composed a few miles above Tintern Abbey' (1805), and 'Descriptive Sketches' (1793). With Coleridge, he wrote *Lyrical Ballads* (1798). He became Poet Laureate in 1843.

DUNCAN WU is Professor of English Language and Literature and a Fellow of St Catherine's College, Oxford.

Also edited by Duncan Wu from Carcanet

William Wordsworth: The Earliest Poems 1785-1790

Wordsworth's Poets

Edited by Duncan Wu

CARCANET

First published in Great Britain in 2003 by
Carcanet Press Limited
Alliance House
Cross Street
Manchester M2 7AQ

Introduction, selection and editorial
apparatus copyright © Duncan Wu 2003
The right of Duncan Wu to be identified
as the editor of this work has been asserted
by him in accordance with the Copyright,
Designs and Patents Act of 1988

The publisher acknowledges financial assistance
from Arts Council England

Typeset in 10pt Plantin by Bryan Williamson, Frome
Printed and bound in England by SRP Ltd, Exeter

Contents

Introduction

What did Wordsworth read for pleasure? This book is an attempt to provide an answer. It contains poetry and prose which received some kind of endorsement from him, either by direct comment, or by being copied into his notebooks for preservation. On occasion he was very specific about what he liked in the work at hand, going so far as to single out individual lines or stanzas; in all such cases his comments are provided. The various works appear in order of Wordsworth's encounter with them, insofar as that can be deduced.

As this anthology contains only literature of which he approved, the experience of reading (and compiling) it provides an object lesson in Wordsworthian values. Many of its contents are here because he regarded them as truthful articulations of human emotion, unfettered by the artificial language in writing of his day. When commending them he refers to such things as intensity of 'feeling' and 'purity' of diction: Thomson for instance is distinguished by 'a true love and feeling for Nature' (p. 109); Gray's journal is written with 'unaffected simplicity' (p. 43); Mickle was possessed of 'genuine poetic feelings' (p. 112); Cowper and Burns were among 'those in modern times who have been the most successful in painting manners and passions' (p. 48); Bishop Percy followed the path of 'true simplicity and genuine pathos' (p. 61). Bad poetry was distinguished by its bogusness: Macaulay was 'false in style, and in everything else'; George Lyttelton's *Monody* on his wife lacks 'stamina of thought and feeling'; Dryden's language was 'neither of the imagination nor of the passions'.

In view of this, it may be helpful were something to be said about his aesthetics as they bear on my principles of selection, which are founded on a tenet to which Wordsworth always remained true: 'poetry is passion', he wrote in a note to 'The Thorn' (1800), 'it is the history or science of feelings'. Words, he believed, 'ought to be weighed in the balance of feeling, and not measured by the space which they occupy on paper'. 'Passion' and 'feeling' have been vulgarised and devalued in the two centuries since Wordsworth wrote that. By setting them at the heart of his work he meant to claim truth to psychological reality as his subject. If that now seems unremarkable it is because we take for granted the revolution wrought by him; it takes a leap of imagination to understand how, in his day, such notions were radical, vaguely improper and, to many, absurd. For instance:

> Did Mr Wordsworth really imagine that his favourite doctrines were likely to gain anything in point of effect or authority by being put into the mouth of a person accustomed to higgle about tape, or brass sleeve-buttons?

scoffed Francis Jeffrey when attacking the Pedlar in Wordsworth's *Excursion* in 1814. The correct answer is 'yes'. Wordsworth's poems attribute depths of emotion to working-class people as a shock tactic, prompting the well-heeled folk who comprised the principal readership of poetry to abandon attitudes of the kind espoused by Jeffrey. It was a revolution in the politics of the poem. By describing the pain and courage of such characters as Martha Ray, Betty Foy, and Simon Lee, Wordsworth aimed, as he told Charles James Fox (Whig leader in the House of Commons):

> to shew that men who do not wear fine cloaths can feel deeply . . . The poems are faithful copies from nature; and I hope, whatever effect they may have upon you, you will at least be able to perceive that they may excite profitable sympathies in many kind and good hearts, and may in some small degree enlarge our feelings of reverence for our species, and our knowledge of human nature, by shewing that our best qualities are possessed by men whom we are too apt to consider, not with reference to the points in which they resemble us, but to those in which they manifestly differ from us.

Jeffrey understood this, but lacked the vision to see beyond his own doctrines (largely adapted from Scottish Enlightenment thinkers). Though it is now clear what a huge failure that was, Jeffrey's rejection of Wordsworth seemed at the time no more than common sense, and his dismissal of *The Excursion* as 'mystical verbiage' was picked up by other reviewers and echoed down subsequent decades. For years Wordsworth's poetry would provide the occasion for jokes about philosophical peasants and talking horses; not until he was in his seventies did he see a time when it was accepted without ridicule. He resented that, but had known he would need patience; the reading public had to be weaned away from the watered-down imitations of Pope to which they were used. Writing to Lady Beaumont in May 1807, Wordsworth remarked that 'every great and original writer, in proportion as he is great or original, must himself create the taste by which he is to be relished; he must teach the art by which he is to be seen . . . and if this be possible, it must be a work *of time*'.

Living as we do in an age when an understanding of the mind, however crude, is taken for granted in any work of literature, we find it difficult to see how sharply Wordsworth departed from the cultural norm of his day in making the mind his subject. At that time poems – especially those published in journals and newspapers – were concerned typically with neoclassical deities, paraphrases of the Bible, and abstractions such as 'Hope' and 'Pity'. Seldom did they discuss peasant folk, and rarely did they reflect much psychological insight. Why do children lie? Why might randomly seen objects move us to tears? Such questions, which demanded in the first place a clear-sighted understanding of himself, provided Wordsworth with his principal subject-matter.

It was a new kind of poetry – one based on truth to the human heart – and demanded a new language. In a post-Freudian age we are apt to take such language for granted; Wordsworth had to make do with the words he had – crude eighteenth-century implements to articulate complex visions of an interior landscape the contours of which were yet untraced.

I have introduced this anthology by discussing not its contents but the man who, posthumously and by proxy, has selected them. It is necessary because this rough assemblage of prose and verse forms the melting-pot of literary ideas out of which his poetry emerged. Here are the poets and prose writers in whom Wordsworth saw merit for their affinity to his own views. Though regenerated and reconfigured by him, those views were latent – and sometimes not so latent – in works of earlier times. Some were misunderstood in their own day only to be accepted by another; others remain in obscurity. Whatever their separate fates, each earns its place here by dint of its part in the forging of a new poetic.

Wordsworth Reading

> Books! 'tis a dull and endless strife,
> Come, hear the woodland linnet,
> How sweet his music; on my life
> There's more of wisdom in it.
>
> ('The Tables Turned' 9-12)

A century ago, the received view was not merely that Wordsworth read little during his lifetime but that he disapproved of bookishness altogether. This was due in large part to De Quincey who in his *Recollections* claimed that 'Wordsworth rarely resorted to his books (unless, perhaps, to some little pocket edition of a poet which accompanied him in his rambles), except in the evenings, or after he had tired himself by walking'. But De Quincey was a biased witness; embittered by what he felt to be coldness on Wordsworth's part, he ended his life telling tales about his former mentor. His remarks on Wordsworth's reading could not have been more misleading. In recent years scholars have revealed Wordsworth to have been one of the best-read men of the age, particularly in the realm of literature. This was all the more astonishing for someone resident for much of his life in a comparative backwater where books were not easy to come by.

By our standards his breadth of knowledge was staggering. Who now, in the age of copyright libraries, databases and the Internet, can claim to be a reader of Samuel Daniel, Richard Edwardes, Barnaby Googe, Laurence Minot, Giovanni Battista Marino, Pierre Fulcrand de Rosset, Johann Arnold Ebert, Daniel Sennertus, and Thomas Randolph? They were familiar to Wordsworth. At a period when the works of medieval writers were still being 'discovered', he was an admirer of Dante, Langland, Malory, and Chaucer. Italian, French, Latin and medieval scholars could debate with him and expect an informed response; and when Alexander Dyce questioned him on the finer points of Collins' posthumous texts, Wordsworth supplied an accurate bibliographical history still useful to modern-day editors. He was exceptional in both the extent of his reading and the depth of his understanding.

Required at Hawkshead Grammar School to memorise vast tracts of Latin, he had an amazingly retentive mind that could with scant difficulty commit many hundreds of lines of verse to memory; in his fifties he told Barron Field: 'to this day I believe I could repeat with a little previous rummaging of my memory several 1,000 lines of Pope'. As a result he was authoritative when it came to recognising borrowings or echoes; in 1822 Samuel Rogers remarked on this to Dorothy Wordsworth:

> I have lately met with a remarkable instance of your Brother's sagacity – He had always maintained that Gray's line 'And leave us leisure to be good' was not his own – It is in Oldham. 'I have not yet the leisure to be good.'

The ability to hold within his mind the fluctuating colours and sounds of a poem came early and never left him. It was part of his intellectual equipment from an early age, and as a writer his thoughts were shaped by the verbal music in his head. In part, this anthology is a Wordsworthian pattern-book containing the templates on which he drew throughout his career – rhythms, rhymes, images and cadences that coursed through his imagination and into his poetry.

This tells us much about him as a reader. As an adult he could read a poem and react so powerfully to it as to feel its impact throughout his nervous system, sometimes for a lengthy period: in 1799 he said that he could not read Burns' 'Despondency' 'without the deepest agitation'; in 1800 he told Hazlitt that he 'could read the description of Satan in Milton till he felt a certain faintness come over his mind from a sense of beauty and grandeur'; in 1802 a reading of *Paradise Lost* caused him and his sister to 'melt' into tears; and one night she read some short poems of Ben Jonson 'which were too *interesting* for him, and would not let him go to sleep'. This was not affectation – it was literally true. Such sensitivity made him a demanding and rigorously judgemental reader. The faintest shadow of insincerity was condemned, just as its opposite could move him to raptures. His ability to evaluate poetry, to feel it on his pulse, was highly developed, and led him to appreciate many whose work has been long neglected.

In 1815 he wrote that 'the pathetic participates of an *animal* sensation', meaning that words had the power to alter the physical as well as emotional constitution of those who read them. As he commented in the third of his *Essays upon Epitaphs* (composed 1810):

> Words are too awful an instrument for good and evil to be trifled with: they hold above all other external powers a dominion over thoughts. If words be not . . . an incarnation of the thought but only a clothing for it, then surely will they prove an ill gift; such a one as those poisoned vestments, read of in the stories of superstitious times, which had power to consume and to alienate from his right mind the victim who put them on. Language, if it do not uphold, and feed, and leave in quiet, like the power of gravitation or the air we breathe, is a counter-spirit, unremittingly and noiselessly at work to derange, to subvert, to lay waste, to vitiate, and to dissolve.

Frequently misrepresented in his own day, Wordsworth's views on poetry remain widely misunderstood. In truth, his argument was simple. He believed that thoughts, though insubstantial, should be incarnate in the words chosen to express them; by the same token a

13

linguistic false step might suggest incoherence or outright false-hood. Such views explain Wordsworth's uncompromising attitude towards poetry he thought insincere. He criticised Gray's poems because they were not based on observation and were too imitative: 'He wrote English Verses, as he and other Eton school-boys wrote Latin; filching a phrase now from one author, and now from another'. Pope's case is similar: 'Having wandered from humanity in his Eclogues with boyish inexperience, the praise which these compositions obtained tempted him into a belief that Nature was not to be trusted, at least in pastoral Poetry'. In short, the writings of both Pope and Gray were the product not of observation but of study.

Though not an unkind man, Wordsworth did not deceive those close to him about the quality of their writing, even when it would have been politic to do so. Though a good friend, Walter Scott never won Wordsworth's respect as a poet – because, as Wordsworth told Lady Richardson in 1844, his poetry 'does not reach to any intellectual or spiritual emotion; it is altogether super-ficial, and he felt it himself to be so. His descriptions are not true to Nature; they are addressed to the ear, not to the mind'. Scott did not describe what he observed, and as a result fell short of psycho-logical and emotional truth. (I sometimes wonder whether Scott's abandonment of poetic ambition with his last long poem, *Harold the Dauntless* (1817), was related to the consistency of Wordsworth's disapprobation.)

In these cases, and many others, the essence of his argument is that a deception has been practised, whether deliberately or by neglect – that though charmed by technique and style, the reader has been conned, as language has been made the dressing for thoughts lacking foundation in external (or internal) reality. This was a fault he was particularly apt to find among philosophers, as he admitted in the *Essay on Morals*, composed c. 1798:

> The whole secret of this juggler's trick lies not in fitting words to things (which would be a noble employment) but in fitting things to words – I have said that these bald and naked reason-ings are impotent over our habits, they cannot form them; from the same cause they are equally powerless in regulating our judgments concerning the value of men and things.

If the words do not naturally incarnate the objects to which they refer (that is, emotions or ideas), the act of writing is reduced to the level of a superficial game. Doubtless this was the reason why

14

Wordsworth had little patience for German metaphysicians – 'Kant, Schelling, Fichte; Fichte, Schelling, Kant: all this is dreary work and does not denote progress', he commented in 1844. Perhaps he was just as preoccupied with intellectual matters as the Germans, but they seemed to him to avoid, rather than address, spiritual matters.

The notion that the word should be an incarnation of the thought is a reminder of Wordsworth's messianic streak: as he saw it, he had been summoned by forces larger than himself to perform an almost religious function. 'What is a Poet?' he asked in the Preface to *Lyrical Ballads*, 'He is a man speaking to men',

> a man pleased with his own passions and volitions, and who rejoices more than other men in the spirit of life that is in him; delighting to contemplate similar volitions and passions as manifested in the goings-on of the Universe, and habitually impelled to create them where he does not find them.

To all intents and purposes, he is a mediator between his readers and 'the goings-on of the Universe' – a hieratic role that has attracted little notice from critics, perhaps because it is camouflaged as a rhetorical point. It is nothing of the kind – its function is to assert the connection between poetry and the divine. You can present such arguments only if you believe in the sacramental function of poetic discourse; just as he reviled those who failed that test, Wordsworth held in high regard those who passed it. This volume is a memorial to them.

Take for instance James Graham, 1st Marquis of Montrose, 'Great, good, and just' – little read today, but valued by Wordsworth because of the way in which

> His soul labours; – the most tremendous event in the history of the Planet, namely, the Deluge, is brought before his imagination by the physical image of tears, – a connection awful from its very remoteness and from the slender bond that unites its ideas . . . The whole is instinct with spirit, and every word has its separate life; like the Chariot of the Messiah, and the wheels of that Chariot, as they appeared to the imagination of Milton aided by that of the Prophet Ezekiel.

Wordsworth is not always clear, partly because he is attempting to discuss something that defies description. But insofar as language will allow, he attributes visionary power to Graham – the same as that possessed by the blind Milton as he described conflict in heaven

15

in *Paradise Lost*. The essence of his argument is that the experience of composition is in the first place a spiritual one: 'His soul labours'. And as it did so, Graham's imagination generated connections that bridged the gap between the human and the divine.

At a distance of two centuries, we cannot know as much as we would like about Wordsworth's responses to the literature that passed through his hands. I have been compelled to rely on various forms of evidence: for instance, he and his circle were in the habit of copying into notebooks passages of prose and poetry they wished to preserve – they even had a Commonplace Book containing works gathered from a bewildering array of sources which scholars continue to trace. This was a sensible measure for people with a small library who were not in the habit of collecting books. On those occasions it is reasonable to assume that their reason for making the transcription was that they liked the passage in question and wished to preserve it for future reference – hence the appearance in these pages of Marvell's 'Horatian Ode', Kirke White's 'To the Herb Rosemary', Cowper's 'Yardley-Oak' and Blake's 'The Tiger'. Elsewhere there is no option but to rely on anecdotal evidence – accounts of readings by Wordsworth at which those present were moved or impressed, or repeated allusions that may be taken to indicate Wordsworth's high opinion of the work at hand.

Wordsworth and Books

> To introduce Wordsworth into one's library is like letting a bear into a tulip garden.
>
> (Southey to De Quincey)

On 16 June 1811 Dorothy Wordsworth told Catherine Clarkson: 'yesterday we were all employed in bearing the Books out of the Barn, and arranging them'. Unfortunately we have no idea what titles she was referring to. Nor do we know which were stored in the 'large book-case' in the Rydal Mount study in September 1813. On occasion we catch glimpses of Wordsworth's shelves, as with the list of books sent by Richard Wordsworth of Branthwaite to Dove Cottage in 1805, or the scan of the Rydal Mount library shelves in the 'Essay, Supplementary to the Preface', but these are too brief to be illuminating. In some ways the retrospective glance offered by

De Quincey of the sitting-room at Dove Cottage is more informative than anything given by Wordsworth:

> The two or three hundred volumes of Wordsworth occupied a little, homely painted bookcase, fixed into one of two shallow recesses formed on each side of the fireplace by the projection of the chimney in the little sitting-room upstairs.

I would give a good deal to know what those volumes were; some are known but most remain guesses, speculations, chimeras – and opium-tinged ones at that. The full contents of Wordsworth's library at any one time remain impossible to pin down, because he left so little evidence for us to go on.

Perhaps this is only to be expected: not until the Rydal Mount years did he take his library seriously enough to make an inventory of its contents. That was symptomatic of his attitude, something of which book-snobs like De Quincey were wryly contemptuous; compared with Southey's, De Quincey recalled, those in Wordsworth's possession were

> ill bound, or not bound at all – in boards, sometimes in tatters; many were imperfect as to the number of volumes, mutilated as to the number of pages: sometimes, where it seemed worth while, the defects being supplied by manuscript; sometimes not: in short, everything showed that the books were for use, and not for show; and their limited amount showed that their possessor must have independent sources of enjoyment to fill up the major part of his time.

Elsewhere De Quincey retails an anecdote in which he describes Wordsworth opening the uncut pages of a volume by Edmund Burke using a knife recently used to spread butter onto a piece of dry toast: 'he tore his way into the heart of the volume with his knife, that left its greasy honours behind it upon every page: and are they not there to this day? . . . I mention the case at all, only to illustrate the excess of Wordsworth's outrages on books, which made him, in Southey's eyes, a mere monster'. Scholars have exhausted themselves attempting to track down the volume mentioned by De Quincey, but to no avail.

True or not, De Quincey's remarks highlight Wordsworth's pragmatism when it came to books. Writing to Walter Scott in November 1806 he said that he preferred books to be 'of a Pocket size. Any Poetry which I like, I wish for in that size, to which no doubt yours will one day descend' – the equivalent of today's paperbacks. That is not to say that he was in any sense unappreciative of the bibliographical significance of early volumes. James Muirhead recorded the pride with which he showed him his first edition of *The Seasons*, and the note in his copy of Martin's *Voyage to St Kilda* shows that he prized it for its rarity (see p. 128). All the same, though erudite in textual matters, he acquired such items as exceptions to his usual book-buying habits.

Many of the poems and prose passages in this anthology come from books never owned by Wordsworth. In general he bought one only if he had perused it elsewhere and came across a reasonably priced working copy. There must be many authors whose works he read, but about whom he made no comment, or none that has come down to us. And there must be others which he read but failed, for whatever reason, to buy. This explains why, as late as 1808, Dorothy reported to De Quincey that her brother lacked 'Clarendon – Burnet – any of the elder Histories – translations from the Classics chiefly – historical – Plutarch's Lives, – Thucydides, *Tacitus* (I think he said) – (by the bye, he *has* a translation of Herodotus), Lord Bacon's Works – Milton's prose Works – in short, any of the good elder writers'. These were listed not because Wordsworth had not read them, but because he *had*: he had failed, thus far, to buy his own copies.

When it came to acquiring books, Wordsworth was adept at drawing on the goodwill of others. Besides De Quincey, numerous friends, relatives and acquaintances were asked to send them: his brothers Richard and John, Sir George and Lady Beaumont (see for instance p. 226), Charles Lamb and Coleridge – even such publishers as Thomas Norton Longman, Joseph Cottle and Daniel Stuart.

Wordsworth was from an early age a resourceful user of libraries both public and private. At an early age he had the run of the Hawkshead Grammar School library, endowed by the founders of the school, to which boys were encouraged to donate books after leaving (as he did). When he and Dorothy set up house, first at Racedown Lodge in Dorset and then at Alfoxden House in Somerset, they were fortunate on both occasions in finding residences notable for their well-stocked libraries.

In the Lake District, though distant from publishers and printing presses, Wordsworth used the book clubs at Grasmere and Kendal, and was lucky in having at hand several friends who were more serious about collecting books than he was – most obviously Coleridge. The 'library-cormorant' was a more acquisitive collector than Wordsworth, and devoured their contents more rapidly. His library was accordingly more extensive. The numerous volumes acquired during his residence in Nether Stowey were eventually shipped to the

Lakes when he settled in Keswick, among them Percy's *Reliques* and Anderson's *British Poets*, copies of which he owned before Wordsworth. During his on–off residence in the Lakes Coleridge was a frequent visitor to Dove Cottage, and many of his books and manuscripts passed into Wordsworth's keeping permanently. During work on *The Friend*, most of which was produced during his residence with the Wordsworths at Allan Bank, Coleridge amassed a large quantity of volumes many of which remained there when the two men fell out.

Coleridge rented Greta Hall in Keswick from William Jackson, who thoughtfully stocked it with a number of old books, though not necessarily the ones Coleridge would have chosen for himself. On 1 November 1800 he told Josiah Wedgwood that Jackson 'has collected nearly 500 volumes of our most esteemed modern Writers, such as Gibbon, Hume, Johnson, etc. etc.' Somewhat less respectfully he confided to another correspondent that 'in *my* Library you will find all the Poets and Philosophers, and many of our best old Writers – below in our Parlor, belonging to my Landlord, but in my possession, are almost all the usual Trash of the Johnsons, Gibbons, Robertsons, etc. with the Encyclopaedia Britannica, etc. etc.' As a regular visitor, Wordsworth had regular access to this collection, along with those retained by other inmates of Greta Hall.

The most prominent among them was Robert Southey, whose personal library was one of the richest and most extensive in the near vicinity. Southey acquired books at an astonishing rate, and had been doing so for years. The greater part of his existing library reached Keswick in 1808, when Duck Row was established to house twenty-two packages of books. On 5 May Southey told his friend Charles Danvers:

> I have had a range of shelves run up along one side of the passage which connects the two houses from the floor to the ceiling. It holds about 1,350 volumes, and is denominated Duck Row, though there is only the dark end to which that name can properly be applied, those which are in the light being Drakes. There must be yet a small stand of shelves on the upper landing-place to hold about 200 which are still kicking to windward, and to receive droppers-in.

This proved far from adequate, and he was compelled to construct more and more shelves and bookcases for decades to come. Although Wordsworth was initially wary of him – the disillusioned Coleridge had queried his reputation – they became firm friends after the death of Wordsworth's brother John in 1805, when

Southey showed great sensitivity and kindness at the height of his grief. As Dorothy told Lady Beaumont, Southey 'wept with us in our sorrow, and for that cause I think I must always love him'. From that time onwards Southey and Wordsworth were regular guests in each other's homes, and Wordsworth's access to books increased. Southey showed or lent him Malory's *Morte D'Arthur* and Henry Kirke White's 'To the Herb Rosemary' (see pp. 179, 204); doubtless he enabled Wordsworth to read other works in these pages.

De Quincey liked to pretend that Wordsworth read little but poetry; that is not so. Southey had a strong interest in current affairs, and besides drawing on his large stock of literary works, Wordsworth borrowed political tracts and history books from him. In 1810, at a time when Sir George Beaumont regarded him as too much of a 'democrat' to be acceptable among his friends, Wordsworth followed Napoleon's fortunes avidly. He was addicted to newspapers, including the *Morning Post*, the *Morning Chronicle*, the *Courier* and the *Times* (often sent on to Grasmere by Southey when he had finished with them), and thought at one point of becoming a journalist. Conversation with Coleridge, and involvement with *The Friend*, fuelled his political interests.

There may have been other libraries available to Wordsworth, both public and private, of which we know nothing. But what we do know is sufficient to reveal that although he lived for much of his life in a relatively obscure part of the country, he exercised resourcefulness and ingenuity in obtaining books he either needed or wanted, even if he could not own them. His interests were by no means circumscribed by what was on his shelves: if he wanted to read about a particular subject, or to obtain a particular title, he did so by all means necessary.

Principles of Selection

Items in this anthology are presented chronologically in order of reading, insofar as that may be ascertained, and introduced by headnotes providing Wordsworth's comments on the writer or work at hand. It would be a sad task and hard, even in several volumes of these dimensions, to attempt fully to represent the breadth and depth of his knowledge of English literature; nonetheless it is my hope that much of what he regarded highly is included here. His remarks on prose and poetry – scattered throughout his correspondence, prose works, poetry, and reported observations on literature (some hitherto unpublished) – have been dragooned into service as I have compiled this selection. Doubtless I have omitted works which he loved but about which he said little or nothing. Likewise, some items are here on the strength of cursory remarks that do no more than hint at a positive judgement – or which testify to a liking that may have waned with the passing of time. I can say only that I have endeavoured to take such factors into account, and trust that I have been faithful to Wordsworth's opinions at the time at which they were expressed.

As a means of rationalising the selection it has been necessary to exclude, or at least restrict, certain classes of item. I have preferred poetry to prose, though prose extracts are included where of exceptional interest. Writings of prominent members of the Wordsworth circle – Coleridge, Lamb, Southey and Scott – are excluded, as they are already widely circulated. It would be a fascinating project to edit the poems of Coleridge or Southey in the form in which they were first known to Wordsworth – perhaps someone will undertake it one day – but as there is not sufficient room to do it satisfactorily here, it seemed best not attempted. Finally, I decided at an early stage not to include works in languages other than English. This was advisable not least because, in order to make them viable, it would have been necessary to provide translations, effectively doubling their length. Although their omission makes this a partial account of Wordsworth's reading (especially as it has meant dropping works in French, Italian, Latin, and German), it has helped to enable a much fuller treatment of works in English than would otherwise have been possible.

All texts are edited directly from sources known to Wordsworth. In some cases they are edited from books he owned, or from manuscript copies made by him. As they comprise principal sources – and provide copy-texts – for some of the items here, Wordsworth's books and notebooks deserve a word of comment. All are retained and preserved by the Wordsworth Trust in Grasmere where I have consulted them.

Wordsworth Library MS 16 is a red leather bound notebook in use during 1798. It contains a copy in Dorothy Wordsworth's hand of an extract from Marlowe's *Edward II* (p.177), probably copied from Dodsley's *Select Collection of Old Plays* (1744).

Wordsworth Library MS 38 is a small blue pocket notebook used for drafting of *The Prelude* in spring 1804. It contains a transcription of Marvell's 'Horatian Ode' in Wordsworth's hand, probably dating from September 1802, which follows the text published by

21

Captain Edward Thompson in his edition of Marvell's *Works* (1776) (see p. 148). Wordsworth was working from Charles Lamb's copy of Thompson's edition, as he and Dorothy spent the first three weeks of September 1802 in London, frequently in Lamb's company.

Wordsworth's Commonplace Book (MS 26) is a quarto notebook of 145 pages containing a number of copies of prose and poems in an array of hands. Scholars are still in the process of identifying these works and sources for them. I have taken the appearance of some texts in the Commonplace Book as sufficient justification for inclusion here: namely, the extract from Malory's *Morte D'Arthur* (p. 179); Burns' 'Go fetch to me a pint o' wine' (p. 181); Thomas Wilkinson's 'I love to be alone' and 'Lines written on a Paper wrapt round a Moss-Rose pulled on New Years Day, and sent to M. Wilson' (pp. 186, 188); the extract from Richard Edwardes, 'Amantium Irae' (p. 211); John Mayne, 'By Logan's streams that rin sae deep' (p. 212); and William Blake's poems (pp. 231-4).

Wordsworth's copy of Charlotte Smith's *Elegiac Sonnets* (1789) is the source for the text of the sonnets on pp. 142-3. It was apparently purchased jointly with his cousin John Myers, for Wordsworth added their names on the page headed 'Subscribers' Names omitted by mistake, or received too late for insertion in the list'. He copied two sonnets by Smith on page 84 of the volume, probably when he visited in November 1791.

The extract from Bartram's *Travels* (p. 165) is edited from the copy belonging to Wordsworth and Coleridge. Emmeline Fisher's two poems, 'On a sound somewhat resembling thunder' and 'Secrecy' (pp. 285-6), are edited from her mother's transcriptions, sent to Wordsworth in 1837.

Conclusion

This anthology is a kind of biography, because the history of a writer's reading is necessarily determined by the circumstances of his day to day existence – the accessibility of libraries public and private; the willingness of friends and relatives to send books; even the generosity of booksellers and publishers. It is a biography in another sense too. It tells the story of a reader passionately engaged with the problems of writing, and the challenge of clarifying, if not solving, those problems through the act of reading. Perhaps it is not too much of an exaggeration to suggest that the story told by this book is that of the growth of a poet's mind.

Acknowledgements

For advice and encouragement during work on this book I am grateful to Philip Hobsbaum, Roger Robinson, and Paul F. Betz. The resources of the Bodleian Library, St Catherine's College Library, the English Faculty Library in Oxford, and the Wordsworth Library in Grasmere were essential to the completion of this work, and I am indebted to librarians at those institutions. I am grateful to Stephen Burley for help clarifying some texts. It has been a pleasure to work again with Michael Schmidt and his staff at Carcanet Press. My wife Caroline bravely countenanced the all-embracing presence of this book during summer 2002.

A Note on the Texts

Texts of works known to Wordsworth fall into one or two categories: those edited from printed sources, and those edited from his transcriptions.

Those from printed sources retain the accidentals and orthography of the copy-text except in the case of obvious errors or solecisms, which I have not hesitated silently to correct. Where italics are used for reasons other than that of emphasis (as for example in the case of proper nouns), I have converted them to roman. Some copy-texts contain footnotes; these are retained where they carry points of information necessary to a full understanding of the work. In some instances (most notably Collins's 'Ode on the Superstitions of the Highlands of Scotland'), I have dispensed with notes by eighteenth-century editors about textual matters.

Texts transcribed by Wordsworth into his notebooks are collated with their printed sources. This has been necessary because when copying he frequently made alterations – repunctuating; omitting lines, sentences, stanzas; even rewriting. In all cases where the copy-text is Wordsworth's transcription, I have preferred Wordsworth's readings to those of the equivalent printed source. Where divergences are marked, I have made a note of the variations either in notes or in the prefatory headnote. Mistranscriptions and other slips of the pen are silently corrected; punctuation and orthography are preserved unless they are erroneous. In some cases, most notably two sonnets from Charlotte Smith (see pp. 142-3) it has been necessary, in view of the absence of punctuation in the transcription, to supply it from printed sources. Throughout the volume ampersands are changed to 'and'.

John Milton, 'Morning Hymn' from *Paradise Lost*; William Shakespeare, 'Hamlet and Ghost' from *Hamlet*; Edmund Spenser, 'The Bower of Bliss' from *The Faerie Queene*

Date of Reading: between 1774 and 1779

According to Christopher Wordsworth Jr, 'the Poet's father set him very early to learn portions of the works of the best English poets by heart, so that at an early age he could repeat large portions of Shakespeare, Milton, and Spenser'. These 'portions', presumably memorised prior to Wordsworth's departure for Hawkshead Grammar School in 1779, were probably taken from such children's anthologies as Enfield's *Speaker* and Knox's *Elegant Extracts*, from which the following texts are edited.

Milton precedes Shakespeare and Spenser because in January 1847 Wordsworth told Mrs Davy that his poetry 'was earlier a favourite with him than that of Shakespeare' – a comment given some support by his comment to John James Tayler in 1826 that 'Spenser, Shakspeare, and Milton are his favourites among the English poets, especially the latter, whom he almost idolises'.

The 'Morning Hymn' from *Paradise Lost* was by Wordsworth's childhood one of its most widely anthologised passages, and one of which he would remain fond. When visiting Hackett, a remote cottage above Colwith, in October 1810, he recited it to his family, as Dorothy reported to Catherine Clarkson:

> The weather was heavenly, when we were there, and the first morning we sate in hot sunshine on a crag, twenty yards from the door, while William read part of the 5th Book of the Paradise Lost to us. He read The Morning Hymn, while a stream of white vapour, which covered the Valley of Brathay, ascended slowly and by degrees melted away. It seemed as if we had never before felt deeply the power of the Poet – 'Ye mists and exhalations, etc., etc.!'

'The Morning Hymn' is edited here from Enfield's *Speaker*, as is my selection from *Hamlet*, which Enfield entitles 'Hamlet and Ghost'. In 1827 Wordsworth told his nephew, Christopher Wordsworth Jr, that 'the opening of "Hamlet" is full of exhausting interest. There is more mind in "Hamlet" than in any other play, more knowledge of human nature. The first act is incomparable.' Wordsworth's endorsement of Shakespeare's handling of psychology is characteristic, and when he commended Act I of the play he was thinking partly of Hamlet's disturbed reaction to the appearance of the Ghost. Having heard about a contemporary production of *Hamlet*, he told Sir George Beaumont in May 1805:

> I never saw Hamlet acted my self nor do I know what kind of play they make of it. I think I have heard that some parts which I consider as among the finest are omitted; in particular, Hamlet's wild language after the Ghost has disappeared.

Those 'finest' parts are, of course, included in 'Hamlet and Ghost'.

In 1815 Wordsworth described Spenser as 'a great power' whose genius was of 'a gentler nature' to that of Milton. Enfield included nothing from him, but Knox's *Elegant Extracts* contains what has always been a standard anthology piece – 'The Bower of Bliss'. In 1812, the journalist John Payne Collier recorded that Wordsworth described it as:

> unrivalled in our own, or perhaps in any language, in spite of some pieces of description imitated from the great Italian poets. The allegory, he said, was miraculous and miraculously maintained, yet with the preservation of the liveliest interest in the impersonations of Sir Guyon and the Palmer, as the representatives of virtue and prudence. I collected, however, that Spenser was not in all respects a great favourite with Wordsworth, dealing, as he does so much, in description, and comparatively little in reflection. I may be mistaken, but this was my impression.

Wordsworth's love of Spenser's poetry deepened with time, as was the case with each of these writers. He paid tribute to him in *The Prelude*, when he remembered reading his poetry as an undergraduate at Cambridge:

> And that gentle Bard,
> Chosen by the Muses for their Page of State,
> Sweet Spenser, moving through his clouded heaven
> With the moon's beauty, and the moon's soft pace;
> I call'd him Brother, Englishman, and Friend.
> (*The Thirteen-Book Prelude* iii 279-83)

John Milton, 'Morning Hymn'
(*Paradise Lost* Book 5)

These are thy glorious works, Parent of good!
Almighty! thine this universal frame,
Thus wond'rous fair! thyself how wond'rous then!
Unspeakable! who fitt'st above these heav'ns,
To us invisible, or dimly seen   5
In these thy lowliest works; yet these declare
Thy goodness beyond thought, and pow'r divine.
Speak ye who best can tell, ye sons of light,
Angels; for ye behold him, and with songs
And choral symphonies, day without night,   10
Circle his throne rejoicing; ye in heav'n.
On earth join all ye creatures to extol
Him first, him last, him midst, and without end.
Fairest of stars, last in the train of night,
If better thou belong not to the dawn,   15
Sure pledge of day, that crown'd the smiling morn
With thy bright circlet, praise him in thy sphere,
While day arises, that sweet hour of prime.
Thou sun, of this great world both eye and soul,
Acknowledge him thy greater; sound his praise   20
In thy eternal course, both when thou climb'st,
And when high noon hast gain'd, and when thou fall'st.
Moon, that now meets the orient sun, now fly'st
With the fix'd stars, fix'd in their orb that flies;
And ye five other wand'ring fires, that move   25
In mystic dance not without song, resound
His praise, who out of darkness call'd up light.
Air, and ye elements, the eldest birth
Of nature's womb, that in quaternion run
Perpetual circle, multiform, and mix,   30
And nourish all things; let your ceaseless change
Vary to our great Maker still new praise.
Ye mists and exhalations, that now rise
From hill or streaming lake, dusky or gray,
Till the sun paint your fleecy skirts with gold,   35
In honour to the world's great Author rise,
Whether to deck with clouds th' uncolour'd sky,
Or wet the thirsty earth with falling showers,
Rising or falling still advance his praise.

1774-9

His praise, ye winds, that from four quarters blow, 40
Breathe soft or loud; and wave your tops, ye pines,
With every plant, in sign of worship wave.
Fountains, and ye that warble, as ye flow,
Melodious murmurs, warbling tune his praise.
Join voices all ye living souls; ye birds, 45
That singing up to heaven-gate ascend,
Bear on your wings and in your notes his praise.
Ye that in waters glide, and ye that walk
The earth, and stately tread, or lowly creep;
Witness if I be silent, morn or even, 50
To hill or valley, fountain or fresh shade,
Made vocal by my song, and taught his praise.
Hail, universal Lord; be bounteous still
To give us only good; and if the night
Have gather'd aught of evil, or conceal'd, 55
Disperse it, as now light dispels the dark.

William Shakespeare, 'Hamlet and Ghost'
(*Hamlet* Act I)

HAM. Angels and ministers of grace defend us!
Be thou a spirit of health, or goblin damn'd,
Bring with thee airs from heav'n, or blasts from hell,
Be thy intent wicked or charitable,
Thou com'st in such a questionable shape, 5
That I will speak to thee. I'll call thee Hamlet,
King, Father, Royal Dane; oh! answer me!
Let me not burst in ignorance; but tell,
Why thy canoniz'd bones, hearsed in earth,
Have burst their cerements? why the sepulchre, 10
Wherein we saw thee quietly inurn'd,
Hath op'd his ponderous and marble jaws,
To cast thee up again? What may this mean?
That thou, dead corse, again in complete steel,
Revisit'st thus the glimpses of the moon, 15
Making night hideous, and us fools of nature
So horribly to shake our disposition

With thoughts beyond the reaches of our souls?
Say, why is this? wherefore? what should we do?
GHOST. Mark me. –
HAM.   I will.
GHOST.   My hour is almost come,   20
When I to sulphurous and tormenting flames
Must render up myself.
HAM.   Alas, poor ghost!
GHOST. Pity me not, but lend thy serious hearing
To what I shall unfold.
HAM.   Speak, I am bound to hear.
GHOST. So art thou to revenge when thou shalt hear.   25
HAM. What?
GHOST.   I am thy father's spirit,
Doom'd for a certain term to walk the night,
And for the day, confin'd to fast in fire,
Till the foul crimes done in my days of nature
Are burnt and purg'd away. But that I am forbid   30
To tell the secrets of my prison-house,
I could a tale unfold, whose lightest word
Would harrow up thy soul, freeze thy young blood,
Make thy two eyes, like stars, start from their spheres,
Thy knotty and combined locks to part,   35
And each particular hair to stand on end
Like quills upon the fretful porcupine:
But this eternal blazon must not be
To ears of flesh and blood; list, list, oh list!
If thou did'st ever thy dear father love –   40
HAM. O heav'n!
GHOST. Revenge his foul and most unnatural murther.
HAM. Murther?
GHOST. Murther most foul, as in the best it is;
But this most foul, strange, and unnatural.   45
HAM. Haste me to know it, that I, with wings as swift
As meditation, or the thoughts of love,
May fly to my revenge.
GHOST.   I find thee apt;
And duller should'st thou be, than the fat-weed
That roots itself in ease on Lethe's wharf,   50
Would'st thou not stir in this. Now, Hamlet, hear;
'Tis giv'n out, that, sleeping in my orchard,
A serpent stung me. So the whole ear of Denmark

29   *1774-9*

Is by a forged process of my death
Rankly abus'd: but know, thou noble youth,   55
The serpent that did sting thy father's life
Now wears his crown.
HAM.   Oh, my prophetic soul! my uncle!
GHOST. Ay, that incestuous, that adulterate beast,
With witchcraft of his wit, with trait'rous gifts,
(O wicked wit, and gifts, that have the power   60
So to seduce!) won to his shameful lust
The will of my most seeming virtuous queen.
Oh Hamlet, what a falling off was there!
But soft! methinks I scent the morning air –
Brief let me be: Sleeping within mine orchard,   65
My custom always in the afternoon,
Upon my secure hour thy uncle stole
With juice of cursed hebony in a phial,
And in the porches of mine ear did pour
The leperous distilment. –   70
Thus was I, sleeping, by a brother's hand,
Of life, of crown, of queen, at once bereft;
Cut off even in the blossoms of my sin;
No reck'ning made! but sent to my account
With all my imperfections on my head!   75
HAM. Oh horrible! oh horrible! most horrible!
GHOST. If thou hast nature in thee, bear it not;
But howsoever thou pursu'st this act,
Taint not thy mind, nor let thy soul contrive
Against thy mother aught; leave her to heav'n,   80
And to those thorns that in her bosom lodge,
To prick and sting her. Fare thee well at once!
The glow-worm shows the matin to be near,
And 'gins to pale his ineffectual fire.
Adieu, adieu, adieu: remember me.   85
HAM. Oh, all you host of heav'n! oh earth! what else!
And shall I couple hell? oh fie! hold my heart!
And you, my sinews, grow not instant old,
But bear me stiffly up. Remember thee!
Ay, thou poor ghost, while memory holds a seat   90
In this distracted globe; remember thee!
Yea, from the tablet of my memory
I'll wipe away all trivial fond records,
All saws of books, all forms, all pressures past,

That youth and observation copied there;   95
And thy commandment all alone shall live
Within the book and volume of my brain,
Unmix'd with baser matter.

Edmund Spenser, 'Bower of Bliss'
(*The Faerie Queene* Book II, Canto xii)

Thence passing forth, they shortly do arrive
Whereat the Bower of Bliss was situate;
   A place pick'd out by choice of best alive,
That nature's work by art can imitate;
In which whatever in this worldly state   5
   Is sweet and pleasing unto living sense,
Or that may daintiest fantasie aggrate,
   Was poured forth with plentiful dispense,
And made there to abound with lavish affluence.

Goodly it was enclosed round about,   10
As well their enter'd guests to keep within,
   As those unruly beasts to hold without;
Yet was the fence thereof but weak and thin:
Nought fear'd their force that fortilage to win,
   But wisdom's powre and temperance's might,   15
By which the mightiest things efforced bin:
   And eke the gate was wrought of substance light,
Rather for pleasure than for battery or fight.

It framed was of pretious yvory,
That seem'd a work of admirable wit;   20
   And therein all the famous historie
Of Jason and Medæa was ywrit;
Her mighty charmes, her furious loving fit,
   His goodly conquest of the golden fleece,
His falsed faith, and love to lightly flit,   25
   The wondred Argo, which in vent'rous peece
First thro' the Euxian seas bore all the flow'r of Greece.

Ye might have seen the frothy billowes fry
Under the ship, as thorough them she went,
   That seemed the waves were into yvory,   30
Or yvory into the waves were sent:
And other where the snowy substance sprent,
   With vermell, like the boyes bloud therein shed,
A pitious spectacle did represent;
   And otherwhiles with gold besprinkeled,   35
It seem'd th' enchanted flame which did Creüsa wed.

All this and more might in this goodly gate
Be read; that ever open stood to all
   Which thither came; but in the porch there sate
A comely personage of stature tall,   40
And semblance pleasing more than natural,
   That travellers to him seem'd to entice;
His looser garments to the ground did fall,
   And flew about his heels in wanton wise,
Not fit for speedy pace or manly exercise . . .   45

The foe of life, that good envies to all,
   That secretly doth us procure to fall,
Through guileful semblaunce which he makes us see,
He of this gardin had the governall,
   And Pleasure's porter was devis'd to be,   50
Holding a staffe in hand for more formalitie . . .

Thus being entred, they behold around
A large and spatious plaine on ev'ry side
   Strow'd with pleasaunce, whose faire grassie ground
Mantled with green, and goodly beautifide   55
With all the ornaments of Floraes pride,
   Wherewith her mother Art, as half in scorne
Of niggard Nature, like a pompous bride,
   Did deck her, and too lavishly adorne,
When forth from virgin bowre she comes in th' early morne.   60

Thereto the heavens always joviall,
Lookt on them lovely, still in stedfast state,
   Ne suffer'd storme nor frost on them to fall,
Their tender buds or leaves to violate,
Nor scorching heat, nor cold intemperate,   65

T' afflict the creatures which therein did dwell;
But the milde air with season moderate
   Gently attempred and dispos'd so well,
That still it breathed forth sweet spirit and wholesome smell.

More sweet and wholesome than the pleasant hill   70
Of Rhodopè, on which the nymph that bore
   A giant-babe, her selfe for griefe did kill;
Or the Thessalian Tempè, where of yore
Faire Daphne Phœbus' heart with love did gore;
   Or Ida, where the Gods lov'd to repaire,   75
When-ever they their heavenly bowres forlore;
   Or sweet Parnasse, the haunt of muses faire;
Or Eden, if that aught with Eden mote compare . . .

Till that he came unto another gate,
No gate, but like one, beeing goodly dight   80
   With boughes and branches, which did broad dilate
Their clasping armes, in wanton wreathings intricate.

So fashioned a porch with rare divise,
Archt over head with an embracing vine,
   Whose bunches hanging downe, seem'd to entice   85
All passers by to taste their lushious wine,
And did themselves into their hands incline,
   As freely offering to be gathered:
Some deep empurpled as the hyacint,
   Some as the rubine, laughing sweetly red,   90
Some like faire emerauldes not yet well ripened.

And them amongst, some were of burnisht gold,
So made by art, to beautifie the rest,
   Which did themselves emongst the leaves enfold,
As lurking from the view of covetous guest,   95
That the weak boughes, with so rich load opprest,
   Did bow adown as over-burthened . . .

There the most dainty paradise on ground,
It self doth offer to his sober eye,
   In which all pleasures plentiously abound,   100
And none does others happiness envie:
The painted flowres, the trees upshooting hie,
   The dales for shade, the hills for breathing place,

33   *1774-9*

The trembling groves, the crystall running by;
   And that which all fair works doth most aggrace,   105
The art which wrought it all appeared in no place.

   One would have thought (so cunningly the rude
And scorned parts were mingled with the fine)
   That Nature had for wantonness ensude
Art, and that Art at Nature did repine;   110
So striveing each the other to undermine,
   Each did the other's worke more beautify;
So differing both in willes, agreed in fine:
   So all agreed through sweet diversitie,
This garden to adorne with all varietie.   115

   And in the midst of all, a fountaine stood,
Of richest substance that on earth might be,
   So pure and shiny, that the silver flood
Through every channell running, one might see;
Most goodly it with pure imageree   120
   Was over-wrought, and shapes of naked boyes,
Of which some seem'd with lively jollitee
   To fly about, playing their wanton toyes,
Whiles others did themselves embay in liquid joyes.

   And over all, of purest gold, was spred   125
A trayle of ivie in his native hew:
   For the rich metall was so coloured,
That wight that did not well advised view,
Would surely deem it to be ivie true:
   Lowe his lascivious armes adowne did creep,   130
That themselves dipping in the silver dew,
   Their fleecie flowres they tenderly did steepe,
Which drops of crystall seem'd for wantonness to weepe.

   Infinite streames continually did well
Out of this fountaine, sweet and faire to see,   135
   The which into an ample lauer fell,
And shortly grew to so great quantitie,
That like a little lake it seem'd to bee;
   Whose depth exceeded not three cubits height,
That through the waves one might the bottom see,   140
   All pav'd beneath with jasper shining bright
That seem'd the fountaine in that sea did sayle upright.

Elizabeth Carter, *Ode to Spring* (1756)

Suggested date of reading: by 1779

> The first verses from which he remembered to have received
> great pleasure, were Miss Carter's 'Poem on Spring', a poem in
> the six-line stanza, which he was particularly fond of, and had
> composed much in, for example, 'Ruth'.
>
> (John Duke Coleridge, 1836)

As a boy Wordsworth encountered 'Ode to Spring' in Anne Fisher's
children's anthology, *The Pleasing Instructor* (1756), from which the
text here is edited. Fisher's collection also contained Gray's *Elegy*,
Parnell's *The Hermit*, and Thomson's *Hymn to the Seasons*, which he
probably also read there for the first time. The most likely time for
him to have read it is during his early childhood at his father's house
in Cockermouth.

Born in 1717, Carter had been a friend of Dr Johnson (who
regarded her as the finest exponent of ancient Greek he had ever
met), and she would remain a prominent intellectual figure until
her death in 1806. She is the first of a number of women writers
whose poetry Wordsworth held in high esteem; others include
Charlotte Smith (pp. 41-2, 141-3), Helen Maria Williams (p. 96),
Anna Laetitia Barbauld (p. 274), Anne Finch, Countess of
Winchelsea (pp. 101-6), and Margaret Cavendish, Duchess of
Newcastle (p. 270).

Ode to Spring

Youth of the Year, delightful Spring!
Thy blest Return on genial Wing
   Inspires my languid Lays;
No more I sleep in Sloth supine,
While all Creation at thy Shrine   5
   Its annual Tribute pays.

Escap'd from Winter's freezing Pow'r
Each Blossom greets thee, and each Flow'r;
    And, foremost of the Train,
By Nature (artless Handmaid) drest,   10
The Snow-drop comes in lillied Vest
    Prophetic of thy Reign.

The Lark now strains her tuneful Throat
And ev'ry loud, and sprightly Note
    Calls Echo from her Cell;   15
Be warn'd, ye Maids, that listen round,
A beauteous Nymph became a Sound,
    The Nymph, who lov'd too well.

The bright-hair'd Sun, with Warmth benign,
Bids Tree and Shrub, and swelling Vine   20
    Their infant Buds display;
Again the Streams refresh the Plains,
Which Winter bound in icy Chains,
    And sparkling bless his Ray.

Life-giving Zephyrs breathe around,   25
And instant glows th' enamell'd Ground
    With Nature's varied Hues;
Not so returns our Youth decay'd,
Alas! nor Air, nor Sun, nor Shade
    The Spring of Life renews.   30

The Sun's too quick revolving Beam
A-pace dissolves the human Dream,
    And brings th' appointed Hour;
Too late we catch his parting Ray,
And mourn the idly wasted Day,   35
    No longer in our Pow'r.

Then happiest he, whose lengthen'd Sight
Pursues by Virtue's constant Light
    A Hope beyond the Skies;
Where frowning Winter ne'er shall come,   40
But rosy Spring for ever bloom,
    And Suns eternal rise.

Thomas Chatterton, *Ælla* (1778): 'Mynstrelles Songe'

Suggested date of reading; by 1783

> I thought of Chatterton, the marvellous Boy,
> The sleepless Soul that perish'd in its pride . . .
> > ('Resolution and Independence' 43-4)

As a schoolboy Wordsworth read the copy of Chatterton's *Miscellanies in Prose and Verse* (1778) owned by his Hawkshead schoolmaster, William Taylor (who died in 1783). It survives today at the Armitt Library, Ambleside, and bears a presentation inscription by Edmund Irton:

> To the Revd. William Taylor, Master of the Free Grammar School at Hawkshead, to mark my appreciation of his luminous and pertinent reflections on the poets of our time, and especially the unhappy boy whose genius is evident in many of the pieces contained in this slender volume.

This confirms that Taylor enjoyed verse by 'the poets of our time', and took pleasure in passing on his enthusiasm to his pupils. We can be sure that among the poems Wordsworth admired as a schoolboy was the 'Mynstrelles Songe', frequently anthologised. He quotes three lines from it in a notebook draft for a poem of his own, composed January 1788:

> Mie love ys dedde
> Gon to his deathe-bedde
> Al under the wyllowe tree[1]

Chatterton had a permanent place in Wordsworth's pantheon of great but neglected poets who, like Collins and Kirke White, were undervalued, stricken by depression, and taken before their time: 'We Poets in our youth begin in gladness; / But thereof comes in the end despondency and madness.' Not that Wordsworth viewed Chatterton as destroyed by poverty or neglect – in fact, he seems to have regarded his early demise as having been in some sense his own fault. Asked in 1819 to contribute to a fund for a memorial to him, Wordsworth replied:

---

[1] *Early Poems and Fragments, 1785-1797* ed. Carol Landon and Jared Curtis (Ithaca, NY, 1997), p. 570.

I would readily assist, according to my means, in erecting a Monument to the memory of Chatterton, who with transcendent genius was cut off by his own hand while he was yet a Boy in years; this, could he have anticipated the tribute, might have soothed his troubled spirit; as an expression of general belief in the existence of those powers which he was too impatient and too proud to develop.

And when in 1837 Sir William Rowan Hamilton asked about the idea of using public funds to help writers Wordsworth remarked of Chatterton and Burns: 'I do think that in the temperament of the two I have mentioned there was something which however favourable had been their circumstances, however much they had been encouraged and supported, would have brought on their ruin.'

Wordsworth's love of Chatterton's verse never diminished. On 13 September 1833 Eliza Fletcher, a young admirer, reported that he 'expressed the highest admiration for Chatterton's genius and thinks had he lived he would have been the greatest of English Poets except Shakespeare.'

Here is the 'Mynstrelles Song' from Chatterton's 1778 volume, in the form in which Wordsworth first encountered it.

Mynstrelles Songe

O! synge untoe mie roundelaie,
O! droppe the brynie teare wythe mee,   845
Daunce ne moe atte hallie daie,
Lycke a reynynge[1] ryver bee;
    Mie love ys dedde,
    Gon to hys death-bedde,
    Al under the wyllowe tree.   850

---

[1] Running

Blacke hys cryne² as the wyntere nyghte,
Whyte hys rode³ as the sommer snowe,
Rodde hys face as the mornynge lyghte,
Cale he lyes ynne the grave belowe;
  Mie love ys dedde,   855
  Gon to hys deathe-bedde,
  Al under the wyllowe tree.

Swote hys tyngue as the throstles note,
Quycke ynn daunce as thoughte canne bee,
Defte hys taboure, codgelle stote,   860
O! hee lyes bie the wyllowe tree:
  Mie love ys dedde,
  Gonne to hys deathe-bedde,
  Alle underre the wyllowe tree.

Harke! the ravenne flappes hys wynge,   865
In the briered delle belowe;
Harke! the dethe-owle loude dothe synge,
To the nyghte-mares as heie goe;
  Mie love ys dedde,
  Gonne to hys deathe-bedde,   870
  Al under the wyllowe tree.

See! the whyte moone sheenes onne hie;
Whyterre ys mie true loves shroude;
Whyterre yanne the mornynge skie,
Whyterre yanne the evenynge cloude;   875
  Mie love ys dedde,
  Gon to hys death-bedde,
  Al under the wyllowe tree.

Heere, uponne mie true loves grave,
Schalle the baren fleurs be layde,   880
Nee one hallie Seyncte to save
Al the celness of a mayde.
  Mie love ys dedde,
  Gon to hys death-bedde,
  Alle under the wyllowe tree.   885

---

² hair ³ complexion

Wythe mie hondes I'lle dente the brieres
Rounde his hallie corse to gre,
Ouphante fairie, lyghte youre fyres,
Heere mie boddie stylle schalle bee.
       Mie love ys dedde,   890
       Gon to hys death-bedde,
       Al under the wyllowe tree.

Comme, wythe acorn-coppe & thorne,
Drayne mie hartys blodde awaie;
Lyfe & all yttes goode I scorne,   895
Daunce bie nete, or feaste by daie.
       Mie love ys dedde,
       Gon to hys death-bedde,
       Al under the wyllowe tree.

Waterre wytches, crownede wythe reytes[4],   900
Bere mee to yer leathalle tyde.
I die; I comme; mie true love waytes.
Thos the damselle spake, and dyed.

---

[4] Water-flags

Charlotte Smith, *Elegiac Sonnets* (1784): *To the South Downs, To Night*

Date of reading: 1784

> She wrote little, and that little unambitiously, but with true feeling for rural nature, at a time when nature was not much regarded by English Poets; for in point of time her earlier writings preceded, I believe, those of Cowper and Burns.
>
> (Wordsworth, note to 'Stanzas suggested in a Steamboat off St Bees' Heads', 1835)

After the premature death of his teacher, William Taylor, young Wordsworth was fortunate in having as schoolmaster Thomas Bowman who, like his predecessor, kept up with contemporary poetry. He lent Wordsworth a copy of Charlotte Smith's *Elegiac Sonnets* soon after publication in 1784. So much did he enjoy the volume that in 1789, during his second year as a Cambridge under-graduate, Wordsworth subscribed to the fifth edition with his cousin John Myers. Their copy survives at the Wordsworth Library in Grasmere bearing the ownership inscription 'Wm Wordsworth St John's'. He was never to lose his love of Smith's poetry; in January 1836 he referred to her as 'my old Friend Charlotte Smith, who was the first *Modern* distinguished in that Composition' (that is, the sonnet).

'To the South Downs' was probably her most famous work, and Wordsworth alluded to it in his own *An Evening Walk* (see my *The Earliest Wordsworth: Poems 1785-1790* (Carcanet, 2002), p. 63); in 1830 he advised Alexander Dyce to include 'To Night' in an anthology of women poets. Both are edited here from Wordsworth's copy of the 1789 edition.

Sonnet V

Ah! hills belov'd! – where once, an happy child,
　　Your beechen shades, 'your turf, your flowers among,'
I wove your blue-bells into garlands wild,
　　And woke your echoes with my artless song.
Ah! hills belov'd! – your turf, your flow'rs remain;　　　5
　　But can they peace to this sad breast restore,
For one poor moment soothe the sense of pain,
　　And teach a breaking heart to throb no more?
And you, Aruna! – in the vale below,
　　As to the sea your limpid wives you bear,　　　10
Can you one kind Lethean cup bestow,
　　To drink a long oblivion to my care?
Ah! no! – when all, e'en Hope's last ray is gone,
There's no oblivion – but in death alone!

Sonnet XXXIX

I love thee, mournful sober-suited night,
　　When the faint moon, yet lingering in her wane,
And veil'd in clouds, with pale uncertain light
　　Hangs o'er the waters of the restless main.
In deep depression sunk, the enfeebled mind　　　5
　　Will to the deaf, cold elements complain,
　　And tell the embosom'd grief, however vain,
To sullen surges and the viewless wind.
Tho' no repose on thy dark breast I find,
　　I still enjoy thee – cheerless as thou art;　　　10
　　For in thy quiet gloom, the exhausted heart
Is calm, tho' wretched; hopeless, yet resign'd.
While, to the winds and waves its sorrows given,
May reach – tho' lost on earth – the ear of Heaven!

Thomas Gray, *Journal of the Lakes* (1775) (extract)

Suggested date of reading: 1784

Gray, the poet, followed; he died soon after his forlorn and melancholy pilgrimage to the Vale of Keswick, and the record left behind him of what he had seen and felt in this journey, excited that pensive interest with which the human mind is ever disposed to listen to the farewell words of a man of genius. The journal of Gray feelingly showed how the gloom of ill health and low spirits had been irradiated by objects, which the Author's powers of mind enabled him to describe with distinctness and unaffected simplicity. Every reader of this journal must have been impressed with the words which conclude his notice of the Vale of Grasmere: –

> Not a single red tile, no flaring gentleman's house or garden-wall, breaks in upon the repose of this little unsuspected paradise; but all is peace, rusticity, and happy poverty, in its neatest and most becoming attire.
>
> (Wordsworth, *Description of the Scenery of the Lakes* (1822))

Gray's account of his tour through the Lakes is an inspired, pioneering work of travel literature, available not just in his posthumous *Works* (1775) but in Thomas West's popular *Guide to the Lakes* (from the second edition of 1780 onwards, where it was entitled 'Mr Gray's Journal'), a copy of which Wordsworth had at his disposal as a schoolboy. One of its earliest literary visitors, Gray helped turn Grasmere into a tourist attraction, a haunt of writers and artists, all of whom wanted to witness for themselves the numinous landscape he described.

Shortly after setting up house in Dove Cottage with Dorothy in 1799, Wordsworth composed a poetic response to Gray in which he remembered his first glimpse of Grasmere from Red Bank some time in the early 1780s – from the southern end of the valley, rather than from the north, where Gray had his first sight of 'this little unsuspected paradise':

> Once on the brow of yonder Hill I stopped,
> While I was yet a School-boy (of what age
> I cannot well remember, but the hour
> I well remember though the year be gone),

And with a sudden influx overcome
At sight of this seclusion, I forgot
My haste – for hasty had my footsteps been,
As boyish my pursuits – and sighing said,
'What happy fortune were it here to live!
And if I thought of dying, if a thought
Of mortal separation could come in
With paradise before me, here to die.'

('Home at Grasmere' MS B, 1-12)

In the first of these extracts, edited here from the journal as presented in West's *Guide* (3rd ed., 1784), Gray's entry for 3 October 1769 describes, in dramatic terms, 'the jaws of Borrowdale' and the Lodore Falls. That for 8 October – singled out by Wordsworth – describes his journey from Keswick to Grasmere.

❧

Oct. 3.   A heavenly day; rose at seven, and walked out under the conduct of my landlord to Borrowdale; the grass was covered with a hoar-frost, which soon melted and exhaled in a thin bluish smoke; crossed the meadows, obliquely catching a diversity of views among the hills over the lake and islands, and changing prospect at every ten paces. Left Cockshut (which we formerly mounted) and Castle-hill, a loftier and more rugged hill behind me, and drew near the foot of Wallow-crag, whose bare and rocky brow cut perpendicularly down above 400 feet (as I guess, though the people called it much more) awfully overlooks the way. Our path here tends to the left, and the ground gently rising and covered with a glade of scattering trees and bushes on the very margin of the water, opens both ways the most delicious view that my eyes ever beheld. Opposite are the thick woods of Lord Egremont, and Newland valley, with green and smiling fields embosomed in the dark cliffs; to the left the jaws of Borrowdale, with that turbulent chaos of mountain behind mountain, rolled in confusion; beneath you and stretching far away to the right, the shining purity of the lake reflecting rocks, woods, fields, and inverted tops of hills, just ruffled by the breeze, enough to shew it is alive, with the white buildings of Keswick, Crosthwaite church, and Skiddaw for a back-ground at a distance. Behind you the magnificent heights of Wallow-crag: Here the glass played its part divinely; the place is called Carfclose-reeds; and I chose to set down these barbarous names, that any body may enquire on the place and easily find the particular station that I mean. This scene continues to Barrowgate, and a little farther, passing a brook called Barrow-beck, we entered Borrowdale: The crags named Lowdore-banks begin now to impend terribly over your way, and more terribly when you hear that three years since an immense mass of rock tumbled at once from the brow, and barred all access to the dale (for this is the only road) till they could work their way through it. Luckily no one was passing by at the time of this fall; but down the side of the mountain, and far into the lake, lie dispersed the huge fragments of this ruin in all shapes and in all directions; Something farther we turned aside into a coppice, ascending a little in front of Lowdore water-fall; the height appeared to be about 200 feet, the quantity of water not great, though (these three days excepted) it had rained daily in the hills for near two months before: But then the stream was nobly broken, leaping from rock to rock, and foam-ing with fury. On one side a towering crag that spired up to equal, if not overtop the neighbouring cliffs (this lay all in shade and dark-ness:) On the other hand a rounder, broader, projecting hill, shagged with wood, and illuminated by the sun, which glanced side-ways on the upper part of the cataract. The force of the water wear-ing a deep channel in the ground, hurries away to join the lake. We descended again and passed the stream over a rude bridge. Soon after we came under Gowdar-crag, a hill more formidable to the eye, and to the apprehension, than that of Lowdore; the rocks at top deep-cloven perpendicularly by the rains, hanging loose and nodding forwards, seen just starting from their base in shivers. The whole way down, and the road on both sides is strewed with piles of the fragments strangely thrown across each other, and of a dreadful bulk; the place reminds me of those passes in the Alps, where the guides tell you to move on with speed, and say nothing, lest the agitation of the air should loosen the snows above, and bring down a mass that would overwhelm a caravan. I took their counsel here and hastened on in silence . . .

We returned leisurely home the way we came, but saw a new landscape; the features indeed were the same in part, but many new ones were disclosed by the mid day sun, and the tints were intirely changed; take notice this was the best, or perhaps the only day for going up Skiddaw, but I thought it better employed; it was perfectly serene, and hot as midsummer.

In the evening I walked alone down to the lake, by the side of Crow-park, after sunset, and saw the solemn colouring of the night draw on, the last gleam of sunshine fading away on the hill tops, the deep serene of the waters, and the long shadows of the mountains thrown across them, till they nearly touched the hithermost shore. At a distance were heard the murmurs of many water-falls, not audible in the day-time; I wished for the moon; but she was dark to me and silent,

Hid in her vacant interlunar cave.

Oct. 8. I left Keswick, and took the Ambleside road in a gloomy morning; and about two miles from the town mounted an eminence called Castle-rig, and the sun breaking out, discovered the most inchanting view I have yet seen of the whole valley behind me, the two lakes, the river, the mountains all in their glory; so that I had almost a mind to have gone back again. The road in some few parts is not completed, yet good country road, through sound but narrow and stony lanes, very safe in broad day light. This is the case about Causeway-foot, and among Naddle-fells to Langthwaite. The vale you go in has little breadth; the mountains are vast and rocky, the fields little and poor, and the inhabitants are now making hay, and see not the sun by two hours in a day so long as at Keswick. Came to the foot of Helvellyn, along which runs an excellent road, looking down from a little height on Leathes-water (called also Thirlmere, or Wythburn-water) and soon descending on its margin. The lake looks black from its depth, and from the gloom of the vast crags that scowl over it, though really clear as glass; it is narrow, and about three miles long, resembling a river in its course; little shining torrents hurrying down the rocks to join it, but not a bush to overshadow them, or cover their march; all is rock and loose stones up to the very brow, which lies so near your way, that not above half the height of Helvellyn can be seen.

Next I passed by the little chapel of Wythburn, out of which the sunday congregation were then issuing; soon after a beck near Dunmail-raise, where I entered Westmorland a second time; and now began to see Helm-crag, distinguished from its rugged neighbours, not so much by its height as by the strange broken outlines of its top, like some gigantic building demolished, and the stones that composed it flung across each other in wild confusion. Just beyond it, opens one of the sweetest landscapes that art ever attempted to imitate. The bosom of the mountains spreading here into a broad bason discovers in the midst Grasmere-water; its margin is hollowed into small bays, with bold eminences; some of rock some of turf, that half-conceal, and vary the figure of the little lake they command: from the shore, a low promontory pushes itself far into the water, and on it stands a white village with the parish church rising in the midst of it: hanging inclosures, corn-fields and meadows green as an emerald, with their trees and hedges, and cattle, fill up the whole space from the edge of the water: And just opposite to you is a large farm-house at the bottom of a steep smooth lawn, embosomed in old woods which climb half way up the mountains side, and discover above them a broken line of crags that crown the scene. Not a single red tile, no gentlemen's flaring house, or garden walls, break in upon the repose of this little unsuspected paradise; but all is peace, rusticity, and happy poverty, in its neatest most becoming attire.

William Cowper, *The Task* Book VI (1785) (extract)

Date of Reading: shortly after July 1785

> You know how I love and quote, not even Shakespeare and
> Milton, but Cowper, Burns, etc. As to the modern poets –
> Byron, Scott, etc. – I do not quote them because I do not love
> them.
>
> (Wordsworth to Henry Crabb Robinson, 1836)

Cowper's blank verse poem in six books was a best-seller in its day,
remaining so until well into the nineteenth century. Wordsworth
remained a fervent admirer from the time he was introduced to it by
his schoolmaster at Hawkshead, Thomas Bowman, shortly after
publication in July 1785. When in the Advertisement to *Lyrical
Ballads* (1798) Wordsworth and Coleridge praised 'those in
modern times who have been the most successful in painting
manners and passions' they were referring to Cowper and Burns; in
conversation with friends, Coleridge remarked that 'Burns and
Cowper were the only modern writers that deserve the name of
poet'. This remained Wordsworth's view for the rest of his life;
thinking of his early debt to Burns and Cowper, he commented in
1842:

> It gives me pleasure, venial I trust, to acknowledge at this late
> day, my obligations to these two great Authors, both then and at
> a later period, when my taste and natural tendencies were under
> an injurious influence from the dazzling manner of Darwin, and
> the extravagance of the earlier Dramas of Schiller and that of
> other German Writers.

This extract from *The Task* comes from Book VI, 'The Winter
Walk at Noon', which includes a reflection on the power of memo-
ry, and a characteristic attack on book-learning as opposed to the
insights gained from meditative thought. Wordsworth ran a varia-
tion on the same theme in 'Expostulation and Reply' and 'The
Tables Turned'.

There is in souls a sympathy with sounds,
And as the mind is pitch'd the ear is pleas'd
With melting airs or martial, brisk or grave.
Some chord in unison with what we hear
Is touched within us, and the heart replies.   5
How soft the music of those village bells
Falling at intervals upon the ear
In cadence sweet! now dying all away,
Now pealing loud again and louder still,
Clear and sonorous as the gale comes on.   10
With easy force it opens all the cells
Where mem'ry slept. Wherever I have heard
A kindred melody, the scene recurs,
And with it all its pleasures and its pains.
Such comprehensive views the spirit takes,   15
That in a few short moments I retrace
(As in a map the voyager his course)
The windings of my way through many years,
Short as in retrospect the journey seems,
It seem'd not always short; the rugged path   20
And prospect oft so dreary and forlorn
Moved many a sigh at its disheart'ning length.
Yet feeling present evils, while the past
Faintly impress the mind, or not at all,
How readily we wish time spent revoked,   25
That we might try the ground again, where once
(Through inexperience as we now perceive)
We miss'd that happiness we might have found.
Some friend is gone, perhaps his son's best friend
A father, whose authority, in show   30
When most severe, and must'ring all its force,
Was but the graver countenance of love.
Whose favour like the clouds of spring, might low'r
And utter now and then an awful voice,
But had a blessing in its darkest frown,   35
Threat'ning at once and nourishing the plant.
We loved, but not enough the gentle hand
That reared us. At a thoughtless age allured
By ev'ry gilded folly, we renounced

His shelt'ring side, and wilfully forewent   40
That converse which we now in vain regret.
How gladly would the man recall to life
The boy's neglected fire! a mother too,
That softer friend, perhaps more gladly still
Might he demand them at the gates of death.   45
Sorrow has since they went subdued and tamed
The playful humour, he could now endure,
(Himself grown sober in the vale of tears)
And feel a parent's presence no restraint.
But not to understand a treasure's worth   50
'Till time has stol'n away the slighted good,
Is cause of half the poverty we feel,
And makes the world the wilderness it is.
The few that pray at all pray oft amiss,
And seeking grace t' improve the prize they hold   55
Would urge a wiser suit, than asking more.
    The night was winter in his roughest mood,
The morning sharp and clear. But now at noon,
Upon the southern side of the slant hills,
And where the woods fence off the northern blast,   60
The season smiles resigning all its rage
And has the warmth of May. The vault is blue
Without a cloud, and white without a speck
The dazzling splendour of the scene below.
Again the harmony comes o'er the vale,   65
And through the trees I view th' embattled tow'r
Whence all the music. I again perceive
The soothing influence of the wafted strains,
And settle in soft musings as I tread
The walk still verdant under oaks and elms,   70
Whose outspread branches overarch the glade.
The roof though moveable through all its length
As the wind sways it, has yet well sufficed;
And intercepting in their silent fall
The frequent flakes, has kept a path for me.   75
No noise is here, or none that hinders thought.
The red-breast warbles still, but is content
With slender notes and more than half suppress'd.
Pleased with his solitude, and flitting light
From spray to spray, where'er he rests he shakes   80
From many a twig the pendent drops of ice,

That tinkle in the wither'd leaves below.
Stillness accompanied with sounds so soft
Charms more than silence. Meditation here
May think down hours to moments. Here the heart 85
May give an useful lesson to the head,
And learning wiser grow without his books.
Knowledge and wisdom, far from being one,
Have oft times no connexion. Knowledge dwells
In heads replete with thoughts of other men, 90
Wisdom in minds attentive to their own.
Knowledge, a rude unprofitable mass,
The mere materials with which wisdom builds,
'Till smooth'd and squared and fitted to its place
Does but incumber whom it seems t' enrich. 95
Knowledge is proud that he has learn'd so much,
Wisdom is humble that he knows no more.
Books are not seldom talismans and spells
By which the magic art of shrewder wits
Holds an unthinking multitude enthrall'd. 100
Some to the fascination of a name
Surrender judgment hood-wink'd. Some the stile
Infatuates, and through labyrinths and wilds
Of error, leads them by a tune entranced.
While sloth seduces more, too weak to bear 105
The insupportable fatigue of thought,
And swallowing therefore without pause or choice
The total grist unsifted, husks and all.
But trees, and rivulets whose rapid course
Defies the check of winter, haunts of deer, 110
And sheep-walks populous with bleating lambs,
And lanes in which the primrose ere her time
Peeps through the moss that cloaths the hawthorn root,
Deceive no student. Wisdom there, and truth,
Not shy as in the world, and to be won 115
By slow solicitation, seize at once
The roving thought, and fix it on themselves.

1785

James Thomson, *The Seasons*: *Winter* (1726) (extract)

Date of reading: by 1785

> Before the morning hour of repairing to school, he has been often seen and heard in the sequestered lane, either alone, or with a favourite companion, repeating aloud beautiful passages from Thomson's Seasons, and sometimes comparing, as they chanced to occur, the actual phenomena of nature with the descriptions given of them by the poet.
>
> (Anon., 'Memoir of William Wordsworth, Esq.', *New Monthly Magazine* (1819))

The Seasons is a strong influence on Wordsworth's schoolboy poetry; it drew his interest, from an early age, to poetry accurately describing natural phenomena. As with many of the poets he read in his schooldays, his love of Thomson's verse never abated. In old age, he praised Thomson for having 'a true love and feeling for Nature, and a greater share of poetical imagination, as distinguished from dramatic, than any man between Milton and him'. He was such an admirer that, after visiting Thomson's school in Jedburgh in 1803, he was inspired to edit his poems; although that ambition was never fulfilled he prepared by acquiring a first edition of *The Seasons* which he interlined with textual variants. When showing it to James Muirhead in 1841 he told him that Thomson was 'one whom Nature had admitted to share in many of her very highest enjoyments and most retired pleasures, and who had received the boon with the keenest feelings and a warm and exquisite sensibility'.

In 1815 he commended Thomson for having written, in *Winter*, 'a work of inspiration; much of it is written from himself, and nobly from himself'. I have accordingly selected an extract from it, edited here from the third edition of 1726. Wordsworth had a particular liking for Thomson's description of the winter storm, and liked his advice, 'Now Shepherds, to your helpless Charge be kind'; he borrowed it for an undergraduate rendering of Virgil's *Georgics*, composed 1788:

> Ah then, when keenly blows the winter's wind,
> Ah then, ye shepherds to your flocks be kind![1]

---

[1] See my *The Earliest Wordsworth: Poems 1785-1790* (Carcanet, 2002), p. 41.

Father of Light, and Life! Thou Good Supreme!   215
O! teach me what is Good! teach me thy self!
Save me from Folly, Vanity and Vice,
From every low Pursuit! and feed my Soul,
With Knowledge, conscious Peace, and Vertue pure,
Sacred, substantial, never-fading Bliss!   220
    Dun, from the livid East, or piercing North,
Thick Clouds ascend, in whose capacious Womb,
A vapoury Deluge lies, to Snow congeal'd:
Heavy, they roll their fleecy World along;
And the Sky saddens with th' impending Storm.   225
Thro' the hush'd Air, the whitening Shower descends,
At first, thin-wavering; till, at last, the Flakes
Fall broad, and wide, and fast, dimming the Day,
With a continual Flow. Blackening, they melt,
Along the mazy Stream. The leafless Woods   230
Bow their hoar' Heads. And e'er the languid Sun,
Faint, from the West, emit his evening Ray,
Earth's universal Face, deep-hid, and chill,
Is all one, dazzling, Waste. The Labourer-Ox
Stands cover'd o'er with Snow, and then demands   235
The Fruit of all his Toil. The Fowls of Heaven,
Tam'd by the cruel Season, croud around
The winnowing Store, and claim the little Boon
That Providence allows. The Red-Breast, sole,
Wisely regardful of th' embroiling Sky,   240
In joyless Fields, and thorny Thickets, leaves
His shivering Fellows, and to trusted Man
His annual Visit pays: New to the Dome,
Against the Window beats; then, brisk, alights
On the warm Hearth, and, hopping o'er the Floor,   245
Eyes all the smiling Family, askance,
And pecks, and starts, and wonders where he is:
Till, more familiar grown, the Table-Crumbs
Attract his slender Feet. The foodless Wilds
Pour forth their brown Inhabitants; the Hare,   250
Tho' timorous of Heart, and hard beset
By Death, in various Forms, dark Snares and Dogs,
And more unpitying Men, the Garden seeks,
Urg'd on by fearless Want. The bleating Kind
Eye the bleak Heavens, and next, the glistening Earth,   255
With Looks of dumb Despair; then sad, dispers'd,

Dig, for the wither'd Herb, thro' Heaps of Snow.
  Now Shepherds, to your helpless Charge be kind;
Baffle the raging Year, and fill their Pens
With Food, at will: Lodge them below the Storm,   260
And watch them strict; for, from the bellowing East,
In this dire Season, oft the Whirlwind's Wing
Sweeps up the Burthen of whole wintry Plains
In one fierce Blast, and o'er th' unhappy Flocks,
Hid in the Hollow of two neighbouring Hills,   265
The billowy Tempest whelms; till, upwards urg'd,
The Valley to a shining Mountain swells,
That curls its Wreaths amid the freezing Sky.

James Beattie, *The Minstrel* (1779) (extracts)

Suggested date of reading: by 1785

Beattie's *Minstrel* was eagerly devoured by Wordsworth when intro-
duced to it by Thomas Bowman at Hawkshead, probably by 1785
– and not surprisingly: Edwin, the minstrel of the title, was so uncan-
nily close to Wordsworth in his tastes and ambitions that Dorothy
took it for a description of her brother. Writing to her best friend
Jane Pollard in July 1793, she remarked:

> 'In truth he was a strange and wayward wight fond of each gen-
> tle' etc. etc. That verse of Beattie's Minstrel always reminds me
> of him, and indeed the whole character of Edwin resembles
> much what William was when I first knew him after my leaving
> Halifax – 'and oft he traced the uplands', etc. etc. etc.

This was not whimsy; Beattie's protagonist is a precursor of the
Wordsworthian hero. The son of a shepherd, Edwin loves the
mountains in which he grew up, and has a mentor, a hermit who
advises him to study science and philosophy. Wordsworth would
follow a similar narrative course in his portrait of the Pedlar in *The
Excursion* (1814). In addition, Beattie's description of the Scottish
mountains provided him with an effective model of nature poetry to
which he would remain indebted throughout his career.

Wordsworth valued *The Minstrel* partly for Beattie's technique –
always correct in its handling of the language, and mindful of
classical antecedents. In a letter of 14 February 1815 to R.P. Gillies
Wordsworth compared Beattie favourably with James Hogg and
Walter Scott; he preferred, he said:

> the *Classical* model of Dr Beattie to the insupportable slovenli-
> ness and neglect of syntax and *grammar* by which Hogg's writ-
> ings are disfigured. It is excusable in him from his education, but
> Walter Scott knows, and ought to do, better. They neither of
> them write a language which has any pretension to be called
> English; and their versification – who can endure it when he
> comes fresh from the Minstrel?

Again, when Wordsworth spoke to the journalist John Payne
Collier, he emphasised Beattie's technique. Wordsworth, Collier
records, spoke 'well of the earlier portion of Beattie's "Minstrel",

not so much for originality of thought, as for the skilful manner in which he employed the nine-line stanza'.

These two extracts come from Book I ('the earlier portion' of the work), describing Edwin's passionate engagement with the natural world and a Gothic vision. They are almost certainly Wordsworth's favourite passages; the first is of course the one mentioned by Dorothy in 1793.

The wight, whose tale these artless lines unfold,
Was all the offspring of this humble pair.
His birth no oracle or seer foretold:
No prodigy appear'd in earth or air,   130
Nor aught that might a strange event declare.
You guess each circumstance of EDWIN's birth;
The parent's transport, and the parent's care;
The gossip's prayer for wealth, and wit, and worth;
And one long summer-day of indolence and mirth.   135

And yet poor Edwin was no vulgar boy;
Deep thought oft seem'd to fix his infant eye.
Dainties he heeded not, nor gaude, nor toy,
Save one short pipe of rudest minstrelsy.
Silent when glad; affectionate, though shy;   140
And now his look was most demurely sad;
And now he laugh'd aloud, yet none knew why.
The neighbours stared and sigh'd, yet bless'd the lad:
Some deem'd him wondrous wise, and some believed him mad.

But why should I his childish feats display?   145
Concourse, and noise, and toil, he ever fled;
Nor cared to mingle in the clamorous fray
Of squabbling imps; but to the forest sped;
Or roam'd at large the lonely mountain's head;
Or, where the maze of some bewilder'd stream   150
To deep untrodden groves his footsteps led,
There would he wander wild, till Phœbus' beam,
Shot from the western cliff, released the weary team.

Th' exploit of strength, dexterity, or speed,
To him nor vanity nor joy could bring.   155
His heart, from cruel sport estranged, would bleed
To work the wo of any living thing,
By trap, or net; by arrow, or by sling;
These he detested, those he scorned to wield:
He wish'd to be the guardian, not the king,   160
Tyrant far less, or traitor of the field.
And sure the sylvan reign unbloody joy might yield.

Lo! where the stripling, wrapt in wonder, roves
Beneath the precipice o'erhung with pine;
And sees, on high, amidst th' encircling groves,   165
From cliff to cliff the foaming torrents shine:
While waters, woods, and winds, in concert join,
And Echo swells the chorus to the skies.
Would Edwin this majestic scene resign
For aught the huntsman's puny craft supplies?   170
Ah! no: he better knows great Nature's charms to prize.

And oft he traced the uplands, to survey,
When o'er the sky advanced the kindling dawn,
The crimson cloud, blue main, and mountain grey,
And lake, dim-gleaming on the smoky lawn;   175
Far to the west the long long vale withdrawn,
Where twilight loves to linger for a while;
And now he faintly kens the bounding fawn,
And villager abroad at early toil.
But, lo! the sun appears! and heaven, earth, ocean, smile.   180

And oft the craggy cliff he loved to climb,
When all in mist the world below was lost.
What dreadful pleasure! there to stand sublime,
Like shipwreck'd mariner on desert coast,
And view th' enormous waste of vapour, tost   185
In billows, lengthening to th' horizon round,
Now scoop'd in gulfs, with mountains now emboss'd!
And hear the voice of mirth and song rebound,
Flocks, herds, and waterfalls, along the hoar profound!

In truth he was a strange and wayward wight,   190
Fond of each gentle, and each dreadful scene.
In darkness, and in storm, he found delight:
Nor less, than when on ocean-wave serene
The southern sun diffused his dazzling shene.
Even sad vicissitude amused his soul: 195
And if a sigh would sometimes intervene,
And down his cheek a tear of pity roll,
A sigh, a tear, so sweet, he wish'd not to control . . .

See, in the rear of the warm sunny shower,
The visionary boy from shelter fly!
For now the storm of summer-rain is o'er,
And cool, and fresh, and fragrant is the sky.   265
And, lo! in the dark east, expanded high,
The rainbow brightens to the setting sun!
Fond fool, that deem'st the streaming glory nigh,
How vain the chace thine ardor has begun!
'Tis fled afar, ere half thy purposed race be run.   270

Yet couldst thou learn, that thus it fares with age,
When pleasure, wealth, or power the bosom warm,
This baffled hope might tame thy manhood's rage,
And Disappointment of her sting disarm.
But why should foresight thy fond heart alarm?   275
Perish the lore that deadens young desire!
Pursue, poor imp, th' imaginary charm,
Indulge gay Hope, and Fancy's pleasing fire:
Fancy and Hope too soon shall of themselves expire.

When the long-sounding curlew from afar   280
Loaded with loud lament the lonely gale,
Young Edwin, lighted by the evening star,
Lingering and listening wander'd down the vale.
There would he dream of graves, and corses pale;
And ghosts that to the charnel-dungeon throng,   285
And drag a length of clanking chain, and wail,
Till silenced by the owl's terrific song,
Or blast that shrieks by fits the shuddering isles along.

Or, when the setting moon, in crimson dyed,
Hung o'er the dark and melancholy deep,   290
To haunted stream, remote from man, he hied,
Where Fays of yore their revels wont to keep;
And there let Fancy rove at large, till sleep
A vision brought to his intranced sight.
And first, a wildly murmuring wind 'gan creep   295
Shrill to his ringing ear; then tapers bright,
With instantaneous gleam, illumed the vault of night.

Anon in view a portal's blazon'd arch
Arose; the trumpet bids the valves unfold;
And forth an host of little warriors march,   300
Grasping the diamond lance, and targe of gold.
Their look was gentle, their demeanour bold,
And green their helms, and green their silk attire;
And here and there, right venerably old,
The long-robed minstrels wake the warbling wire,   305
And some with mellow breath the martial pipe inspire.

With merriment, and song, and timbrels clear,
A troop of dames from myrtle bowers advance;
The little warriors doff the targe and spear,
And loud enlivening strains provoke the dance.   310
They meet, they dart away, they wheel askance;
To right, to left, they thrid the flying maze;
Now bound aloft with vigorous spring, then glance
Rapid along: with many-colour'd rays
Of tapers, gems, and gold, the echoing forests blaze.   315

The dream is fled. Proud harbinger of day,
Who scar'dst the vision with thy clarion shrill,
Fell chanticleer! who oft hast reft away
My fancied good, and brought substantial ill!
O to thy cursed scream, discordant still,   320
Let harmony aye shut her gentle ear:
Thy boastful mirth let jealous rivals spill,
Insult thy crest, and glossy pinions tear,
And ever in thy dreams the ruthless fox appear.

Forbear, my Muse. Let Love attune thy line.   325
Revoke the spell. Thine Edwin frets not so.
For how should he at wicked chance repine,
Who feels from every change amusement flow?
Even now his eyes with smiles of rapture glow,
As on he wanders through the scenes of morn,   330
Where the fresh flowers in living lustre blow,
Where thousand pearls the dewy lawns adorn,
A thousand notes of joy in every breeze are born.

But who the melodies of morn can tell?
The wild brook babbling down the mountain side;   335
The lowing herd; the sheepfold's simple bell;
The pipe of early shepherd dim descried
In the lone valley; echoing far and wide
The clamorous horn along the cliffs above;
The hollow murmur of the ocean-tide;   340
The hum of bees, and linnet's lay of love,
And the full choir that wakes the universal grove.

The cottage-curs at early pilgrim bark;
Crown'd with her pail the tripping milkmaid sings;
The whistling plowman stalks afield; and, hark!   345
Down the rough slope the ponderous waggon rings;
Through rustling corn the hare astonish'd springs;
Slow tolls the village-clock the drowsy hour;
The partridge bursts away on whirring wings;
Deep mourns the turtle in sequester'd bower,   350
And shrill lark carols clear from her aërial tour.

Thomas Percy, *Reliques of Ancient English Poetry* (1765):
The Spanish Lady's Love; William Hamilton of Bangour,
The Braes of Yarrow

Suggested date of reading: by 1785

Thomas Percy's anthology of folk ballads and popular songs was among the most popular collections of its time and first read by Wordsworth when a schoolboy at Hawkshead. It would remain a powerful influence on him throughout his life; in fact, he would turn to it during the 1790s when considering the poetic manner he wished to follow in his mature work. As late as 1842 he ranked it alongside Burns and Cowper, 'whose writings, in conjunction with Percy's Reliques, powerfully counter-acted the mischievous influence of Darwin's dazzling manner, and the extravagance of Schiller's dramas and other German Writers upon my taste and natural tendencies'. Despite its importance to him, Wordsworth was in the habit of borrowing other people's copies – most notably Coleridge's – until he purchased his own, in Hamburg, on 1 October 1798. (His copy is now at Harvard University.)

In his 'Essay, Supplementary to the Preface' (1815) Wordsworth said that the *Reliques* was second in importance only to Thomson's *Seasons*; it was 'collected, new-modelled, and in many instances (if such a contradiction in terms may be used) composed by the Editor, Dr. Percy'. Wordsworth went on to deplore Dr Johnson's attacks on the *Reliques* "mid the little senate to which he gave laws', but commended the fact that Percy, 'while he was writing under a mask . . . had not wanted resolution to follow his genius into the regions of true simplicity and genuine pathos'.

Two of Percy's ballads are included here, both of which Wordsworth singled out for special comment. Of the first, 'The Spanish Lady's Love', he admired 'the form of stanza, as suitable to dialogue'; 'The Braes of Yarrow' by William Hamilton of Bangour is a precursor of Wordsworth's own Yarrow poems, and was widely anthologised – not just in Percy, but in Knox's *Elegant Extracts* and other standard texts. Wordsworth acknowledged its importance in a headnote to 'Yarrow Unvisited' when it appeared in 1807:

> See the various Poems the scene of which is laid upon the Banks of the Yarrow; in particular, the exquisite Ballad of Hamilton, beginning

Busk ye, busk ye my bonny, bonny Bride,
Busk ye, busk ye my winsome Marrow!

The Spanish Lady's Love

This beautiful old ballad most probably took its rise from
one of those descents made on the Spanish coasts in the time
of queen Elizabeth: in all likelihood from that which is cele-
brated in the foregoing ballad.

Printed from an ancient black letter copy, corrected in
part by the Editor's folio MS.

Will you hear a Spanish lady,
How she wooed an English man?
Garments gay as rich as may be
Decked with jewels she had on.
Of a comely countenance and grace was she,   5
And by birth and parentage of high degree.

As his prisoner there he kept her,
In his hands her life did lye;
Cupid's bands did tye them faster
By the liking of an eye.   10
In his courteous company was all her joy,
To favour him in any thing she was not coy.

But at last there came commandment
For to set the ladies free,
With their jewels still adorned,   15
None to do them injury.
Then said this lady mild, Full woe is me,
O let me still sustain this kind captivity!

Gallant captain, shew some pity
To a ladye in distresse;   20
Leave me not within this city,
For to dye in heavinesse:
Thou hast set this present day my body free,
But my heart in prison still remains with thee.

'How should'st thou, fair lady, love me,   25
   Whom thou knowst thy countrys foe?
Thy fair wordes make me suspect thee:
   'Serpents lie where flowers grow.'
All the harm I wishe to thee, most courteous knight,
God grant the same upon my head may fully light.   30

   Blessed be the time and season,
      That you came on Spanish ground;
   If you may our foes be termed,
      Gentle foes we have you found:
With our city, you have won our hearts each one,   35
Then to your country bear away, that is your own.

   'Rest you still, most gallant lady;
      Rest you still, and weep no more;
   Of fair lovers there are plenty,
      Spain doth yield you wonderous store.'   40
Spaniards fraught with jealousy we oft do find,
But English men throughout the world are counted kind.

   Leave me not unto a Spaniard,
      Thou alone enjoyst my heart;
   I am lovely, young and tender,   45
      Love is likewise my desert:
Still to serve thee day and night my mind is prest;
The wife of every English man is counted blest.

   'It would be a shame, fair lady,
      For to bear a woman hence;   50
   English soldiers never carry
      Any such without offence.'
I'll quickly change myself, if it be so,
And like a page will follow thee, where'er thou go,

   'I have neither gold nor silver   55
      To maintain thee in this case,
   And to travel is great charges,
      As you know in every place.'
My chains and jewels every one shall be thy own,
And eke ten thousand pounds in gold that lies unknown.

'On the seas are many dangers,
    Many storms do there arise,
Which will be to ladies dreadful,
    And force tears from watery eyes.'
Well in troth I shall endure extremity,   65
For I could find in heart to lose my life for thee.

'Courteous ladye, leave this fancy,
    Here comes all that breeds the strife;
I in England have already
    A sweet woman to my wife;   70
I will not falsify my vow for gold nor gain,
Nor yet for all the fairest dames that live in Spain.'

O how happy is that woman
    That enjoys so true a friend!
Many happy days God send her;   75
    Of my suit I make an end:
On my knees I pardon crave for my offence,
Which did from love and true affection first commence.

Commend me to thy lovely lady,
    Bear to her this chain of gold;   80
And these bracelets for a token;
    Grieving that I was so bold:
All my jewels in like sort bear thou with thee,
For they are fitting for thy wife, but not for me.

I will spend my days in prayer.   85
    Love and all his laws defye;
In a nunnery will I shrowd mee,
    Far from any companye:
But ere my prayers have an end, be sure of this,
To pray for thee and for thy love I will not miss.   90

Thus farewell, most gallant captain!
    Farewell too my heart's content!
Count not Spanish ladies wanton,
    Though to thee my love was bent:
Joy and true prosperity goe still with thee!   95
The like fall ever to thy share, most fair ladìe.

The Braes of Yarrow,

IN IMITATION OF THE ANCIENT SCOTS MANNER,

– was written by William Hamilton of Bangour, esq; who died March 25, 1754, aged 50. It is printed from an elegant edition of his Poems published at Edinburgh, 1760: 12mo.

A. Busk ye, busk ye, my bonny bonny bride,
  Busk ye, busk ye, my winsome marrow,
 Busk ye, busk ye, my bonny bonny bride,
  And think nae mair on the Braes of Yarrow.

B. Where gat ye that bonny bonny bride?   5
  Where gat ye that winsome marrow?
A. I gat her where I dare na weil be seen,
  Puing the birks on the Braes of Yarrow.

 Weep not, weep not, my bonny bonny bride,
  Weep not, weep not, my winsome marrow,   10
 Nor let thy heart lament to leive
  Puing the birks on the Braes of Yarrow.

B. Why does she weep, thy bonny bonny bride?
  Why does she weep thy winsome marrow?
 And why dare ye nae mair weil be seen   15
  Puing the birks on the Braes of Yarrow?

A. Lang maun she weep, lang maun she, maun she weep,
  Lang maun she weep with dule and sorrow,
 And lang maun I nae mair weil be seen
  Puing the birks on the Braes of Yarrow.   20

 For she has tint her luver, luver dear,
  Her luver dear, the cause of sorrow,
 And I hae slain the comliest swain
  That eir pu'd birks on the Braes of Yarrow.

 Why rins thy stream, O Yarrow, Yarrow, reid?   25
  Why on thy braes heard the voice of sorrow?
 And why you melancholious weids
  Hung on the bonny birks of Yarrow?

           1785

What's yonder floats on the rueful rueful flude?
   What's yonder floats? O dule and sorrow!   30
O 'tis he the comely swain I slew
   Upon the duleful Braes of Yarrow.

Wash, O wash his wounds, his wounds in tears,
   His wounds in tears with dule and sorrow,
And wrap his limbs in mourning weids,   35
   And lay him on the Braes of Yarrow.

Then build, then build, ye sisters, sisters sad,
   Ye sisters sad, his tomb with sorrow,
And weep around in waeful wise
   His hapless fate on the Braes of Yarrow.   40

Curse ye, curse ye, his useless, useless shield,
   My arm that wrought the deed of sorrow,
The fatal spear that pierc'd his breast,
   His comely breast on the Braes of Yarrow.

Did I not warn thee, not to, not to luve?   45
   And warn from fight? but to my sorrow
Too rashly bauld a stronger arm
   Thou met'st, and and fel'st on the Braes of Yarrow.

Sweet smells the birk, green grows, green grows the grass,
   Yellow on Yarrow's bank the gowan,   50
Fair hangs the apple frae the rock,
   Sweet the wave of Yarrow flowan.

Flows Yarrow sweet? as sweet, as sweet flows Tweed,
   As green its grass, its gowan as yellow,
As sweet smells on its braes the birk,   55
   The apple frae its rock as mellow.

Fair was thy luve, fair fair indeed thy luve,
   In flow'ry bands thou didst him fetter;
Tho' he was fair, and weil beluv'd again
   Than me he never luv'd thee better.   60

Busk ye, then busk, my bonny bonny bride,
  Busk ye, busk ye, my winsome marrow,
Busk ye, and luve me on the banks of Tweed,
  And think nae mair on the Braes of Yarrow.

C.   How can I busk a bonny bonny bride?   65
  How can I busk a winsome marrow?
How luve him upon the banks of Tweed,
  That slew my luve on the Braes of Yarrow?

O Yarrow fields, may never never rain,
  Now dew thy tender blossoms cover,   70
For there was basely slain my luve,
  My luve, as he had not been a lover.

The boy put on his robes, his robes of green,
  His purple vest, 'twas my awn sewing:
Ah! wretched me! I little, little ken'd   75
  He was in these to meet his ruin.

The boy took out his milk-white milk-white steed,
  Unheedful of my dule and sorrow;
But ere the toofall of the night
  He lay a corps on the Braes of Yarrow.   80

Much I rejoyc'd that waeful waeful day;
  I sang, my voice the woods returning:
But lang ere night the spear was flown,
  That slew my luve, and left me mourning.

What can my barbarous barbarous father do,   85
  But with his cruel rage pursue me?
My luver's blood is on thy spear,
  How can'st thou, barbarous man, then woe me?

My happy sisters may be, may be proud
  With cruel, and ungentle scoffin',   90
May bid me seek on Yarrow's Braes
  My luver nailed in his coffin.

My brother Douglas may upbraid, upbraid,
 And strive with threatning words to muve me:
My luver's blood is on thy spear,   95
 How canst thou ever bid me luve thee?

Yes, yes, prepare the bed, the bed of luve,
 With bridal sheets my body cover,
Unbar, ye bridal maids, the door,
 Let in the expected husbande lover.   100

But who the expected husband husband is?
 His hands, methinks, are bath'd in slaughter,
Ah me! what ghastly spectre's yon,
 Comes in his pale shroud, bleeding after?

Pale as he is, here lay him, lay him down,   110
 O lay his cold head on my pillow;
Take aff, take aff these bridal weids,
 And crown my careful head with willow.

Pale tho' thou art, yet best, yet best beluv'd,
 O could my warmth to life restore thee!   115
Yet lye all night between my breists,
 No youth lay ever there before thee.

Pale, pale indeed, O luvely luvely youth,
 Forgive, forgive so foul a slaughter,
And lye all night between my breists,   120
 No youth shall ever lye there after.

A.   Return, return, O mournful, mournful bride,
 Return and dry thy useless sorrow,
Thy luver heeds nought of thy sighs,
 He lyes a corps in the Braes of Yarrow.   125

Sneyd Davies, *Against Indolence. An Epistle*

Suggested date of reading: by 1785

On 22 June 1830 Wordsworth wrote to Alexander Dyce about Sir Egerton Brydges' reported obsession with the 'excellencies' of Sneyd Davies:

> Of some of these Poets whom he would include in a new Corpus I am utterly ignorant; but one of them has produced an exceedingly pleasing poem with a very original air. It begins 'There was a time my dear Cornwallis, when'. I first met with it in Dr Enfield's Exercises of Elocution or Speaker, I forget which. It is by Davies, and well merits preservation.

Wordsworth refers to 'Against Indolence. An Epistle', published in Enfield's *Speaker* from the first edition of 1774 onwards. He probably encountered it first as a schoolboy at Hawkshead, where Enfield would have been a standard text.

Born in 1709, Davies was eminent in literary circles in Lichfield until his death in 1769. He wrote poems in Latin, imitations of Horace's epistles, serious and burlesque imitations of Milton, and imitations of Swift. His friend Anna Seward is said to have wept 'tears of delight' at his earnest and tremulous voice, and thought him a spirit 'beatified before his time'. He numbered among his closest friends Frederick Cornwallis, Archbishop of Canterbury – addressee of 'Against Indolence' – whom he met when they were schoolboys together at Eton.

Against Indolence
An Epistle

In frolick's hour, ere serious thought had birth,
There was a time, my dear CORNWALLIS, when
The Muse would take me on her airy wing
And waft to views romantic; there present
Some motley vision, shade and sun: the cliff   5
O'erhanging, sparkling brooks, and ruins grey:
Bade me meanders trace, and catch the form

Of various clouds, and rainbows learn to paint.
   Sometimes Ambition, brushing by, would twitch
My mantle, and, with winning look sublime,   10
Allure to follow. What tho' steep the track,
Her mountain's top would overpay, when climb'd,
The scaler's toil; her temple there was fine,
And lovely thence the prospects. She cou'd tell
Where laurels grew, whence many a wreath antique;   15
But more advis'd to shun the barren twig,
(What is immortal verdure without fruit?)
And woo some thriving art: her numerous mines
Were open to the searcher's skill and pains.
   Caught by th' harangue, heart beat, and flutt'ring pulse   20
Sounded irregular marches to be gone –
What, pause a moment when Ambition calls?
No, the blood gallops to the distant goal,
And throbs to reach it. Let the lame sit still.
When Fortune gentle, at th' hill's verge extreme,   25
Array'd in decent garb, but somewhat thin,
Smiling approach'd; and what occasion, ask'd,
Of climbing: She, already provident,
Had cater'd well, if stomach cou'd digest
Her viands, and a palate not too nice: 30
Unfit, she said, for perilous attempt;
That manly limb requir'd, and sinew tough:
She took, and laid me in a vale remote,
Amid the gloomy scene of fir and yew,
On poppy beds, where Morpheus strew'd the ground;   35
Obscurity her curtain round me drew,
And Syren Sloth a dull quietus sung.
   Sithence no fairy lights, no quick'ning ray,
No stir of pulse, nor objects to entice
Abroad the spirits: but the cloyster'd heart   40
Sits squat at home, like pagod in a niche
Obscure, or grandees with nod-watching eye,
And folded arms, in presence of the throne,
Turk, or Indostan. – Cities, forums, courts,
And prating sanhedrims, and drumming wars,   45
Affect no more than stories told to bed
Lethargic, which at intervals the sick
Hears and forgets, and wakes to doze again.
Instead of converse and variety,

The same trite round, the same stale silent scene; 50
Such are thy comforts, blessed Solitude! –
But Innocence is there, but Peace all kind,
And simple Quiet with her downy couch,
Meads lowing, tune of birds, and lapse of streams,
And saunter with a book, and warbling Muse 55
In praise of hawthorns – Life's whole business this!
Is it to bask i' th' sun? if so a snail
Were happy crawling on a southern wall.
   Why sits content upon a cottage sill
At eventide, and blesseth the coarse meal 60
In sooty corner? why sweet slumber wait
Th' hard pallet? Not because from haunt remote
Sequester'd in a dingle's bushy lap:
'Tis labour makes the peasant's sav'ry fare,
And works out his repose: for Ease must ask 65
The leave of Diligence to be enjoy'd.
   Oh! listen not to that enchantress Ease
With seeming smile; her palatable cup
By standing grows insipid; and beware
The bottom, for there's poison in the lees. 70
What health impair'd, and crowds inactive maim'd!
What daily martyrs to her sluggish cause!
Less strict devoir the Russ and Persian claim
Despotic; and as subjects long inur'd
To servile burthen grow supine and tame, 75
So fares it with our sov'reign and her train.
   What tho' with lure fallacious she pretend
From worldly bondage to set free, what gain
Her votaries? What avails from iron chains
Exempt, if rosy fetters bind as fast? 80
   Bestir, and answer your creation's end.
Think we that man, with vig'rous pow'r endow'd
And room to stretch, was destin'd to sit still?
Sluggards are Nature's rebels, slight her laws,
Nor live up to the terms on which they hold 85
Their vital lease. Laborious terms and hard;
But such the tenure of our earthly state!
Riches and fame are Industry's reward;
The nimble runner courses Fortune down,
And then he banquets, for she feeds the bold. 90
   Think what you owe your country, what yourself.

71 *1785*

If splendor charm not, yet avoid the scorn,
That treads on lowly stations. Think of some
Assiduous booby mounting o'er your head,
And thence with saucy grandeur looking down: 95
Think of (Reflection's stab!) the pitying friend
With shoulder shrugg'd and sorry. Think that Time
Has golden minutes, if discreetly seiz'd:
And if some sad example, indolent,
To warn and scare be wanting – think of me.   100

William Collins, *Odes* (1746): *Ode to Evening, Ode on the Death of Mr Thomson*

Suggested date of reading: by 1785

> These three Writers, Thomson, Collins, and Dyer, had more
> poetic Imagination than any of their Contemporaries . . .
> (Wordsworth to Alexander Dyce, 12 January 1829)

Wordsworth's high regard for Collins is underlined by the fact that
at Rydal Mount he possessed a first edition of the *Odes* – rare
enough in its own time, as almost the entire run of 1,000 copies was
destroyed when it failed to sell. 'What sale had Collins' Poems
during his lifetime, or during the fourteen years after his death, and
how great has been the sale since! the product of it if secured to his
family, would have been an independence to them', Wordsworth
lamented in 1808. It was an injustice that he thought about often,
as it was a product of the same legislation that might impoverish his
own family in the event of his own death. (At that time copyright
law allowed an author – or his family – to claim royalties for only 28
years after publication. Wordsworth protested against it intermit-
tently, most publicly with a letter to *The Kendal Mercury* in 1838.)
Again, in the 'Essay, Supplementary to the Preface' 1815, he
lamented Collins' fate: 'The notice which his poems attained during
his lifetime was so small, and of course the sale so insignificant, that
not long before his death he deemed it right to repay to the book-
seller the sum which he had advanced for them, and threw the
edition into the fire.'

Collins' odes were among the earliest poetry Wordsworth read, at
Hawkshead Grammar School or even before. By then (the 1780s)
he was a popular and widely anthologised poet, and it is likely that
Wordsworth encountered the odes in a volume such as Enfield's
Speaker. He would later have ready access to Collins' poetry
through Anderson's *British Poets*, which he acquired in 1800.

Wordsworth praised 'Ode to Evening' for its 'description of
exquisite beauty describing the introduction of Evening', and
borrowed a line from 'Ode on the Death of Mr Thomson' in one of
his earliest sonnets at Cambridge,[1] repeating the allusion in the

---

[1] 'How Rich in Front – with Twilight's Tinge Impressed', *The Earliest
Wordsworth: Poems 1785-1790* ed. Duncan Wu (Carcanet, 2002), p. 53.

'Remembrance of Collins' and 'Lines Written near Richmond upon the Thames', both published in *Lyrical Ballads* (1798). In the 'Essay, Supplementary to the Preface', he commended Collins' elegy for Thomson:

> When Thomson died, Collins breathed forth his regrets in an Elegiac Poem, in which he pronounces a poetical curse upon *him* who should regard with insensibility the place where the Poet's remains were deposited. The Poems of the mourner himself have now passed through innumerable editions, and are universally known; but if, when Collins died, the same kind of imprecation had been pronounced by a surviving admirer, small is the number whom it would not have comprehended.

These texts are edited from Anderson's *British Poets* volume 9 (1795) – the form in which they were known to Wordsworth.

Ode to Evening

If aught of oaten stop, or pastoral song,
May hope, chaste Eve, to soothe thy modest ear,
   Like thy own solemn springs,
   Thy springs, and dying gales;

O nymph reserv'd, while now the bright-hair'd Sun   5
Sits in yon western tent, whose cloudy skirts,
   With brede ethereal wove,
   O'erhang his wavy bed:

Now air is hush'd, save where the weak-ey'd bat,
With short shrill shriek flits by on leathern wing,   10
   Or where the beetle winds
   His small but sullen horn,

As oft he rises 'midst the twilight path,
Against the pilgrim borne in heedless hum;
   Now teach me, maid compos'd,   15
   To breathe some soften'd strain,

Whose numbers stealing through thy darkening vale,
May not unseemly with its stillness suit,
   As, musing slow, I hail
   Thy genial lov'd return!   20

For when thy folding-star arising shows
His paly circlet, at his warning lamp
   The fragrant hours, and elves
   Who slept in buds the day,

And many a nymph who wreathes her brows with sedge,   25
And sheds the freshening dew, and lovelier still,
   The pensive pleasures sweet
   Prepare thy shadowy car.

Then let me rove some wild and heathy scene,
Or find some ruin 'midst its dreary dells,   30
   Whose walls more awful nod
   By thy religious gleams.

Or if chill blustering winds, or driving rain,
Prevent my willing feet, be mine the hut,
   That from the mountain's side,   35
   Views wilds, and swelling floods,

And hamlets brown, and dim-discover'd spires,
And hears their simple bell, and marks o'er all
   Thy dewy fingers draw
   The gradual dusky veil.   40

While Spring shall pour his showers, as oft he wont,
And bathe thy breathing tresses, meekest Eve!
   While Summer loves to sport
   Beneath thy lingering light:

While sallow Autumn fills thy lap with leaves,   45
Or Winter yelling through the troublous air,
   Affrights thy shrinking train,
   And rudely rends thy robes:

So long, regardful of thy quiet rule,
Shall Fancy, Friendship, Science, smiling Peace,   50
    Thy gentlest influence own,
    And love thy favourite name!

Ode
ON THE DEATH OF MR THOMSON

*The Scene of the following Stanzas is supposed to lie
on the Thames, near Richmond.*

In yonder grave a Druid lies
    Where slowly winds the stealing wave!
The year's best sweets shall duteous rise,
    To deck its poet's sylvan grave!

In yon deep bed of whispering reeds   5
    His airy harp[1] shall now be laid,
That he, whose heart in sorrow bleeds,
    May love through life the soothing shade.

Then maids and youths shall linger here,
    And, while its sounds at distance swell,   10
Shall sadly seem in pity's ear
    To hear the woodland pilgrim's knell.

Remembrance oft shall haunt the shore
    When Thames in summer wreaths is drest,
And oft suspend the dashing oar   15
    To bid his gentle spirit rest!

And oft as ease and health retire
    To breezy lawn, or forest deep,
The friend shall view yon whitening[2] spire,
    And 'mid the varied landscape weep.   20

---

[1] The harp of Æolus, of which see a description in the Castle of Indolence.
[2] Mr Thomson was buried in Richmond church.

But thou, who own'st that earthly bed,
   Ah! what will every dirge avail?
Or tears, which love and pity shed,
   That mourn beneath the gliding sail!

Yet lives there one, whose heedless eye   25
   Shall scorn thy pale shrine glimmering near?
With him, sweet bard, may fancy die,
   And joy desert the blooming year.

But thou, lorn stream, whose sullen tide
   No sedge-crown'd sisters now attend,   30
Now waft me from the green hill's side
   Whose cold turf hides the buried friend!

And see, the fairy vallies fade,
   Dun night has veil'd the solemn view!
Yet once again, dear parted shade,   35
   Meek nature's child, again adieu!

The genial meads[3] assign'd to bless
   Thy life, shall mourn thy early doom!
Their hinds and shepherd girls shall dress
   With simple hands thy rural tomb.   40

Long, long, thy stone, and pointed clay
   Shall melt the musing Briton's eyes,
O! vales, and wild woods, shall he say,
   In yonder grave your Druid lies!

---

[3] Mr Thomson resided in the neighbourhood of Richmond some time
before his death.

Robert Burns, *Poems* (Kilmarnock, 1786): *The Vision,*
To a Mouse, Despondency, An Ode, To a Mountain-Daisy,
Epistle to J. L*****k

Date of reading: July 1786

With the Poems of Burns I became acquainted almost immedi-
ately upon their first appearance in 1786 . . . Familiarity with the
dialect of the border Counties of Cumberland and
Westmoreland made it easy for me not only to understand but
to feel them. It was not so with his Contemporary or rather his
Predecessor Cowper, – as appears from one of his letters. This
is to be regretted; for the simplicity the truth and the vigour of
Burns would have strongly recommended him, notwithstanding
occasional coarseness, to the sympathies of Cowper, and
ensured the approval of his judgement.

(Wordsworth, 1842 note to *The Grave of Burns*)

This tribute to Burns and Cowper is consistent with the high regard
Wordsworth and Coleridge expressed for both throughout their
lives. That Wordsworth was one of Burns' first readers is certain; he
was probably lent a copy of the Kilmarnock edition (1786) by his
teacher, Thomas Bowman. Just over a year later, in the summer of
1787, shortly before going up to Cambridge, he obtained a copy of
Burns' poems for Dorothy through the local book club in Penrith,
as she told her best friend, Jane Pollard:

My Br Wm was here at the time I got your Letter, I told him that
you had recommended the book to me, he had read it and
admired many of the pieces very much; and promised to get it
me at the book-club, which he did. I was very much pleased with
them indeed, the one which you mentioned to me is I think very
comical, I mean the address to a Louse; there is one, to a moun-
tain daisy which is very pretty.

Doubtless 'To a Louse' and 'To a Mountain-Daisy' were enjoyed
equally by William; perhaps he directed her attention to them as
well. Burns' choice of humble objects as a fit subject for poetry
registered immediately, like Cowper's mock-heroic treatment of the
everyday ('I sing the sofa'). In later years Wordsworth honoured
them for the fact that, as he said of Burns' poems in 1799, 'every
where you have the presence of human life'. He continued:

The communications that proceed from Burns come to the mind with the life and charm of recognitions. But Burns also is energetic solemn and sublime in sentiment, and profound in feeling. His Ode to Despondency I can never read without the deepest agitation.

When Wordsworth says 'agitation', he means emotional intensity – and to react to a poem thus was the highest compliment he could pay it.

At the same time he was fascinated by the way in which Burns was capable of writing poems – some not very good – that for all their faults appealed to a mass audience. In September 1833, when he was in his sixties, he told Eliza Fletcher that:

> Burns so far as he remembered was the only Poet of *real genius* who may be called a popular poet – and it was not his genius but his vulgarity that made him popular. Shakespear he said was not read by the common people – But Burns was read by all Classes because he had vulgarity enough for the lowest, such as that sort of trash 'An honest man for a' that'. – sentiments that a man of good manners would not descend to – and he had nature pathos and elevation for persons of the highest and most refined taste.

Wordsworth would always be impressed that Burns could write 'trash' such as 'For a' that and a' that' and 'Scots wha' hae',[1] that nonetheless found a home in the minds of 'common people', as well as poems that embodied Wordsworthian ideals of 'nature pathos and elevation'. Like many, he hankered after such success, but was never to find it.

The poems in the Kilmarnock volume remained favourites throughout his life, and it is from there that the present texts are edited. One of the things he admired about them was the way in which Burns created a character for himself in them, as he said in his *Letter to a Friend of Robert Burns* (1816):

> On the basis of his human character he has reared a poetic one, which with more or less distinctness presents itself to view in

---

[1] Some of his harshest comments were reserved for it; he once told Felicia Hemans that 'Scots wha' hae' was 'overrated! – trash! – stuff! – miserable inanity! without a thought – without an image! etc. etc. etc. – then he recited the piece in a tone of unutterable scorn; and concluded with a *Da Capo* of "wretched stuff"'.

almost every part of his earlier, and, in my estimation, his most valuable verses. This poetic fabric, dug out of the quarry of genuine humanity, is airy and spiritual: – and though the materials, in some parts, are coarse, and the disposition is often fantastic and irregular, yet the whole is agreeable and strikingly attractive.

The Vision

DUAN FIRST[1]

The sun had clos'd the winter-day,
The Curlers quat their roaring play,
And hunger'd Maukin taen her way
   To kail-yards green,
While faithless snaws ilk step betray   5
   Whare she has been.

The Thresher's weary flingin-tree,
The lee-lang day had tir'd me;
And when the Day had clos'd his e'e,
   Far i' the West,   10
Ben i' the Spence, right pensivelie,
   I gaed to rest.

There, lanely, by the ingle-cheek,
I sat and ey'd the spewing reek,
That fill'd, wi' hoast-provoking smeek,   15
   The auld, clay biggin;
And heard the restless rattons squeak
   About the riggin.

---

[1] Duan, a term of Ossian's for the different divisions of a digressive Poem. (Burns' note)

All in this mottie, misty clime,
I backward mus'd on wasted time,   20
How I had spent my youthfu' prime,
                    An' done nae-thing,
But stringing blethers up in rhyme
                    For fools to sing.

    Had I to guid advice but harket,   25
I might, by this, hae led a market,
Or strutted in a Bank and clarket
                    My Cash-Account;
While here, half-mad, half-fed, half-sarket,
                    Is a' th' amount.   30

    I started, mutt'ring blockhead! coof!
And heav'd on high my wauket loof,
To swear by a' yon starry roof,
                    Or some rash aith,
That I, henceforth, would be rhyme-proof   35
                    Till my last breath –

    When click! the string the snick did draw;
And jee! the door gaed to the wa';
And by my ingle-lowe I saw,
                    Now bleezan bright,   40
A tight, outlandish Hizzie, braw,
                    Come full in sight.

    Ye need na doubt, I held my whisht;
The infant aith, half-form'd, was crusht;
I glowr'd as eerie's I'd been dusht,   45
                    In some wild glen;
When sweet, like modest Worth, she blusht,
                    And stepped ben.

    Green, slender, leaf-clad Holly-boughs
Were twisted, gracefu', round her brows,   50
I took her for some SCOTTISH MUSE,
                    By that same token;
And come to stop those reckless vows,
                    Would soon been broken.

1786

A 'hare-brain'd, sentimental trace'   55
Was strongly marked in her face;
A wildly-witty, rustic grace
        Shone full upon her;
Her eye, ev'n turn'd on empty space,
        Beam'd keen with Honor.   60

   Down flow'd her robe, a tartan sheen,
Till half a leg was scrimply seen;
And such a leg! my BESS, I ween,
        Could only peer it;
Sae straught, sae taper, tight and clean,   65
        Nane else came near it.

   Her Mantle large, of greenish hue,
My gazing wonder chiefly drew;
Deep lights and shades, bold-mingling, threw
        A lustre grand;   70
And seem'd, to my astonish'd view,
        A well-known Land.

   Here, rivers in the sea were lost;
There, mountains to the skies were tost:
Here, tumbling billows mark'd the coast,   75
        With surging foam;
There, distant shone, Art's lofty boast,
        The lordly dome.

   Here, DOON pour'd down his far-fetch'd floods;
There, well-fed IRWINE stately thuds: 80
Auld, hermit AIRE staw thro' his woods,
        On to the shore;
And many a lesser torrent scuds,
        With seeming roar.

   Low, in a sandy valley spread,   85
An ancient BOROUGH rear'd her head;
Still, as in Scottish Story read,
        She boasts a Race,
To ev'ry nobler virtue bred,
        And polish'd grace.   90

With musing-deep, astonished stare,
I view'd the heavenly-seeming Fair;
A whisp'ring throb did witness bear
        Of kindred sweet,
When with an elder Sister's air   95
        She did me greet.

'All hail! my own inspired Bard!
In me thy native Muse regard!
Nor longer mourn thy fate is hard,
        Thus poorly low!   100
I come to give thee such reward,
        As we bestow.

Know, the great Genius of this Land,
Has many a light, aerial band,
Who, all beneath his high command,   105
        Harmoniously,
As Arts or Arms they understand,
        Their labors ply.

They SCOTIA's Race among them share;
Some fire the Sodger on to dare;   110
Some rouse the Patriot up to bare
        Corruption's heart:
Some teach the Bard, a darling care,
        The tuneful Art.

'Mong swelling floods of reeking gore,   115
They ardent, kindling spirits pour;
Or, mid the venal Senate's roar,
        They, sightless, stand,
To mend the honest Patriot-lore,
        And grace the hand.   120

Hence, FULLARTON, the brave and young;
Hence, DEMPSTER's truth-prevailing tongue;
Hence, sweet harmonious BEATTIE sung
        His "Minstrel lays;"
Or tore, with noble ardour stung,   125
        The Sceptic's bays.

1786

To lower Orders are assign'd,
The humbler ranks of Human-kind,
The rustic Bard, the lab'ring Hind,
        The Artisan;   130
All chuse, as, various they're inclin'd,
        The various man.

When yellow waves the heavy grain,
The threat'ning Storm, some, strongly, rein;
Some teach to meliorate the plain,   135
        With tillage-skill;
And some instruct the Shepherd-train,
        Blythe o'er the hill.

Some hint the Lover's harmless wile;
Some grace the Maiden's artless smile;   140
Some soothe the Lab'rer's weary toil,
        For humble gains,
And make his cottage-scenes beguile
        His cares and pains.

Some, bounded to a district-space,   145
Explore at large Man's infant race,
To mark the embryotic trace,
        Of rustic Bard;
And careful note each op'ning grace,
        A guide and guard.   150

Of these am I – COILA my name;
And this district as mine I claim,
Where once the Campbells, chiefs of fame,
        Held ruling pow'r:
I mark'd thy embryo-tuneful flame,   155
        Thy natal hour.

With future hope, I oft would gaze,
Fond, on thy little, early ways,
Thy rudely-caroll'd, chiming phrase,
        In uncouth rhymes,   160
Fir'd at the simple, artless lays
        Of other times.

I saw thee seek the sounding shore,
Delighted with the dashing roar;
Or when the North his fleecy store   165
            Drove thro' the sky,
I saw grim Nature's visage hoar,
            Struck thy young eye.

Or when the deep-green-mantl'd Earth,
Warm-cherish'd ev'ry floweret's birth,   170
And joy and music pouring forth,
            In ev'ry grove,
I saw thee eye the gen'ral mirth
            With boundless love.

When ripen'd fields, and azure skies,   175
Call'd forth the Reaper's rustling noise,
I saw thee leave their ev'ning joys,
            And lonely stalk,
To vent thy bosom's swelling rise,
            In pensive walk.   180

When youthful Love, warm-blushing, strong,
Keen-shivering shot thy nerves along,
Those accents, grateful to thy tongue,
            Th' adored Name,
I taught thee how to pour in song,   185
            To soothe thy flame.

I saw thy pulse's maddening play,
Wild-send thee Pleasure's devious way,
Misled by Fancy's meteor-ray,
            By Passion driven;   190
But yet the light that led astray,
            Was light from Heaven.

I taught thy manners-painting strains,
The loves, the ways of simple swains,
Till now, o'er all my wide domains,   195
            Thy fame extends;
And some, the pride of Coila's plains,
            Become thy friends.

Thou canst not learn, nor I can show,
To paint with Thomson's landscape-glow;   200
Or wake the bosom-melting throe,
        With Shenstone's art;
Or pour, with Gray, the moving flow,
        Warm on the heart.

Yet all beneath th'unrivall'd Rose,   205
The lowly Daisy sweetly blows;
Tho' large the forest's Monarch throws
        His army shade,
Yet green the juicy Hawthorn grows,
        Adown the glade.   210

Then never murmur nor repine;
Strive in thy humble sphere to shine;
And trust me, not Potosi's mine,
        Nor Kings regard,
Can give a bliss o'ermatching thine,   215
        A rustic Bard.

To give my counsels all in one,
Thy tuneful flame still careful fan;
Preserve the dignity of Man,
        With Soul erect;   220
And trust, the UNIVERSAL PLAN
        Will all protect.

And wear thou this' – She solemn said,
And bound the Holly round my head:
The polish'd leaves, and berries red,   225
       · Did rustling play;
And, like a passing thought, she fled,
        In light away.

To a Mouse

On turning her up in her Nest, with the Plough, November, 1785

Wee, sleeket, cowran, tim'rous beastie,
  O, what a panic's in thy breastie!
Thou need na start awa sae hasty,
        Wi' bickering brattle!
I wad be laith to rin an' chase thee,   5
        Wi' murd'ring pattle!

  I'm truly sorry Man's dominion
Has broken Nature's social union,
An' justifies that ill opinion,
        Which makes thee startle,   10
At me, thy poor, earth-born companion,
        An' fellow-mortal!

  I doubt na, whyles, but thou may thieve;
What then? poor beastie, thou maun live!
A daimen-icker in a thrave   15
        'S a sma' request:
I'll get a blessin wi' the lave,
        An' never miss't!

  Thy wee-bit housie, too, in ruin!
It's silly wa's the win's are strewin!   20
An' naething, now, to big a new ane,
        O' foggage green!
An' bleak December's winds ensuin,
        Baith snell an' keen!

  Thou saw the fields laid bare an' wast,   25
An' weary Winter comin fast,
An' cozie here, beneath the blast,
        Thou thought to dwell,
Till crash! the cruel coulter past
        Out thro' thy cell.   30

1786

That wee-bit heap o' leaves an' stibble,
Has cost thee monie a weary nibble!
Now thou's turn'd out, for a' thy trouble,
      But house or hald,
To thole the Winter's sleety dribble,   35
      An' cranreuch cauld!

   But Mousie, thou art no thy-lane,
In proving foresight may be vain:
The best laid schemes o' Mice an' Men,
      Gang aft agley,   40
An' lea'e us nought but grief an' pain,
      For promis'd joy!

   Still, thou art blest, compar'd wi' me!
The present only toucheth thee:
But Och! I backward cast my e'e,   45
      On prospects drear!
An' forward, tho' I canna see,
      I guess an' fear!

Despondency, An Ode

I

Oppress'd with grief, oppress'd with care,
A burden more than I can bear,
   I set me down and sigh:
O Life! Thou art a galling load,
Along a rough, a weary road,   5
   To wretches such as I!
Dim-backward as I cast my view,
   What sick'ning Scenes appear!
What Sorrows yet may pierce me thro',
   Too justly I may fear!   10
     Still caring, despairing,
       Must be my bitter doom;
    My woes here, shall close ne'er,
     But with the closing tomb!

II

Happy! ye sons of Busy-life,   15
Who, equal to the bustling strife,
   No other view regard!
Ev'n when the wished end's deny'd,
Yet while the busy means are ply'd,
   They bring their own reward: 20
Whilst I, a hope-abandon'd wight,
   Unfitted with an aim,
Meet ev'ry sad-returning night,
   And joyless morn the same.
      You, bustling and justling,   25
        Forget each grief and pain;
      I, listless, yet restless,
        Find ev'ry prospect vain.

III

How blest the Solitary's lot,
Who, all-forgetting, all-forgot,   30
   Within his humble cell,
The cavern wild with tangling roots,
Sits o'er his newly-gather'd fruits,
   Beside his crystal well!
Or haply, to his ev'ning thought,   35
   By unfrequented stream,
The ways of men are distant brought,
   A faint-collected dream:
      While praising, and raising
        His thoughts to Heaven on high,   40
      As wand'ring, meand'ring,
        He views the solemn sky.

IV

Than I, no lonely Hermit plac'd
Where never human footstep trac'd,
   Less fit to play the part,   45
The lucky moment to improve,
And just to stop, and just to move,
   With self-respecting art:
But ah! those pleasures, Loves and Joys,
   Which I too keenly taste,   50

The Solitary can despise,
  Can want, and yet be blest!
    He needs not, he heeds not,
      Or human love or hate;
    Whilst I here, must cry here,   55
      At perfidy ingrate!

V

Oh, enviable, early days,
When dancing thoughtless Pleasure's maze,
  To Care, to Guilt unknown!
How ill exchang'd for riper times,   60
To feel the follies, or the crimes,
  Of others, or my own!
Ye tiny elves that guiltless sport,
  Like linnets in the bush,
Ye little know the ills ye court,   65
  When Manhood is your wish!
    The losses, the crosses,
      That active man engage;
    The fears all, the tears all,
      Of dim declining Age!   70

To a Mountain-Daisy

On turning one down, with the Plough, in April 1786

Wee, modest, crimson-tipped flow'r,
Thou's met me in an evil hour;
For I maun crush amang the stoure
    Thy slender stem:
To spare thee now is past my pow'r,   5
    Thou bonie gem.

Alas! it's no thy neebor sweet,
The bonie Lark, companion meet!
Bending thee 'mang the dewy weet!
    Wi's spreckl'd breast,   10
When upward-springing, blythe, to greet
    The purpling East.

Cauld blew the bitter-biting North
Upon thy early, humble birth;
Yet chearfully thou glinted forth   15
        Amid the storm,
Scarce rear'd above the Parent-earth
        Thy tender form.

The flaunting flow'rs our Gardens yield,
High-shelt'ring woods and wa's maun shield,   20
But thou, beneath the random bield
        O' clod or stane,
Adorns the histie stibble-field,
        Unseen, alane.

There, in thy scanty mantle clad,   25
Thy snawie bosom sun-ward spread,
Thou lifts thy unassuming head
        In humble guise;
But now the share uptears thy bed,
        And low thou lies!   30

Such is the fate of artless Maid,
Sweet flow'ret of the rural shade!
By Love's simplicity betray'd,
        And guileless trust,
Till she, like thee, all soil'd, is laid   35
        Low i' the dust.

Such is the fate of simple Bard,
On Life's rough ocean luckless starr'd!
Unskilful he to note the card
        Of prudent Lore,   40
Till billows rage, and gales blow hard,
        And whelm him o'er!

Such fate to suffering worth is giv'n,
Who long with wants and woes has striv'n,
By human pride or cunning driv'n   45
        To Mis'ry's brink,
Till wrench'd of ev'ry stay but HEAV'N,
        He, ruin'd, sink!

1786

Ev'n thou who mourn'st the Daisy's fate,
That fate is thine —— no distant date;   50
Stern Ruin's plough-share drives, elate,
   Full on thy bloom,
Till crush'd beneath the furrows weight,
   Shall be thy doom!

Epistle to J. L*****k,
AN OLD SCOTCH BARD

April 1st, 1785.

While briers an' woodbines budding green,
An' Paitricks scraichan loud at e'en,
And morning Poossie whiddan seen,
   Inspire my Muse,
This freedom, in an unknown frien',   5
   I pray excuse.

On Fasteneen we had a rockin,
To ca' the crack and weave our stockin;
And there was muckle fun and jokin,
   Ye need na doubt;   10
At length we had a hearty yokin,
   At sang about.

There was ae sang, amang the rest,
Aboon them a' it pleas'd me best,
That some kind husband had addrest,   15
   To some sweet wife:
It thirl'd the heart-strings thro' the breast,
   A' to the life.

I've scarce heard ought describ'd sae weel,
What gen'rous, manly bosoms feel;   20
Thought I, 'Can this be Pope, or Steele,
   Or Beattie's wark;'
They tald me 'twas an odd kind chiel
   About Muirkirk.

It pat me fidgean-fain to hear't,   25
An' sae about him there I spier't;
Then a' that kent him round declar'd,
        He had ingine.
That nane excell'd it, few cam near't,
        It was sae fine.   30

    That set him to a pint of ale,
An' either douse or merry tale,
Or rhymes an' sangs he'd made himsel,
        Or witty catches,
'Tween Inverness and Tiviotdale,   35
        He had few matches.

    Then up I gat, an swoor an aith,
Tho' I should pawn my pleugh an' graith,
Or die a cadger pownie's death,
        At some dyke-back,   40
A pint an' gill I'd gie them baith,
        To hear your crack.

    But first an' foremost, I should tell,
Amaist as soon as I could spell,
I to the crambo-jingle fell,   45
        Tho' rude an' rough,
Yet crooning to a body's sel,
        Does weel eneugh.

    I am nae Poet, in a sense,
But just a Rhymer like by chance,   50
An' hae to Learning nae pretence,
        Yet, what the matter?
Whene'er my Muse does on me glance,
        I jingle at her.

    Your Critic-folk may cock their nose,   55
And say, 'How can you e'er propose,
You wha ken hardly verse frae prose,
        To make a sang?'
But by your leaves, my learned foes,
        Ye're maybe wrang.   60

        1786

What's a' your jargon o' your Schools,
Your Latin names for horns an' stools;
If honest Nature made you fools,
           What sairs your Grammars?
Ye'd better taen up spades and shools,   65
           Or knappin-hammers.

A set o' dull, conceited Hashes,
Confuse their brains in Colledge-classes!
They gang in Stirks, and come out Asses,
           Plain truth to speak;   70
An' syne they think to climb Parnassus
           By dint o' Greek!

Gie me ae spark o' Nature's fire,
That's a' the learning I desire;
Then tho' I drudge thro' dub an' mire   75
           At pleugh or cart,
My Muse, tho' hamely in attire,
           May touch the heart.

O for a spunk o' ALLAN's glee,
Or FERGUSON's, the bauld an' slee,   80
Or bright L*****K's, my friend to be,
           If I can hit it!
That would be lear eneugh for me,
           If I could get it.

Now, Sir, if ye hae friends enow,   85
Tho' real friends I b'lieve are few,
Yet, if your catalogue be fow,
           I'se no insist;
But gif ye want ae friend that's true,
           I'm on your list.   90

I winna blaw about mysel,
As ill I like my fauts to tell;
But friends an' folk that wish me well,
           They sometimes roose me;
Tho' I maun own, as monie still,   95
           As far abuse me.

There's ae wee faut they whiles lay to me.
I like the lasses – Gude forgie me!
For monie a Plack they wheedle frae me,
        At dance or fair: 100
Maybe some ither thing they gie me
        They weel can spare.

But MAUCHLINE Race or MAUCHLINE Fair,
I should be proud to meet you there;
We'se gie ae night's discharge to care,   105
        If we forgather,
An' hae a swap o' rhymin-ware,
        Wi' ane anither.

The four-gill chap, we'se gar him clatter,
An' kirs'n him wi' reekin water;   110
Syne we'll sit down an' tak our whitter,
        To chear our heart;
An' faith, we'se be acquainted better
        Before we part.

Awa ye selfish, warly race,   115
Wha think that havins, sense an' grace,
Ev'n love an' friendship should give place
        To catch-the-plack!
I dinna like to see your face,
        Nor hear your crack.   120

But ye whom social pleasure charms,
Whose hearts the tide of kindness warms,
Who hold your being on the terms,
        'Each aid the others,'
Come to my bowl, come to my arms,   125
        My friends, my brothers!

But to conclude my lang epistle,
As my auld pen's worn to the grissle;
Twa lines frae you wad gar me fissle,
        Who am, most fervent,   130
While I can either sing, or whissle,
        Your friend and servant.

           1786

Helen Maria Williams, *Poems* (1786): *To Twilight*

Suggested date of reading: summer 1786

When it was published in June 1786, Thomas Bowman lent Williams' *Poems* to Wordsworth; inspired by them, the sixteen-year-old schoolboy addressed a sonnet to its author, which became his first published poem – 'Sonnet, on Seeing Miss Helen Maria Williams Weep at a Tale of Distress' (*European Magazine*, March 1787).[1] As a poet of sensibility Williams wrote about emotion in a way that intrigued her young admirer, and encouraged him to think further about how to write about states of mind.

Wordsworth always remembered at least one of the poems of the 1786 volume: in 1833 he suggested that Alexander Dyce include it in an anthology of women poets: 'Miss Williams's Sonnet upon Twilight is pleasing', he said. It had been reprinted in Williams' *Poems on Various Subjects* (1823); Wordsworth's copy has now disappeared, but the Rydal Mount auction catalogue records that it contained an ownership inscription: 'Sent to me by the Author from Paris – W.W.' For more on Wordsworth's meeting with Williams, see page 138.

'To Twilight' is here edited from the 1786 volume, where Wordsworth first encountered it.

To Twilight

Meek Twilight! soften the declining day,
    And bring the hour my pensive spirit loves;
When, o'er the mountain slow descends the ray
    That gives to silence the deserted groves.
Ah, let the happy court the morning still,   5
    When, in her blooming loveliness array'd,
She bids fresh beauty light the vale, or hill,
    And rapture warble in the vocal shade.

---

[1] See *The Earliest Wordsworth: Poems 1785-1790* (Carcanet, 2002), p.10.

Sweet is the odour of the morning's flower,
 And rich in melody her accents rise;   10
Yet dearer to my soul the shadowy hour,
 At which her blossoms close, her music dies –
For then, while languid nature droops her head,
She wakes the tear 'tis luxury to shed.

John Dyer, *The Ruins of Rome* (1740) (extract)

Suggested date of reading: by July 1787

> The character of Dyer, as a patriot, a citizen, and a tender-hearted friend of humanity, was, in some respects, injurious to him as a poet . . . In point of *imagination*, and purity of style, I am not sure that he is not superior to any writer in verse since the time of Milton.
>
> (Wordsworth to Lady Beaumont, November 1811)

Dr Johnson strongly criticised Dyer, and his strictures were echoed by other eighteenth-century writers, so that in commending him Wordsworth was out of line with current critical thought. In fact, from his schooldays onwards he remained an admirer of Dyer's landscape poem *Grongar Hill*, *The Fleece* (a Virgilian poem on tending sheep), and *The Ruins of Rome*, composed and published after Dyer's visit to Italy. In response to the negative view of Dyer put about by Johnson, Wordsworth dedicated a sonnet to him in 1811:

> Bard of the Fleece, whose skilful Genius made
> That Work a living landscape fair and bright;
> Nor hallowed less with musical delight
> Than those soft scenes through which thy Childhood stray'd,
> Those southern Tracts of Cambria, 'deep embayed,
> By green hills fenced, by Ocean's murmur lulled;'
> Though hasty Fame hath many a chaplet culled
> For worthless brows, while in the pensive shade
> Of cold neglect she leaves thy head ungraced,
> Yet pure and powerful minds, hearts meek and still,
> A grateful few, shall love thy modest Lay
> Long as the Shepherd's bleating flock shall stray
> O'er naked Snowdon's wide aerial waste;
> Long as the thrush shall pipe on Grongar Hill.

In later years Wordsworth said that his favourite passage in *The Ruins of Rome* was that in which 'the poet hears the voice of Time'; it was, he said, 'A beautiful instance of the modifying and *investive* power of imagination', and he copied it into the album he gave to Lady Mary Lowther in 1819, from which the present text is edited.

The Ruins of Rome

Fallen, fallen, a silent heap! . . .
        Behold the pride of pomp,
The throne of nations, fall'n! obscured in dust;
Even yet majestical: the solemn scene
Elates the soul, while now the rising sun   5
Flames on the ruins in the purer air
Towering aloft upon the glittering plain,
Like broken rocks, a vast circumference!
Rent palaces, crush'd columns, rifled moles,
Fanes roll'd on fanes, and tombs on buried tombs!   10
  Deep lies in dust the Theban obelisk
Immense along the waste; minuter art,
Gliconian forms, or Phidian, subtly fair,
O'erwhelming; as the vast leviathan
The finny brood, when near Irene's shore   15
Outstretch'd unwieldy, his island length appears
Above the foamy flood. Globose and huge,
Gray-mouldering temples swell, and wide o'ercast
The solitary landscape, hills and woods,
And boundless wilds; while the vine-mantled brows   20
The pendant goats unveil, regardless they
Of hourly peril, though the clefted domes
Tremble to every wind. The pilgrim oft,
At dead of night, mid his orisons hears
Aghast, the voice of time-disparting towers,   25
While murmurs sooth each awful interval
Of ever-falling waters; shrouded Nile,
Eridanus, and Tiber with his twins,
And palmy Euphrates; who with dropping locks
Hang o'er their urns, and mournfully among   30
The plaintive-echoing ruins pour their streams.
. . . .

  So Time ordains, who rolls the things of pride
From dust again to dust. Behold that heap
Of mould'ring urns (their ashes blown away,
Dust of the mighty) the same story tell;   40
And at its base, from whence the serpent glides
Down the green desart street, yon hoary monk
Laments the same, the vision as he views
The solitary, silent, solemn scene,

Where Cæsars, heroes, peasants, hermits, lie,   45
Blended in dust together; where the slave
Rests from his labours; where the insulting proud
Resigns his power; the miser drops his hoard;
Where human folly sleeps. – There is a mood,
(I sing not to the vacant and the young)   50
There is a kindly mood of melancholy
That wings the soul, and points her to the skies;
When tribulation clothes the child of man,
When age descends with sorrow to the grave,
'Tis sweetly-soothing sympathy to pain,   55
A gently-wak'ning call to health and ease.
How musical, when all-composing Time,
Here sits upon his throne of ruins hoar
While winds and tempests sweep his various lyre,
How sweet the diapason!   60

Anne Finch, Countess of Winchelsea, *Miscellany Poems*
(1713): *Petition for an Absolute Retreat,*
Song ('Would we attain the happiest state'),
A Nocturnal Reverie, Life's Progress

Suggested date of reading: by July 1787

> There is one poetess to whose writings I am especially partial,
> the Countess of Winchelsea. I have perused her poems fre-
> quently, and should be happy to name such passages as I think
> most characteristic of her genius, and most fit to be selected.
>
> (Wordsworth to Alexander Dyce, October 1829)

Six months after writing this Wordsworth told Dyce that Finch's
'Petition for an Absolute Retreat' and 'A Nocturnal Reverie' were
of 'superior merit'. He had been an admirer of her since at least his
undergraduate years, and probably encountered her poems at
school. He returned to them regularly, usually in the copy of her
Miscellany Poems (1713) which he owned. In 1814 he advised
Robert Anderson to include her in an additional volume of his
British Poets (1792-5), and the following year commended 'A
Nocturnal Reverie' for being the only poem of its time (except for
Pope's *Windsor Forest*) to contain a 'new image of external nature'.

When compiling a collection of poems in manuscript for Lady
Mary Lowther in 1819, he began with a series of passages drawn
from Finch; the texts below are edited from his transcripts. He is
characteristically selective about what he copies. The complete text
of 'Petition for an Absolute Retreat' runs to 293 lines, of which
Wordsworth transcribes 1-25, 32-47, and 104-25. 'Song' ('Would
we attain the happiest state') is entitled 'Moral Song' by Finch, and
not divided into quatrains. Wordsworth omits four lines from 'A
Nocturnal Reverie', which occur between lines 16 and 17 (after
'dusky brakes'):

> When scatter'd Glow-worms, but in Twilight fine,
> Shew trivial Beauties watch their Hour to shine;
> Whil'st Salisb'ry stands the Test of every Light,
> In perfect charms, and perfect Virtue bright . . .

'Life's Progress' is nine stanzas long in Finch's text; Wordsworth
selects stanzas 1, 4, 5 and 6.

Petition for an Absolute Retreat

Give me, O indulgent Fate!
Give me yet before I die
A sweet but absolute Retreat,
'Mongst paths so lost and trees so high,
That the world may ne'er invade,   5
Through such windings and such shade,
    My unshaken liberty.

No intruders thither come!
Who visit but to be from home,
None who their vain moments pass,   10
Only studious of their glass
News, that charm to listening ears
That false alarm to hopes and fears,
That common theme for every fop
From the Statesman to the shop   15
In those coverts ne'er be spread.
Of who's deceased or who's to wed
Be no tidings hither brought
But silent as a midnight thought,
Where the world may ne'er invade,   20
Be those windings and that shade:

Courteous Fate! afford me there
A table spread without my care,
With what the neighb'ring fields impart,
Whose cleanliness be all their art;   25
Courteous Fate then give me there
Only plain and wholesome fare.
Fruits indeed (would heaven bestow)
All that did in Eden grow;
All but the *Forbidden Tree*,   30
Would be covetted by me;
Grapes with juice so crowded up,
As breaking through their native cup,
Figs, yet growing, candied o'er,
By the sun's attracting power;   35
Cherries, with the downy peach
All within my easy reach;
Whilst creeping near the humble ground,

Should the strawberry be found
Springing wheresoe'er I strayed   40
Through those windings and that shade.

Give me there (since heaven has shewn
It was not good to be alone)
A partner suited to my mind,
Solitary, pleased, and kind;   45
Who, partially, may something see
Preferred to all the world in me;
Slighting by my humble side
Fame and splendor, wealth and pride.

When but two the earth possesst   50
'Twas their happiest days and best;
They by business, nor by wars,
They by no domestic cares,
From each other e'er were drawn,
But in some grove or flowery lawn,   55
Spent the swiftly-flying time
Spent their own and natures prime
In love; that only passion given
To perfect man whilst friends with heaven. –
Rage and jealousies and hate,   60
Transports of his fallen state,
When by Satan's wiles betrayed
Fly those windings and that shade.

Song

Would we attain the happiest state,
    That is design'd us here
No joy a rapture must create
    No grief beget despair.

No injury fierce anger raise,   5
    No honour tempt to pride
No vain desires of empty praise
    Must in the soul abide.

103   *1787*

No charms of youth or beauty move
    The constant settled breast;   10
Who leaves a passage free to love,
    Shall let in all the rest.

In such a heart soft peace will live,
    Where none of these abound;
The greatest blessing heaven does give   15
    Or can on earth be found.

A Nocturnal Reverie

In such a night when every louder wind
Is to its distant cavern safe confined,
And only gentle Zephyr fans his wings,
And lonely Philomel, still waking, sings,
Or from some tree, fam'd for the owl's delight,   5
She, hollowing clear directs the wanderer right:
In such a night when passing clouds give place,
Or thinly veil the heaven's mysterious face;
When in some river, overhung with green,
The waving moon and trembling leaves are seen;   10
When freshened grass now bears itself upright,
And makes cool banks to pleasing rest invite,
Whence springs the woodbine and the bramble-rose,
And where the sleepy cowslip sheltered grows;
Whilst now a paler hue the foxglove takes   15
And chequers still with red the dusky brakes:
When odours which declin'd repelling day,
Thro' temperate air uninterrupted stray;
When darken'd groves their softest shadows wear
And falling waters we distinctly hear;   20
When through the gloom more venerable shows
Some ancient Fabric, awful in repose,
While sunburnt hills their swarthy looks conceal,
And swelling hay-cocks thicken up the vale:
When the loos'd horse now, as his pasture leads,   25
Comes slowly grazing through the adjoining meads,
Whose stealing pace, and lengthen'd shade we fear

'Till torn-up forage in his teeth we hear:
When nibbling sheep at large pursue their food,
And unmolested kine re-chew the cud;   30
When curlews cry beneath the village walls,
And to her straggling brood the partridge calls;
Their short-lived jubilee the creatures keep,
Which but endures while tyrant man does sleep:
When a sedate content the spirit feels,   35
And no fierce light disturbs whilst it reveals;
But silent musings urge the mind to seek
Something too high for syllables to speak;
'Till the free soul to a compos'dness charm'd,
Finding the elements of rage disarm'd,   40
O'er all below a solemn quiet grown,
Joys in the inferior world, and thinks it like her own: –
In such a night let me abroad remain,
Till morning breaks and all's confus'd again;
Our cares, our toils, our clamours are renew'd,   45
Our pleasures, seldom reach'd, again pursued.

Life's Progress

How gaily is our Life begun
    Our life's uncertain race!
Whilst yet that sprightly morning sun,
With which we just set out to run,
    Enlightens all the place.   5

How soft the first Ideas prove,
    Which wander through our minds!
How full the joys, how free the love,
Which doth that early season move;
    As flowers the western winds!   10

Our sighs are then but vernal air;
    But April drops our tears,
Which swiftly passing, all grows fair,
Whilst beauty compensates our care,
    And youth each vapour clears.   15

 1787

But O! too soon alas, we climb;
  Scarce feeling we ascend
The gently-rising hill of Time,
From whence with grief we see that prime,
  And all its sweetness end.   20

William Cowper, *Poems* (1782): *Ode to Peace*

Suggested date of reading: by July 1787

Wordsworth first read Cowper as a schoolboy (see p. 48), and probably read 'Ode to Peace' during his time at Hawkshead. For someone already interested in the challenge of describing psychological states in poetry, it would have been influential, written as it was in the wake of one of Cowper's nervous breakdowns. It was among the works selected for the collection Wordsworth gave to Lady Mary Lowther in Christmas 1819, and is here edited from his transcription.

Ode to Peace

Come, Peace of Mind, delightful guest,
Return and make thy downy nest
   Once more in this sad heart!
Nor riches I, nor power pursue,
Nor hold forbidden joys in view;   5
   We therefore need not part.

Where wilt thou dwell if not with me,
From avarice and ambition free
   And pleasure's fatal wiles?
For whom, alas! dost thou prepare,   10
The sweets which I was wont to share
   The banquet of thy smiles.

The great, the gay, shall they partake
The heaven that thou alone canst make?
   And wilt thou quit the stream   15
That murmurs through the dewy mead,
The grove and the sequester'd shed,
   To be a guest with them?

For thee I panted; thee I prized,
For thee I gladly sacrificed   20
   Whate'er I lov'd before;
And shall I see thee start away
And, helpless, hopeless, hear thee say –
   Farewell! we meet no more!

James Thomson, *Hymn on Solitude*

Suggested date of reading: by July 1787

Thomson's 'Hymn on Solitude' (first published 1729) was a favourite eighteenth-century anthology piece which Wordsworth probably encountered first as a schoolboy. Its comparison of the relative merits of town and country is reworked in Coleridge's 'Frost at Midnight', 'This Lime-Tree Bower my Prison', and Wordsworth's 'Tintern Abbey'.

In a letter of December 1806 Wordsworth quoted its conclusion (lines 23-30 of the text below), referring to 'these beautiful lines'. And that high opinion was reiterated in conversation with John Duke Coleridge on 10 October 1836, when he suggested that he preferred the 'Hymn' to *The Seasons*:

> Thomson he spoke of as a real poet, though it appeared less in his 'Seasons' than in his other poems. He had wanted some judicious advisor to correct his taste; but every person he had to deal with only served to injure it. He had, however, a true love and feeling for Nature, and a greater share of poetical imagination, as distinguished from dramatic, than any man between Milton and him. As he stood looking at Ambleside, seen across the valley, embosomed in wood, and separated from us at sufficient distance, he quoted from Thomson's 'Hymn on Solitude', and suggested the addition, or rather insertion, of a line at the close, where he speaks of glancing at London from Norwood. The line, he said, should have given something of a more favourable impression:
>
> Ambition —— and pleasure vain.

The dash after 'Ambition' in the suggested line is due to the fact that, as Coleridge noted, 'I cannot fill the blank', because he had forgotten exactly what Wordsworth had suggested; the line would presumably have been inserted between lines 29 and 30 of the text below.

The present text is edited from the transcription made by Wordsworth when he included it in the album of manuscript poems compiled for Lady Mary Lowther in 1819. It omits eighteen lines from Thomson's poem, after line 6.

Hymn on Solitude

Hail, mildly-pleasing Solitude,
Companion of the wise and good;
But from whose holy, piercing eye
The herd of fools and villains fly.
  Oh! how I love with thee to walk   5
And listen to thy whisper'd talk,
Thine is the balmy breath of morn,
Just as the dew-bent rose is born;
And while meridian fervors beat,
Thine is the woodland dumb retreat;   10
But chief when evening scenes decay
And the faint landscape swims away,
Thine is the doubtful soft decline,
And that best hour of musing thine.

Descending angels bless thy train   15
The virtues of the sage, and swain;
Plain innocence in white array'd,
Before thee lifts her fearless head:
Religions beams around thee shine,
And clear thy glooms with light divine: 20
About thee sports sweet Liberty;
And wrapt Urania sings to thee.

Oh! let me pierce thy secret cell!
And in thy deep recesses dwell.
Perhaps from Norwood's oak-clad hill,   25
When meditation has her fill,
I just may cast my careless eyes
Where London's spiry turrets rise;
Think of its crimes, its cares, its pains,
Then shield me in the woods again.   30

James Beattie, *Retirement* (extract)

Suggested date of reading: by July 1787

Wordsworth read 'Retirement' at Hawkshead Grammar School, in the first edition of Beattie's *Original Poems and Translations* (1760), a copy of which may have been in the possession of his teacher Thomas Bowman. He retained a high opinion of it, and included its seventh stanza in the collection of poems given to Lady Mary Lowther in 1819; the text is edited from his transcription.

Thy shades thy silence now be mine,
Thy charms my only theme,
My haunt the hollow cliff whose pine
Waves o'er the gloomy stream,
Whence the scared Owl on pinions grey,   5
Breaks through the rustling boughs,
And down the long vale sails away
To more profound repose.

William Julius Mickle, *Sir Martyn* Canto 2 (extracts)

Suggested date of reading: by July 1787

In 1843 Wordsworth remembered Mickle in connection with 'a small stream called the Wauchope that flows into the Esk near Langholme': 'Mickle who, as it appears from his poem on Sir Martin, was not without genuine poetic feelings, was born and passed his boyhood in this neighbourhood'. That comment may sound reserved, but it is high praise from someone who recognised 'genuine poetic feelings' when he saw them.

Wordsworth had long been an admirer of *Sir Martyn*. In 1795 he had asked a friend to 'make me a present of that vol: of Bells forgotten poetry which contains The minstrel and Sir martyn'. John Bell's *Classical Arrangement of Fugitive Poetry* volume 10 did indeed contain Beattie's *The Minstrel* and Mickle's *Sir Martyn*, gathered in the same volume as a number of other poems written in Spenserians. Wordsworth requested it because he already knew *The Minstrel* and wanted to own a copy; he must have known *Sir Martyn* by 1795 as well, having probably encountered it at Hawkshead.

In 1819, Wordsworth included two extracts from *Sir Martyn* Canto 2 in his compilation of poems for Lady Mary Lowther; the text below is edited from his transcription.

Sir Martyn
CANTO 2 *(extracts)*

Sooth'd by the murmurs of a plaintive stream,   10
    A wild romantic dell its fragrance shed;
Safe from the thunder shower and scorching beam
    Their faery charms the summer bowers display'd;
    Wild by the banks the bashful cowslips spread,
And from the rocks above each ivied seat,   15
    The spotted foxgloves hung the purple head,
And lowly violets kiss'd the wanderer's feet;
Sure never Hybla's bees rov'd through a wild so sweet.

As winds the streamlet serpentine along,
  So leads a solemn walk its bowery way,   20
The pale-leaved palms and darker limes among,
  To where a grotto lone and secret lay;
  The yellow broom, where chirp the linnets gay,
Waves round the cave; and to the blue-streaked skies
  A shattered rock towers up in fragments grey: 25
The she-goat from its height the landscape eyes,
And calls her wander'd young, the call each bank replies.

   .   .   .   .

And now, perch'd proudly on the topmost spray,
  The sooty blackbird chaunts his vespers shrill;
While twilight spreads his robe of sober grey,
And to their bowers the rooks loud cawing wing their way;   270

And bright behind the Cambrian mountains hoar
  Flames the red beam; while on the distant east,
Led by her star, the horned moon looks o'er
  The bending forest, and with rays increast
  Ascends; while trembling on the dappled west   275
The purple radience shifts and dies away;
  The willows with a deeper green imprest
Nod o'er the brooks; the brooks with gleamy ray
Glide on, and holy Peace assumes her woodland sway.

Geoffrey Chaucer, *Troilus and Criseyde* Book V (extract)

Date of reading: 1787 onwards

> When I began to give myself up to the profession of a poet for life, I was impressed with a conviction, that there were four English poets whom I must have continually before me as examples – Chaucer, Shakspeare, Spenser, and Milton. These I must study, and equal *if I could*; and I need not think of the rest.
>
> (Wordsworth to Christopher Wordsworth Jr, c. 1827)

> My love and reverence for Chaucer are unbounded . . .
>
> (Wordsworth, 23 January 1840)

> . . . Beside the pleasant Mills of Trompington
> I laugh'd with Chaucer; in the hawthorn shade
> Heard him (while birds were warbling) tell his tales
> Of amorous passion.
>
> (*The Thirteen-Book Prelude* iii 276-9)

It is easy to imagine the undergraduate Wordsworth on the banks of the Cam where it passes through Trumpington to the south of the city of Cambridge, at that time the location of several watermills, reading Chaucer. The mention of 'amorous passion' is a reminder that he enjoyed Chaucer's writing for all its qualities: in his seventies, he was critical of a modernised rendering of *The Reeve's Tale* because its translator had 'killed the spirit of that humour, gross and farcical, that pervades the original', and when commending Chaucer to Isabella Fenwick, he told her that 'Chaucer was one of the greatest poets the world has ever seen. He is certainly, at times, in his comic tales indecent, but he is never, as far as I know, insidiously or openly voluptuous'.

When asked to write in an autograph album in 1826, he entered what he called 'my favourite autograph for ladies':

> The God of Love, ah benedicité,
> How naughty and how great a Lord is he![1]

Wordsworth's best-documented readings from Chaucer are those mentioned in Dorothy's Grasmere Journal, when there were two copies of the *Works* at Dove Cottage, one each for Dorothy and

---

[1] From Chaucer, *The Knight's Tale* 1785-6.

William. She reveals that between December 1801 and January 1803 either she or her brother (or both) read *Troilus and Criseyde, The Manciple's Tale, The Prioress's Tale, The General Prologue, The Man of Law's Tale, The Miller's Tale,* and *The Knight's Tale* – and probably a good deal else. In December 1801, Wordsworth produced some modernised renderings of *The Manciple's Tale, The Prioress's Tale,* part of *Troilus and Criseyde,* and a poem called *The Cuckoo and the Nightingale,* then believed to be by Chaucer but now attributed to John Clanvowe. They remained in manuscript until 1820 when Wordsworth published a revised version of *The Prioress's Tale* in *The River Duddon* (1820); *The Cuckoo and the Nightingale* and *The Prioress's Tale* appeared in *The Poems of Chaucer, Modernised* (1841).

Extracting from Chaucer is no easy matter; turning to Wordsworth for guidance I have selected the lines in *Troilus and Criseyde* he translated in December 1801, edited from Anderson's *British Poets* volume 1, which was his source – Book V, lines 519-686. These lines, from the final book of the poem, remind us of the tales of 'amorous passion' which Wordsworth so enjoyed as an undergraduate. The noble Trojan warrior, Troilus, who at first scorns love, has fallen for the beautiful young widow, Criseyde, and sleeps with her thanks to the agency of her Uncle Pandarus. However, on a visit to the Greek camp to see her father, she forgets Troilus and begins an affair with his arch-rival Diomede. In Wordsworth's extract Troilus begins to understand what has happened and to lament his loss.

On morow as sone as day began to clere
This Troilus gan of his slepe to abreide,   520
And to Pandarus his owne brothir dere,
For love of God, ful pitously he seide,
As go we sene the paleis of Creseide,
For sens we yet maie have none othir fest
So let us sene her paleis at the lest!   525

And therwithal his meinè for to blende
A cause he fonde into the toun to go,
And to Creseid'is paleis they gone wende;

115   *1787*

But Lorde! this sely Troilus was wo,
Him thought his sorouful hert brast atwo, 530
For when he saw her doris sperrid all
Wel nigh for sorow adoun he gan to fall.

Therwith when he was ware, and gan behold
How shet was every window of the place,
As frost him thought his hert began to cold, 535
For whiche with chaungid dedly palè face
Withoutin worde he forth by gan to pace,
And as God would he gan so fast to ride
That no wight of his countinaunce aspide.

Than saide he thus; O paleis desolate! 540
O house of housis whilom best ydight!
O paleis empty and disconsolate!
O thou lanterne, of which queint is the light!
O paleis whilom day, that now art night!
Wel oughtist thou to fal and I to die 545
Sens she is went that wont was us to gie.

O paleis whilom croune of housis al!
Enluminid with sunne of allè blisse,
O ring, of whiche the rubie is out fall!
O cause of wo that cause hast ben of blisse! 550
Yet sens I may no bet faine would I kisse
Thy coldè doris, durst I for this route;
And farwel shrine of whiche the saint is out.

Therwith he cast on Pandarus his eie
With chaungid face, and pitous to beholde, 555
And whan he might his time aright aspie
Aie as he rode to Pandarus he tolde
His newe sorow, and eke his joyis olde,
So pitously, and with so ded an hewe,
That every wight might on his sorow rewe. 560

Fro thinnis forth he ridith up and doune,
And every thing came him to remembraunce
As he rode forth by placis of the toune
In whiche he whilom had all his plesaunce;
Lo! yondir saw I mine owne lady daunce, 565

And in that temple with her eyin clere
Me captive caught first my right lady dere:

And yondir have I herde ful lustily
My dere hert Creseide laugh, and yondir play
Sawe I her onis eke ful blisfully,   570
And yondir onis to me gan she saie,
Now, gode swete! lovith me wel I you praye
And yonde so godely gan she me beholde
That to the deth mine hert is to her holde:

And at the cornir in the yondir house   575
Herde I mine aldirlevist lady dere
So womanly with voice melodiouse
Singin so wel, so godely and so clere,
That in my soule yet me thinkith I here
The blisful sowne, and in that yondir place   580
My lady first me toke unto her grace.

Than thought he thus, O blisfull Lorde Cupide
Whan I the processe have in memorie
How thou me hast weried on every side
Men might a boke make of it like a storie;   585
What nede is the to seke on me victorie
Sens I am thine and wholly at thy will?
What joy hast thou thine ownè folke to spill?

Wel hast thou, Lorde, iwroke on me thine ire
Thou mighty God, and dredful for to greve;   590
Now mercy, Lorde! thou wost wel I desire
Thy grace moste of allè lustis leve;
And live and die I wol in thy beleve,
For whiche I ne' aske in guerdon but a bone,
That thou Creseide aien me sendè sone.   595

Distrainin her hert as fast to returne
As thou doest mine to longin her to se,
Than wote I wel that she n'il nat sojourne:
Now blisful Lorde! so cruil thou ne be
Unto the blode of Troie, I praiè the,   600
As Juno was unto the blode Thebane,
For whiche the folke of Thebis caught ther bane.

And aftir this he to the yatis wente
Ther as Creseide out rode a full gode paas,
And up and doun there made he many' a wente,   605
And to him selfe ful oft he said, Alas!
Fro hennis rode my blisse and my solas:
As wouldè blisful God now for his joie
I might her sene ayen comin to Troie!

And to the yondir hil I gan her gide,   610
Alas! and there I toke of her my leve,
And yonde I saw her to her fathir ride,
For sorow of whiche mine hert shal to cleve,
And hithir home I came whan it was eve,
And here I dwel, out cast from allè joie,   615
And shal, til I maie sene her efte in Troie.

And of him selfe imaginid he ofte
To ben defaitid, pale, and woxin lesse
Than he was wonte, and that men saidin softe
What may it be? who can the sothè gesse   620
Why Troilus hath al this hevinesse?
And al this n'as but his melancolie,
That he had of him selfe suche fantasie.

Anothir time imaginin he would
That evèry wight that went by the wey   625
Had of him routhe, and that thei sainè should
I am right sory Troilus wol dey:
And thus he drove a daie yet forth or twey,
As ye have herde: suche life gan he to lede
As he that stode betwixin hope and drede: 630

For which him likid in his songis shewe
Th' encheson of his wo as he best might,
And made a songe of wordis but a fewe,
Somwhat his wofull herte for to light,
And whan he was from every mann'is sight   635
With softè voice he of his lady dere,
That absent was, gan sing as ye maie here:

O sterre! of which I lost have all the light;
With hertè sore wel ought I to bewaile

That evir derke in turment, night by night,   640
Towarde my deth with winde I stere and saile;
For whiche the tennith night if that I faile
The giding of thy bemis bright an houre
My ship and me Carybdis woll devoure.

   This songè when he thus songin had sone   645
He fil aien into his sighis olde,
And every night, as was his wont to done,
He stode the bright mone to beholde,
And all his sorowe he to the mone tolde,
And said, Iwis whan thou art hornid newe   650
I shal be glad if al the world be trewe.

   I saw thine hornis olde eke by that morow
Whan hennis rode my bright lady dere,
That cause is of my turment and my sorow,
For whichè, o bright Lucina the clere!   655
For love of God ren fast about thy sphere,
For whan thine hornis newe ginnin to spring
Than shal she come that maie my blisse ybring.

   The daie is more and lengir every night
Than thei ben wont to be, thim thoughtè tho,   660
And that the sunnè went his course unright
By lengir waie than it was wonte to go,
And said, Iwis I drede me evirmo
The sunn'is sonne Phaeton be on live;
And that his fathir's carre amisse he drive.   665

   Upon the wallis fast eke would he walke,
And on the Grekis host he would yse,
And to him selfe right thus he would ytalke;
Lo! yondir is mine ownè lady fre,
Or ellis yondir there the tentis be,   670
And thence comith this ayre that is so sote,
That in my soule I fele it doth me bote.

   And hardily this winde that more and more
Thus stoundèmele encresith in my face
Is of my ladies depè sighis sore;   675
I preve it thus, for in none othir space

Of al this toun, save onely in this place,
Fele I no winde that sounith so like paine,
It saith Alas! why twinid be we twaine?

This longè time he drivith forth right thus,   680
Til fully passid was the ninthè night,
And aie beside him was this Pandarus,
That besily did allè his full might
Him to comfort and make his hertè light,
Yeving him hope alway the tenthè morow   685
That she shal comen and stintin al his sorow.

William Collins, *An Ode on the Popular Superstitions of the Highlands of Scotland* (1788)

Date of reading: May 1788

On rare occasions Wordsworth would reveal to select correspondents that he was not merely a great lover of fine literature but an accomplished bibliographer. One such is his letter to Alexander Dyce of 19 October 1828 describing the textual history of Collins' 'Ode on the Popular Superstitions of the Highlands' – still useful to modern editors of the poem:

> In 1779, according to Dr Anderson, or according to Boswell, 1781 – Johnson's Lives of the Poets was published, and made known to the literary world that Collins had composed an Ode on the Popular Superstitions of the Highlands of Scotland, which the Wartons who had seen it thought the best of his works. In 1784 Dr Carlyle read from a MS. in Collins's own handwriting this Ode, of which a Stanza and a half were wanting, and in 1788 the Ode was first printed from Dr Carlyle's copy, with Mr Mackenzie's supplemental lines – and was extensively circulated through the English newspapers, in which I remember to have read it with great pleasure upon its first appearance.

We do not know for certain where Wordsworth read that first published text, as it appeared simultaneously in a range of titles, but we can make a good guess. One of the 'English newspapers' to publish the poem in 1788 was the *European Magazine*, a periodical of which, while a schoolboy at Hawkshead, Wordsworth was a regular reader – in fact, his first published poem appeared in its pages (in 1786, when he was sixteen).[1] He is likely to have kept up with the *European* during his years as an undergraduate at Cambridge; by May 1788, when Collins' 'new' poem appeared there, Wordsworth was nearing the end of his freshman year. It would have appealed to him not just as an admirer of Collins, but because he loved gothic poetry, and had an interest in St Kilda where the poem is partly set (see footnote 11, p. 128).

---

[1] See *The Earliest Wordsworth: Poems 1785-1790* ed. Duncan Wu (Carcanet, 2002), p. 10.

Here is the text published by the *European Magazine* in May 1788, when as Wordsworth recalls it was prefaced by a letter by Alexander Carlyle, explaining that it had been edited from Collins' manuscript; that a gap from lines 70 to 94 had been filled by Henry Mackenzie; and that the poem as a whole had been addressed to another Scottish writer, John Home.

An Ode on the Popular Superstitions of the Highlands of Scotland, considered as the Subject of Poetry

By WILLIAM COLLINS

I

Home, thou return'st from Thames, whose Naiads long
    Have seen thee ling'ring, with a fond delay,
Mid those soft friends, whose hearts, some future day,
    Shall melt, perhaps, to hear thy tragic song.
Go, not unmindful of that cordial youth,   5
    Whom, long endear'd, thou leav'st by Lavant's side;
Together let us wish him lasting truth,
    And joy untainted with his destin'd bride.
Go! nor regardless, while these numbers boast
    My short-lived bliss, forget my social name;   10
But think far off how, on the southern coast,
    I met thy friendship with an equal flame!
Fresh to that soil thou turn'st, whose ev'ry vale
    Shall prompt the poet, and his song demand:
To thee thy copious subjects ne'er shall fail;   15
    Thou need'st but take the pencil to thy hand,
And paint what all believe who own thy genial land.

II

There must thou wake perforce thy Doric quill,
    'Tis Fancy's land to which thou sett'st thy feet;
Where still, 'tis said, the fairy people meet   20
    Beneath each birken shade on mead or hill.
There each trim lass that skims the milky store,

To the swart tribes their creamy bowl allots;
By night they sip it round the cottage-door,
    While airy minstrels warble jocund notes.   25
There every herd, by sad experience, knows
    How, wing'd with fate, their elf-shot arrows fly;
When the sick ewe her summer food foregoes,
    Or, stretch'd on earth, the heart-smit heifers lie.
Such airy beings awe th' untutor'd swain: 30
    Nor thou, though learn'd, his homelier thoughts neglect;
Let thy sweet Muse the rural faith sustain:
    These are the themes of simple, sure effect,
That add new conquests to her boundless reign,
And fill, with double force, her heart-commanding strain.   35

III

Ev'n yet preserv'd, how often may'st thou hear,
    Where to the Pole the Boreal mountains run,
Taught by the father to his listening son
    Strange lays, whose power had charm'd a Spenser's ear.
At ev'ry pause, before thy mind possest,   40
    Old Runic bards shall seem to rise around,
With uncouth lyres, in many-colour'd vest,
    Their matted hair with boughs fantastic crown'd:
Whether thou bid'st the well-taught hind repeat
    The choral dirge that mourns some chieftain brave,   45
When ev'ry shrieking maid her bosom beat,
    And strew'd with choicest herbs his scented grave;
Or whether, sitting in the shepherd's shiel,[1]
    Thou hear'st some sounding tale of war's alarms;
When, at the bugle's call, with fire and steel,   50
    The sturdy clans pour'd forth their bony swarms,
And hostile brothers met to prove each other's arms.

IV

'Tis thine to sing, how framing hideous spells
    In Sky's lone isle the gifted wizzard sits,

---

[1] A kind of hut, built for a summer habitation to the herdsmen, when the cattle are sent to graze in distant pastures. (Carlyle's note)

Waiting in wintry cave his wayward fits;[2]   55
    Or in depth of Uist's dark forest dwells:
How they, whose sight such dreary dreams engross,
    With their own visions oft astonish'd droop,
When o'er the wat'ry strath or quaggy moss
    They see the gliding ghosts unbodied troop.   60
Or if in sports, or on the festive green,
    Their piercing[3] glance some fated youth descry,
Who, now perhaps in lusty vigour seen
    And rosy health, shall soon lamented die.
For them the viewless forms of air obey,   65
    Their bidding heed, and at their beck repair.
They know what spirit brews the stormful day,
    And heartless, oft like moody madness stare
To see the phantom train their secret work prepare.

V

Or on some bellying rock that shades the deep,[4]   70
    They view the lurid signs that cross the sky,
Where, in the west, the brooding tempests lie,
    And hear their first, faint, rustling pennons sweep.
Or in the arched cave, where deep and dark
    The broad, unbroken billows heave and swell,   75
In horrid musings rapt, they sit to mark
    The labouring moon; or lift the nightly yell
Of that dread spirit, whose gigantic form
    The seer's entranced eye can well survey,
Through the dim air who guides the driving storm,   80
    And points the wretched bark its destin'd prey.
Or him who hovers, on his flagging wing,
    O'er the dire whirlpool, that, in ocean's waste,
Draws instant down whate'er devoted thing
    The failing breeze within its reach hath plac'd –   85
The distant seaman hears, and flies with trembling haste.

---

[2] Collins had written, *Lodg'd in the wintry cave with* – and had left the line
imperfect: Altered, and the chasm supplied by Dr Carlyle. (Carlyle's note)
[3] A blank in the manuscript. The word *piercing* supplied by Dr Carlyle.
(Carlyle's note)
[4] A leaf of the manuscript, containing the fifth stanza, and one half of the
sixth, is here lost. The chasm is supplied by Mr Mackenzie. (Carlyle's note)

VI

Or, if on land the fiend exerts his sway,
   Silent he broods o'er quicksand, bog, or fen,
Far from the shelt'ring roof and haunts of men,
   When witched darkness shuts the eye of day,   90
And shrouds each star that wont to cheer the night;
   Or, if the drifted snow perplex the way,
With treach'rous gleam he lures the fated wight,
   And leads him flound'ring on, and quite astray.
What though far off, from some dark dell espied,   95
   His glimm'ring mazes cheer th' excursive sight,
Yet turn, ye wand'rers, turn your steps aside,
   Nor trust the guidance of that faithless light;
For watchful, lurking, 'mid th' unrustling reed,
   At those mirk hours the wily monster lies,   100
And listens oft to hear the passing steed,
   And frequent round him rolls his sullen eyes,
If chance his savage wrath may some weak wretch surprise.

VII

Ah, luckless swain, o'er all unblest indeed!
   Whom late bewilder'd in the dank, dark fen,   105
Far from his flocks and smoking hamlet then!
   To that sad spot 'his wayward fate shall lead:'[5]
On him enrag'd, the fiend, in angry mood,
   Shall never look with pity's kind concern,
But instant, furious, raise the whelming flood   110
   O'er its drown'd bank, forbidding all return.
Or, if he meditate his wish'd escape
   To some dim hill that seems uprising near,
To his faint eye the grim and grisly shape,
   In all its terrors clad, shall wild appear.   115
Meantime, the wat'ry surge shall round him rise,
   Pour'd sudden forth from ev'ry swelling source.
What now remains but tears and hopeless sighs?
   His fear-shook limbs have lost their youthly force,
And down the waves he floats, a pale and breathless corse.   120

---

[5] A blank in the manuscript. The line filled up by Dr Carlyle. (Carlyle's note)

         1788

VIII

For him, in vain, his anxious wife shall wait,
   Or wander forth to meet him on his way,
For him, in vain, at to-fall of the day,
   His babes shall linger at th' unclosing gate.
Ah, ne'er shall he return! Alone, if night   125
   Her travell'd limbs in broken slumbers steep,
With dropping willows drest, his mournful sprite
   Shall visit sad, perchance, her silent sleep:
Then he, perhaps, with moist and wat'ry hand,
   Shall fondly seem to press her shudd'ring cheek,   130
And with his blue swoln face before her stand,
   And, shiv'ring cold, these piteous actions speak:
Pursue, dear wife, thy daily toils pursue
   At dawn or dusk, industrious as before;
Nor e'er of me one hapless thought renew,   135
   While I lie welt'ring on the ozier'd shore,
Drown'd by the Kaelpie's[6] wrath, nor e'er shall aid thee more!

IX

Unbounded is thy range; with varied stile
   Thy Muse may, like those feath'ry tribes which spring
From their rude rocks, extend her skirting wing   140
   Round the moist marge of each cold Hebrid isle,
To that hoar pile which still its ruin shows:[7]
   In whose small vaults a pigmy-folk is found,
Whose bones the delver with his spade upthrows,
   And culls them, wond'ring, from the hallow'd ground!   145
Or thither where beneath the show'ry west

---

[6] A name given in Scotland to a supposed spirit of the waters. (Carlyle's note)

[7] On the largest of the *Flannan Islands* (isles of the Hebrides) are the ruins of a chapel dedicated to St Flannan. This is reckoned by the inhabitants of the Western Isles a place of uncommon sanctity. One of the Flannan Islands is termed the *Isle of Pigmies*; and Martin says, there have been many small bones dug up here, resembling in miniature those of the human body. (Carlyle's note)

1788

The mighty kings of three fair realms are laid:[8]
Once foes, perhaps, together now they rest,
  No slaves revere them, and no wars invade:
Yet frequent now, at midnight's solemn hour,   150
  The rifted mounds their yawning cells unfold,
And forth the monarchs stalk with sov'reign pow'r
  In pageant robes, and wreath'd with sheeny gold,
And on their twilight tombs aerial council hold.

                              X
But O! o'er all, forget not KILDA's race.[9]   155
  On whose bleak rocks, which brave the wasting tides,
Fair Nature's daughter, Virtue, yet abides.
  Go, just as they, their blameless manners trace!
Then to my ear transmit some gentle song
  Of those whose lives are yet sincere and plain,   160
Their bounded walks the rugged cliffs along,
  And all their prospect but the wint'ry main.
With sparing temp'rance, at the needful time,
  They drain the sainted[10] spring; or, hunger-prest,
Along th' Atlantic rock undreading climb,   165
  And of its eggs despoil the Solan's nest.

---

[8] The island of *Iona* or *Icolmkill*. See Martin's Description of the Western
Islands of Scotland. That author informs us, that forty-eight kings of
Scotland, four kings of Ireland, and five of Norway, were interred in the
church of St. Ouran in that island. There were two churches and two
monasteries founded there by St Columbus about AD 565. Bed. *Hist.*
Eccl l.3. Collins has taken all his information respecting the Western Isles
from Martin; from whom he may likewise have derived his knowledge of
the popular superstitions of the Highlanders, with which this Ode shews so
perfect an acquaintance. (Carlyle's note)
[9] The character of the inhabitants of St Kilda, as here described, agrees
perfectly with the accounts given by Martin and by Macauley, of the
people of that island. It is the most westerly of all the Hebrides, and is
above 130 miles distant from the main land of Scotland. (Carlyle's note)
[10] In his letter to Alexander Dyce of October 1828, Wordsworth
contrasted the reading in his text with the less correct one given in later
editions: 'Is "sainted" a word supplied by Dr Carlyle? as wells were
formerly dedicated to saints it is surely much preferable to "scented",
which besides being used before is nonsense'.

Thus blest in primal innocence they live,
 Suffic'd and happy with their frugal fare,
Which tasteful toil and hourly danger give.
 Hard is their shallow soil, and bleak and bare,   170
Nor ever vernal bee was heard to murmur there![11]

XI

Nor need'st thou blush, that such false themes engage
 Thy gentle mind, of fairer stores possest;
For not alone they touch the village breast,
 But fill'd in elder time th' historic page.   175
There SHAKESPEARE's self, with ev'ry garland crown'd,
 In musing hour, his wayward sisters found,
And with their terrors drest the magic scene.
From them he sung, when 'mid his bold design,
 Before the Scot afflicted and aghast,   180
The shadowy kings of BANQUO's fated line
 Through the dark cave in gleamy pageant past.
Proceed, nor quit the tales which, simply told,
 Could once so well my answering bosom pierce;
Proceed, in forceful sounds and colours bold   185
 The native legends of thy land rehearse;
To such adapt thy lyre and suit thy powerful verse.

---

[11] In his letter to Alexander Dyce of October 1828, Wordsworth praised this line and speculated on its source: 'By the bye, I am almost sure that that very agreeable line "Nor ever vernal bee was heard to murmur there" is from Martin's account of St Kilda, not from his volume on the Western Islands, but a separate pamphlet which he published on St Kilda, and which I once possessed, but have unfortunately mislaid.' Wordsworth's copy of Martin Martin's *A Voyage to St Kilda* (4th ed., 1753) is now at St John's College, Cambridge. On pages 63-4, Wordsworth has written: 'This separate pamphlet which I suppose to be exceedingly scarce is furthermore valuable as containing particulars of St Kilda which are not found in the account of that place given by the same author in his volume concerning the Western Isles. Collins the poet had read this pamphlet.' Wordsworth owned it during his undergraduate years at Cambridge.

XII

In scenes like these, which, daring to depart
  From sober truth, are still to nature true,
And call forth fresh delight to Fancy's view,   190
  Th' Heroic Muse employ'd her TASSO's art!
How have I trembled, when at TANCRED's stroke,
  In gushing blood the gaping cypress pour'd;
When each live plant with mortal accents spoke,
  And the wild blast upheav'd the vanish'd sword!   195
How have I sat, when pip'd the pensive wind,
  To hear his harp by British FAIRFAX strung.
Prevailing poet, whose undoubting mind
  Believ'd the magic wonders which he sung!
Hence at each sound imagination glows;   200
Hence his warm lay with softest sweetness flows;
  Melting it flows, pure, numerous, strong and clear,
  And fills th' impassion'd heart, and wins th' harmonious ear.

XIII

All hail, ye scenes that o'er my soul prevail,
  Ye spacious friths and lakes which far away   205
Are by smooth ANNAN fill'd, or past'ral TAY,
  Or DON's romantic springs, at distance hail!
The time shall come when I, perhaps, may tread
  Your lowly glens, o'erhung with spreading broom,
Or o'er your stretching heaths by fancy led: 210
  Then will I dress once more the faded bow'r,
Where JONSON sat in DRUMMOND's social shade,[12]
  Or crop from Tiviot's dale each 'classic flower,'
And mourn on Yarrow's banks 'the widow'd maid.'
  Meantime, ye pow'rs, that on the plains which bore   215
The cordial youth, on LOTHIAN's plains attend,
  Where'er he dwell, on hill, or lowly muir,
  To him I lose, your kind protection lend,
And, touch'd with love like mine, preserve my absent friend.

---

[12] Ben Jonson undertook a journey to Scotland a-foot in 1619, to visit the
poet Drummond, at his seat at Hawthornden, near Edinburgh. Drummond
has preserved, in his works, some very curious heads of their conversation.
(Carlyle's note)

John Milton, *Paradise Regained* Book IV (extract)

Date of reading: by 1789

In Book III of *The Prelude* Wordsworth recalls his love of Milton's poetry while at Cambridge, envisioning the undergraduate Milton:

> Yea, our blind Poet, who, in his later day,
> Stood almost single, uttering odious truth,
> Darkness before and danger's voice behind;
> Soul awful! if the earth hath ever lodg'd
> An awful Soul, I seem'd to see him here
> Familiarly, and in his Scholar's dress
> Bounding before me, yet a stripling Youth,
> A Boy, no better, with his rosy cheeks
> Angelical, keen eye, courageous look,
> And conscious step of purity and pride.
>
> (*The Thirteen-Book Prelude* iii 284-92)

The copy of Milton's *Works* which Wordsworth owned as an undergraduate is now at the Wordsworth Library in Grasmere. It is autographed 'Wordsworth Cambridge' and was in use by 1789.

It is reasonable to presume that while an undergraduate Wordsworth read everything by Milton that he had not devoured already – perhaps including *Paradise Regained*. In that poem was a passage he is twice recorded as having praised. In 1827 he told his nephew, Christopher Wordsworth Jr, that 'One of the noblest things in Milton is the description of that sweet, quiet morning in the "Paradise Regained", after that terrible night of howling wind and storm. The contrast is divine.' And nearly ten years later Henry Crabb Robinson recorded:

> On our walk Wordsworth was remarkably eloquent and felici-
> tous in his praise of Milton. He spoke of the *Paradise Regained*
> as surpassing even the *Paradise Lost* in perfection of execution,
> though the theme is far below it and demanding less power.
> He spoke of the description of the storm in it as the finest in all
> poetry . . .
>
> (Henry Crabb Robinson, diary entry, 7 January 1836)

The passage describes the culmination of Christ's temptation by Satan, who has taken him into the wilderness so as to subject him to a night of exposure in a terrible storm. It is edited here from Anderson, *British Poets* volume 5, in which Wordsworth read Milton from 1800 onwards.

                    Darkness now rose,
As day-light sunk, and brought in louring Night   395
Her shadowy offspring, unsubstantial both,
Privation mere of light and absent day.
Our Saviour meek, and with untroubled mind,
After his airy jaunt, though hurried sore,
Hungry and cold, betook him to his rest,   400
Wherever, under some concourse of shades,
Whose branching arms thick intertwin'd might shield
From dews and damps of night his shelter'd head;
But shelter'd slept in vain, for at his head
The Tempter watch'd, and soon with ugly dreams   405
Disturb'd his sleep; and either tropic now
'Gan thunder, and both ends of Heav'n, the clouds
From many a horrid rift abortive pour'd
Fierce rain with lightning mix'd, water with fire
In ruin reconcil'd: nor slept the winds   410
Within their stony caves, but rush'd abroad
From the four hinges of the world, and fell
On the vex'd wilderness, whose tallest pines,
Though rooted deep as high, and sturdiest oaks,
Bow'd their stiff necks, loaden with stormy blasts;   415
Or torn up sheer: ill wast thou shrouded then,
O patient Son of God, yet only stood'st
Unshaken; nor yet stay'd the terror there,
Infernal ghosts, and hellish furies, round
Environ'd thee, some howl'd, some yell'd, some shriek'd, 420
Some bent at thee their fiery darts, while thou
Satst unappall'd in calm and sinless peace.
Thus pass'd the night so foul, till morning fair
Came forth with pilgrim steps in amice gray,
Who with her radiant finger still'd the roar   425
Of thunder, chas'd the clouds, and laid the winds
And gristly spectres, which the Fiend had rais'd

To tempt the Son of God with terrors dire.
And now the sun with more effectual beams
Had cheer'd the face of earth, and dry'd the wet   430
From drooping plant, or dropping tree; the birds,
Who all things now behold more fresh and green,
After a night of storm so ruinous,
Clear'd up their choicest notes in bush and spray
To gratulate the sweet return of morn;   435
Nor yet amidst this joy and brightest morn
Was absent, after all his mischief done,
The Prince of Darkness, glad would also seem,
Of this fair change, and to our Saviour came;
Yet with no new device; they all were spent: 440
Rather by this his last affront resolv'd,
Desp'rate of better course, to vent his rage
And mad despite, to be so oft repell'd.

William Lisle Bowles, *Fourteen Sonnets* (1789): *Sonnet I.*
Written at Tinemouth, Northumberland, Sonnet VI,
Sonnet VII. At a Village in Scotland, Sonnet VIII. To the
River Itchin

Date of reading: spring 1789

When Bowles's Sonnets first appeared, – a thin 4to pamphlet,
entitled *Fourteen Sonnets*, – I bought them in a walk through
London with my dear brother, who was afterwards drowned at
sea.
(Wordsworth in conversation with Alexander Dyce,
some time after 1828)

That walk through London with his brother John (drowned in the
wreck of the *Earl of Abergavenny* in 1805) took place probably in the
spring of 1789 shortly after publication of *Fourteen Sonnets*.
Wordsworth was then in his third undergraduate year at Cambridge;
his enthusiastic reading is reflected in the fact that he immediately
wrote a series of Cambridge sonnets in the Bowlesian manner. (See
The Earliest Wordsworth: Poems 1785-1790 (Carcanet, 2002), pp.
53-5.) His enthusiasm for the sonnet form is reflected in readings
of Russell, Williams and Smith, which also date from this period
(see subsequent entries).

The selection of sonnets that follows, from *Fourteen Sonnets*
(1789), includes Bowles' most famous, 'To the River Itchin', which
looks back to Warton's 'To the River Lodon', and would inspire
Coleridge's 'To the River Otter' (probably composed in 1796).

Sonnet I

WRITTEN AT TINEMOUTH, NORTHUMBERLAND,
AFTER A TEMPESTUOUS VOYAGE

As slow I climb the cliff's ascending side,
Much musing on the track of terror past
   When o'er the dark wave rode the howling blast,
Pleas'd I look back, and view the tranquil tide,
     That laves the pebbled shore; and now the beam   5

133 *1789*

Of evening smiles on the grey battlement,
And yon forsaken tow'r, that time has rent.
  The lifted oar far off with silver gleam
Is touch'd, and the hush'd billows seem to sleep.
    Sooth'd by the scene, ev'n thus on sorrow's breast   10
    A kindred stillness steals and bids her rest;
Whilst the weak winds that sigh along the deep,
    The ear, like lullabies of pity, meet,
    Singing her saddest notes of farewell sweet.

Sonnet VI

Evening, as slow thy placid shades descend,
Veiling with gentlest hush the landscape still,
    The lonely battlement, and farthest hill
And wood; I think of those that have no friend;
    Who now perhaps, by melancholy led,   5
From the broad blaze of day, where pleasure flaunts,
Retiring, wander 'mid thy lonely haunts
    Unseen; and mark the tints that o'er thy bed
Hang lovely, oft to musing fancy's eye
    Presenting fairy vales, where the tir'd mind   10
    Might rest, beyond the murmurs of mankind,
Nor hear the hourly moans of misery.
    Ah! beauteous views, that hope's fair gleams the while,
    Should smile like you, and perish as they smile!

Sonnet VII

AT A VILLAGE IN SCOTLAND

O North! as thy romantick vales I leave,
And bid farewell to each retiring hill,
    Where thoughtful fancy seems to linger still,
Tracing the broad bright landscape; much I grieve
    That mingled with the toiling croud, no more   5
I shall return, your varied views to mark,
Of rocks amid the sunshine tow'ring dark,

Of rivers winding wild, and mountains hoar,
Or castle gleaming on the distant steep.
  Yet not the less I pray your charms may last,   10
  And many a soften'd image of the past
Pensive combine; and bid remembrance keep
  To cheer me with the thought of pleasure flown,
  When I am wand'ring on my way alone.

Sonnet VIII

To the River Itchin, Near Winton

Itchin, when I behold thy banks again,
Thy crumbling margin, and thy silver breast,
  On which the self-same tints still seem to rest,
Why feels my heart the shiv'ring sense of pain?
  Is it, that many a summer's day has past   5
Since, in life's morn, I carol'd on thy side?
Is it, that oft, since then, my heart has sigh'd,
  As Youth, and Hope's delusive gleams, flew fast?
Is it that those, who circled on thy shore,
Companions of my youth, now meet no more?   10
  Whate'er the cause, upon thy banks I bend
Sorrowing, yet feel such solace at my heart,
  As at the meeting of some long-lost friend,
  From whom, in happier hours, we wept to part.

Thomas Russell, *Sonnets and Miscellaneous Poems*
ed. W. Howley (Oxford, 1789):
Sonnet XIII. Suppos'd to be written at Lemnos

Suggested date of reading: 1789-90; by 1793

Wordsworth's first encounter with Thomas Russell's sonnets was probably at Cambridge, when he was particularly interested in the form, and was imitating Bowles and Charlotte Smith. He seems never to have closely followed Russell's example, but nonetheless admired his poetry throughout his life, commending it to Alexander Dyce in April 1833, saying of 'Sonnet XIII' that 'the last six lines . . . are first-rate'. So well did he know it that in April 1823 he recited it at a gathering at Samuel Rogers' house, as Henry Crabb Robinson recorded: 'Wordsworth also read extracts from Russell's poems, particularly sonnets, of which he thinks very highly'. And as late as 1844 he 'spoke of the Wykehamist Poets – at the end of the last Century – with great commendation – Russell, Headley, Bowles, and Crowe'.

A native of Dorset (the manuscript of his sonnets is now at Dorchester Museum), Russell was indeed a Wykehamist and graduate of New College, Oxford. Eight years Wordsworth's senior, he died in 1788 shortly after correcting his poems for the press. It may have been his early demise that brought him to Wordsworth's attention while at Cambridge. Wordsworth's kindest words about Russell, and 'Sonnet XIII', come from the 1833 letter to Dyce:

> . . . I am well aware that a Sonnet will often be found excellent, where the beginning, the middle, and the end are distinctly marked, and also where it is distinctly separated into *two* parts, to which, as I before observed, the strict Italian model, as they write it, is favorable. Of this last construction of Sonnet, Russell's upon Philoctetes is a fine specimen; the first eight lines give the hardship of the case, the six last the consolation, or the *per-contra*.

In 1833 Wordsworth would bestow on Russell the ultimate compliment of incorporating four lines from his sonnet, 'Could then, the Babes', into one of his own, 'Iona, Upon Landing', with the note: 'The four last lines of this sonnet are adopted from a well-known sonnet of Russel, as conveying my feeling better than any words of my own could do'.

1789-90　　　　　　136

The text is edited from the 1789 volume, where Wordsworth first encountered Russell's poems.

Sonnet XIII

SUPPOS'D TO BE WRITTEN AT LEMNOS

On this lone Isle, whose rugged rocks affright
    The cautious pilot, ten revolving years
    Great Pæan's Son, unwonted erst to tears,
    Wept o'er his wound: alike each rolling light
Of heaven he watch'd, and blam'd its lingering flight,   5
    By day the sea-mew screaming round his cave
    Drove slumber from his eyes, the chiding wave,
    And savage howlings chas'd his dreams by night.
HOPE still was his: in each low breeze, that sigh'd
    Thro' his rude grot, he heard a coming oar,   10
    In each white cloud a coming sail he spied;
Nor seldom listen'd to the fancied roar
    Of Oeta's torrents, or the hoarser tide
    That parts fam'd Trachis from th' Euboic shore.

Helen Maria Williams, *Julia* (1790): *Sonnet to the Moon, Sonnet to Hope*

Date of reading: 1790-1

Wordsworth read Williams' novel *Julia* soon after publication in 1790; he was intending to seek her out on his next visit to Paris (where she lived in exile). Just before sailing in November 1791 he visited another favourite poetess, Charlotte Smith, who lived in Brighton; she furnished him with a letter of introduction for Williams. Unfortunately, by the time he got to Paris, Williams had left the city: 'This circumstance was a considerable disappointment to me', he told his brother.

They were not to meet for nearly thirty years, when Henry Crabb Robinson introduced them in Paris in October 1820. On that occasion Wordsworth was the recipient of a note from Williams in which, writing of herself in the third person, she declared:

> altho' the greatest part of her life has been passed abroad, she has not lost her sensibility to the charm of English poetry – Mr Wordsworth will therefore easily believe how deeply she has felt the power of his compositions and how much she would regret losing an opportunity of being introduced to him . . .
>
> (Helen Maria Williams, note to Wordsworth
> of 10 October 1820)

She had been an admirer of Wordsworth's poems since 4 September 1814 when Robinson and Catherine Clarkson had read some of them to her, as Robinson recorded in his diary: 'Mrs Clarkson and I repeated some sonnets, etc., by Wordsworth, of whom Miss Williams had never heard before'. At their first meeting Wordsworth was able to compliment her by reciting 'To Hope' from memory. That he was able to do this proves he had been an attentive reader of *Julia*, where it previously appeared alongside 'Sonnet to the Moon'.

When she reprinted 'Sonnet to Hope' several years later in her last collected *Poems* (1823) Williams placed it at the beginning of the sonnet section with the following note: 'I commence the Sonnets with that to Hope, from a predilection in its favour, for which I have a proud reason: it is that of Mr Wordsworth, who lately honoured me with his visits while at Paris, having repeated it to me from memory, after a lapse of many years.'

In 1830 Wordsworth advised Alexander Dyce to include Williams' sonnets in an anthology of women poets: 'If a 2nd edition of your Specimens should be called for, you might add from H.M. Williams the Sonnet to the Moon, and that to Twilight'. Three years later he repeated this suggestion: 'Miss Williams's Sonnet upon Twilight is pleasing; that upon Hope of great merit' (for 'To Twilight' see p. 96). All three were reprinted in Williams' *Poems* (1823), a copy of which she had sent him on publication; Wordsworth's copy has disappeared, but the Rydal Mount auction catalogue records that it contained an ownership inscription: 'Sent to me by the Author from Paris – W.W.'

These texts are edited from *Julia* (1790), where Wordsworth first read them.

&

Sonnet to the Moon

The glitt'ring colours of the day are fled –
Come, melancholy orb! that dwell'st with night,
Come! and o'er earth thy wand'ring lustre shed,
Thy deepest shadow and thy softest light.
To me congenial is the gloomy grove,   5
When with faint rays the sloping uplands shine;
That gloom, those pensive rays, alike I love,
Whose sadness seems in sympathy with mine!
But most for this, pale orb! thy light is dear,
For this, benignant orb! I hail thee most,   10
That while I pour the unavailing tear,
And mourn that hope to me, in youth is lost!
Thy light can visionary thoughts impart,
And lead the Muse to sooth a suff'ring heart.

Sonnet to Hope

Oh, ever skill'd to wear the form we love!
To bid the shapes of fear and grief depart,
Come, gentle Hope! with one gay smile remove
The lasting sadness of an aching heart.
Thy voice, benign enchantress! let me hear;   5
Say that for me some pleasures yet shall bloom!
That fancy's radiance, friendship's precious tear,
Shall soften, or shall chase, misfortune's gloom. –
But come not glowing in the dazzling ray
Which once with dear illusions charm'd my eye!   10
Oh strew no more, sweet flatterer! on my way
The flowers I fondly thought too bright to die.
Visions less fair will sooth my pensive breast,
That asks not happiness, but longs for rest!

Charlotte Smith, 'Oh thou that sleep'st where hazel bands entwine', 'On this lone island whose unfruitful breast'

Date of reading: November 1791

> I was detained at Brighthelmstone from Tuesday till Saturday Evening which time must have past in a manner extremely disagreeable, if I had not bethought me of introducing myself to Mrs Charlotte Smith, she received me in the politest manner, and shewed me every possible civility.
>
> (Wordsworth to Richard Wordsworth, 19 December 1791)

On his way to France in November 1791 Wordsworth called on Smith at her home in Brighton, partly to obtain a letter of introduction to Helen Maria Williams, whom he intended to meet in Paris (see p. 138). In the letter to his brother Richard it sounds almost like a chance encounter but in fact had probably been planned and anticipated for weeks. Brighton was at that time a hotbed of pro-Revolutionary activity, and Wordsworth probably wanted to allay fears that he was getting too deeply immersed in it – which, of course, he was.

The 'civility' Smith showed him indicates that among other things he saw manuscripts of her forthcoming novel *Celestina* (1791), from which he copied two sonnets into the back of his copy of her *Elegiac Sonnets* (1789), now retained at the Wordsworth Library in Grasmere (see p. 41). Besides *Celestina* they were later published in *Elegiac Sonnets* (6th ed., 1792). They are here edited from Wordsworth's unpunctuated transcription, with pointing added from Smith's 1792 printed text for ease of reading. Wordsworth's copies differ in a number of details from those which went into print, and are consistently closer to the earliest printed versions in *Celestina* – confirming that he was working from manuscripts. I have supplied some of the more interesting variants in footnotes.

In the first, the heroine Celestina De Mornay, who is nineteen, expresses despair at the loss of her lover, George Willoughby; when published in *Elegiac Sonnets* it was entitled 'Supposed to have been written in a church-yard, over the grave of a young woman of nineteen'. In the second, Celestina, separated from her friends during the exploration of the Hebrides, reverts to thoughts of Willoughby; in *Elegiac Sonnets* it was entitled 'Supposed to have been written in the Hebrides'.

Wordsworth's *Descriptive Sketches* (1793), composed in France 1791-2, alludes to part of the second of these sonnets, where Celestina sees 'ospreys, cormorants and sea mews' on the 'lone island':

> Mid stormy vapours ever driving by,
> Where ospreys, cormorants, and herons cry,
> Where hardly giv'n the hopeless waste to chear,
> Deny'd the bread of life the foodful ear . . .

(Descriptive Sketches 318-20)

Oh thou that[1] sleep'st where hazel bands entwine
The vernal grass with paler violets dress'd;
I would, sweet maid! thy humble bed were mine,
And mine thy calm and enviable rest.
For never more by human ills oppress'd   5
Shall thy soft spirit fruitlessly repine:
Thou can'st not now thy fondest hope[2] resign
Ev'n in the hour that should have made thee bless'd.
Light lies the turf upon thy virgin breast;
And lingering here, to love and sorrow true,   10
The youth who once thy simple heart possess'd
Shall mingle tears with April's earliest[3] dew;
While still for him shall faithful memory save
Thy form and virtues from the silent grave.

---

[1] **that** 'who' in printed texts.
[2] **hope** 'hopes' in *Elegiac Sonnets*.
[3] **earliest** 'early' in printed texts.

On this lone island whose unfruitful breast
Feeds but the summer shepherd's little flock
With scanty herbage from the half cloath'd rock
Where ospreys, cormorants and sea mews rest;
Even in a scene so desolate and rude   5
I could with thee for months and years be bless'd;
And of thy tenderness and love possess'd,
Find all my world in this lone[1] solitude!
When the bright suns[2] these northern waves illume,
With thee admire the light's reflected charms,   10
And when drear winter spreads his cheerless gloom,
Still find Elysium in thy sheltering arms:
For thou to me canst sovereign bliss impart,
Thy mind my empire – and thy throne my heart.[3]

---

[1] **lone** 'wild' in *Elegiac Sonnets*.
[2] **the bright suns** 'summer suns' in *Elegiac Sonnets*.
[3] **thy throne my heart** 'my throne thy heart' in published texts.
Wordsworth's reading makes sense, and far from being a scribal error
could represent an early reading later revised by Smith.

Joseph Fawcett, *The Art of War* (1795) (extract)

Date of reading: soon after March 1795

An old man in his seventies, Wordsworth looked back on his time in London immediately following the execution of Louis XVI and the outbreak of war with France, when he was moving in radical circles, and remembered 'several persons with whom I had been connected':

> The chief of these was, one may *now* say, *a* Mr Fawcett, a preacher at a dissenting meeting-House at the Old Jewry. It happened to me several times to be one of his congregation through my connection with Mr Nicholson of Cateaton Street, Strand, who, at a time when I had not many acquaintances in London, used often to invite me to dine with him on Sundays, and I took that opportunity (Mr N. being a Dissenter) of going to hear Fawcett who was an able and eloquent man. He published a Poem on War, which had a good deal of merit and made me think more about him than I should otherwise have done.

Wordsworth probably read Fawcett's *The Art of War* soon after publication in late March 1795. Even at that time he was interested in extreme mental and psychological states: his current projects, *Adventures on Salisbury Plain* and the *Fragment of a Gothic Tale*, dealt with the guilt and self-loathing that follow acts of violence. This may have had something to do with the fact that he had been an advocate of regicide at the time of Louis XVI's execution (in January 1793). For that reason the passage selected from Fawcett's long poem is that most likely to have led the young poet to think more about its author than he should otherwise have done: Fawcett's account of a murderer's state of mind.

The Art of War
(extract)

Stript of its trappings, 'tis a deed so dire,
On the first motion of the mind that way,   970
The wretch whom strong temptation draws towards it,
Shrinks from his thought; tries from himself to run;
And is afraid to trust him with himself.
With violent force he calls his thoughts from off
So foul a thing, and tries to chain 'em down.   975
Again and yet again the magnet prize,
Whose strong attraction tugs against the terms
As strongly that repel him, spite of all
His strife to struggle from it, to his mind
Recurs; renews its hold; repeats its pulls: 980
Again and yet again his look returns
To the black work by which it must be won,
Ere his recoiling Reason, less and less
That backward starts, as oftener up it goes
And eyes its fear, with slow consent complies.   985
A deed so dark, that he who has a heart
To wish it done, and wealth a hand to buy,
Culls from the crowd, with penetrating choice,
A face of stone; whose muscles never move
Into a smile; whose heavy, brooding brow,   990
Habitual overhung, his eye's dark den,
Blackens beneath its shade their surly low'r.
A deed, which he who to another moves,
Knows not to name; he has a thing to say,[1]
Which, while he can be seen, he cannot say,   995
Full in his face while looks the staring sun;
Which he must say surrounded by the night;
Which he would say without the use of sound,
Silent infuse into his fellow's breast
By inspiration's spiritual speech;   1000
Which with half utterance he hesitates,
With an unfinish'd voice, unfill'd with breath,
Faint timid tones that fear to leave the lip,
Sounds so like silence, that the hearer doubts

---

[1] Shakespear: King John. (Fawcett's note)

If heard or not; with sentences, concise, 1005
Close clipt and spare, a frugal niggard speech;
All prating superfluities left out,
And issued none but necessary sounds;
Speech bare of words, all hint and skeleton,
In expletives, that plump sleek language out 1010
Meet for the mouth of Pleasure, all uncloath'd,
Suited cadav'rous to the ghastly theme!
A deed, in which the hardier villain's mouth,
That would th' accomplice keep, his words have won,
In his oft-back-retreating must oft 1015
His rallying spirit pour. It is a deed,
Which when determin'd by a tempted wretch,
All his dire fund of fortitude in ill
He must call forth to do, and wind his heart
As high as it will stretch. His choice of time 1020
He fixes on the hour when all the world
Is dead; when with the colour of his act
Darkness accords; and every eye is clos'd.
Between his purpose and his dreadful stroke
Wild is the space within him:² to the scene 1025
Of his dark act, with a light-falling foot,
Ghost-like he glides; and fancifully fears
Lest strange and wondrous voices wake the world
And babble of his business.³ When the blow
His heav'n-forsook and hell-driv'n hand hath struck, 1030
He is 'afraid to think on what he has done;'
That 'twere undone, is his devoutest wish.
Of heaven and earth he feels himself accurst.
With wildest superstition seiz'd, he dreads
That preternat'ral Providence will point 1035
Its finger at his guilt. Whate'er his gain,
He finds that Peace and he have parted, ne'er
To meet again. 'Tis ill for ever with him.
An horrid spectre is before his eyes.
The grave sends back again his ghastly gift; 1040
The shadowy resurrection's grim reproach
Shakes all the trembling pillars of his soul.

---

² Julius Caesar. (Fawcett's note)
³ Macbeth. (Fawcett's note)

He starts, when nothing stirr'd; – 'Who speaks?' – he asks,
When no one spoke; and mutters things unheard
With nimble-moving lips that send no sound.   1045
Disturb'd e'en in the stillest room he lies;
Kept by no noise awake, no sleep he finds,
Or no oblivion finds it. Glad t' escape
From scaring visions, soon in sweats he wakes.
To cheer his midnight hour he must have light   1050
Continual at his couch; the live-long day,
As clings a drowning wretch to him he holds,
(Dreading, as doth that drowning wretch the wave,
Soul-sinking solitude) he closely cleaves
To some companion's side; hunted he seeks   1055
From the keen terrors that his soul pursue
Protection in his presence; when there's near
Nought hostile to him save himself, he fears;
Flees unpursued; and unsuspected, reads
In every eye discernment of his deed.   1060
His life an heavy load upon him lies
He can no longer bear; all wan and worn,
The conscience-wither'd wretch a witness comes
Against himself; and gloomy refuge seeks,
In the dire executioner, from one   1065
More dire within; before his country's bar
When pale he stands, a crowd of curious eyes
The hall of justice choak, with hungry gaze
And gloomy eagerness to mark the case
Of such a monstrous mind! each line to trace,   1070
Where Penetration seeks to track the tread
Of aspect-printing soul; and every look
And motion, with unwearied watchfulness,
Of the prodigious culprit to devour!

Andrew Marvell, *A Drop of Dew, An Horatian Ode upon Cromwell's Return from Ireland*

Date of reading: summer 1795

> Great Men have been among us; hands that penn'd
> And tongues that utter'd wisdom, better none:
> The later Sydney, Marvel, Harrington,
> Young Vane, and others who call'd Milton Friend.
>
> ('Great Men have been among us',
composed May 1802)

Wordsworth was probably introduced to Marvell's poetry by his friend Francis Wrangham in the summer of 1795 while on a visit to Cobham in Surrey (where Wrangham lived). Wrangham was a year older than Wordsworth and like him had been up at Cambridge; he had heard Wordsworth read his early poem, 'Salisbury Plain', and proposed that they embark on a collaborative version of Juvenal's eighth satire.

It was probably for that reason that Wrangham introduced Wordsworth to Marvell's satirical verse, though Wordsworth soon discovered other aspects of his work, not least such religious and political poetry as 'A Drop of Dew' and 'An Horatian Ode'.

'A Drop of Dew' inspired Wordsworth's 'To H.C., Six Years Old', his poignant tribute to Coleridge's son Hartley, composed 1802-4:

> Thou art a Dew-Drop, which the morn brings forth,
> Not doom'd to jostle with unkindly shocks;
> Or to be trail'd along the soiling earth;
> A Gem that glitters while it lives,
> And no forewarning gives;
> But, at the touch of wrong, without a strife
> Slips in a moment out of life.

Wordsworth included 'A Drop of Dew' in the anthology he made for Lady Mary Lowther in 1819, omitting the last four lines. Preferring a complete version I have chosen to edit my text from Captain Edward Thompson's 1776 edition of Marvell.

In c. September 1802 he copied 'An Horatian Ode' into a note-book later used for drafting of *The Prelude*, almost certainly working from Thompson. Charles Lamb owned a copy, and the Wordsworths were seeing the Lambs regularly during the first three weeks of September 1802. Variants between Thompson and Wordsworth reveal a consistent effort to modernise orthography and punctuation – an improvement from the reader's point of view – and in this case I have chosen to edit from Wordsworth's draft.

A Drop of Dew

See, how the orient dew,
Shed from the bosom of the morn,
Into the blowing roses,
Yet careless of its mansion new,
For the clear region where 'twas born,   5
Round in itself incloses:
And in its little globe's extent,
Frames, as it can, its native element.
How it the purple flow'r does slight,
Scarce touching where it lys;   10
But gazing back upon the skys,
Shines with a mournful light,
Like its own tear,
Because so long divided from the sphere
Restless it rolls, and unsecure,   15
Trembling, lest it grows impure;
Till the warm sun pitys its pain,
And to the skys exhales it back again.
So the soul, that drop, that ray,
Of the clear fountain of eternal day,   20
Could it within the human flow'r be seen,
Rememb'ring still its former height,
Shuns the sweet leaves, and blossoms green;
And, recollecting its own light,
Does, in its pure and circling thoughts, express   25
The greater heaven in an heaven less.
In how coy a figure wound,
Every way it turns away;
So the world excluding round,
Yet receiving in the day.   30
Dark beneath, but bright above;
Here disdaining, there in love.

How loose and easy hence to go;
How girt and ready to ascend;
Moving but on a point below,   35
It all about does upwards bend.
Such did the manna's sacred dew distil,
White and entire, although congeal'd and chill;
Congeal'd on earth; but does, dissolving, run
Into the glorys of th' almighty sun.   40

An Horatian Ode Upon Cromwell's Return from Ireland

By Andrew Marvell

The forward youth that would appear
Must now forsake his muses dear,
    Nor in the shadows sing
    His numbers languishing.

Tis time to leave the books in dust,   5
And oyl th' unused armour's rust;
    Removing from the wall
    The corslett of the hall.

So restless Cromwell could not cease
In the inglorious arts of peace,   10
    But through adventrous war
    Urged his active star;

And like the threefork'd lightning first
Breaking the clouds where it was nurst,
    Did thorough his own side   15
    His fiery way divide.

(For tis all one to courage high
The emulous or enemy;
    And with such to enclose
    Is more than to oppose.)   20

Then burning through the air he went
And palaces and temples rent;
    And Cæsar's head at last
    Did through his laurels blast.

Tis madness to resist or blame   25
The face of angry heaven's flame;
    And if we would speak true
    Much to the man is due:

Who from his private gardens, where
He lived reserved, and austere,   30
    As if his highest plot
    To plant the Bergamott,

Could by industrious valour climb
To ruin the great work of time,
    And cast the kingdoms old   35
    Into another mold.

Though justice against fate complain
And plead the antient rights in vain;
    But those do hold or break
    As men are strong or weak.   40

Nature, that hateth emptiness,
Allows of penetration less;
    And therefore must make room
    Where greater spirits come.

What field of all the civil war,   45
Where his were not the deepest scar?
    And Hampton shews what part
    He had of wiser art:

Where, twining subtle fears with hope,
He wove a net of such a scope,   50
        That Charles himself might chase
        To Caresbrook's narrow case.

That thence the royal Actor borne,
The tragic scaffold might adorne,
        While round the armed bands   55
        Did clap their bloody hands:

He nothing common did or mean,
Upon that memorable scene;
        But with his keener eye,
        The axe's edge did try.   60

Nor call'd the gods with vulgar spight
To vindicate his helpless right:
        But bow'd his comely head
        Down, as upon a bed.

This was that memorable hour   65
Which first assured the forced power:
        So when they did design
        The Capitol's first line,

A bleeding head, where they begun,
Did fright the Architects to run;   70
        And yet in that the State
        Foresaw its happy fate.

And now the Irish are ashamed
To see themselves in one year tamed;
        So much one man can do   75
        Who does both act and know.

They can affirm his praises best,
And have, though overcome, confest
        How good he is, how just,
        And fit for highest trust.   80

Nor yet grown stiffer with command,
But still in the Republic's hand,
    How fit he is to sway,
    That can so well obey.

He to the Common's feet presents   85
A Kingdom for his first year's rents:
    And what he may forbears
    His fame, to make it theirs;

And has his sword and spoils ungirt
To lay them at the public's skirt.   90
    So when the Falcon high,
    Falls heavy from the sky,

She, having kill'd, no more does search,
But on the next green bough to perch;
    Where, when he first does lure,   95
    The Falconer has her sure.

What may not then our isle presume
While victory his crest does plume?
    What may not others fear
    If thus he crowns each year?   100

A Cæsar, he, ere long to Gaul,
To Italy an Hannibal,
    And to all states not free
    Shall clymateric be.

The Pict no shelter now shall find   105
Within his party-colour'd mind,
    But from this valour, sad,
    Shrink underneath the plaid;

Happy, if in the tufted brake,
The English Hunter him mistake,   110
    Nor lay his hounds in near
    The Caledonian deer.

1795

But thou, the war's and fortune's, Son,
March indefatigably on;
    And for the last effect   115
    Still keep the sword erect;

Besides the force it has to fright
The spirits of the shady night,
    The same arts that did gain
    A power, must it maintain.   120

William Crowe, *Lewesdon Hill* **(1788) (extract)**

Date of reading: November-December 1795

By November 1795 Wordsworth was living with Dorothy at Racedown Lodge in Dorset, owned by John Prator Pinney, father of their friend Azariah Pinney. Unbeknownst to Azariah's father, the Wordsworths were residing there rent-free – an arrangement that would cause problems for Azariah when his father found out in May 1796.

Based in Bristol, Azariah had access to a number of booksellers who received stock from London, and was able to send the Wordsworths a supply of books old and new – among them, Crowe's *Lewesdon Hill,* which he knew would be of interest to them as it concerned the countryside immediately surrounding Racedown. Wordsworth always expressed fondness for it; in 1810 Henry Crabb Robinson recorded in his diary that *Lewesdon Hill* was 'a poem Wordsworth speaks highly of'. He hung onto the copy sent by Azariah; it was on the shelves at Rydal Mount at the time of his death.

The opening of the poem, which includes an ascent of the hill (a forerunner of the Wordsworthian prospect along the Wye valley in 'Tintern Abbey'), is edited from the text of 1788.

Lewesdon Hill

Up to thy summit, LEWESDON, to the brow
Of yon proud rising, where the lonely thorn
Bends from the rude South-east, with top cut sheer
By his keen breath, along the narrow track
By which the scanty-pastured sheep ascend   5
Up to thy furze-clad summit, let me climb;
My morning exercise; and thence look round
Upon the variegated scene, of hills,
And woods, and fruitful vales, and villages
Half-hid in tufted orchards, and the sea   10
Boundless, and studded thick with many a sail.

Ye dew-fed vapours, nightly balm, exhaled
From earth, young herbs and flowers, that in the morn
Ascend as incense to the Lord of day,
I come to breathe your odours; while they float   15
Yet near this surface, let me walk embathed
In your invisible perfumes, to health
So friendly, nor less grateful to the mind,
Administring sweet peace and cheerfulness.
   How changed is thy appearance, beauteous hill!   20
Thou hast put off thy wintry garb, brown heath
And russet fern, thy seemly-colour'd cloak
To bide the hoary frosts and dripping rains
Of chill December, and art gaily robed
In livery of the spring: upon thy brow   25
A cap of flowery hawthorn, and thy neck
Mantled with new-sprung furze and spangles thick
Of golden bloom: nor lack thee tufted woods
Adown thy sides: Tall oaks of lusty green,
The darker fir, light ash, and the nesh tops   30
Of the young hazel join, to form thy skirts
In many a wavy fold of verdant wreath.
So gorgeously hath Nature drest thee up
Against the birth of May; and, vested so,
Thou dost appear more gracefully array'd   35
Than Fashion's worshippers; whose gaudy shews,
Fantastical as are a sick man's dreams,
From vanity to costly vanity
Change ofter than the moon. Thy comely dress,
From sad to gay returning with the year,   40
Shall grace thee still till Nature's self shall change.
   These are the beauties of thy woodland scene
At each return of spring: yet some delight
Rather to view the change; and fondly gaze
On fading colours, and the thousand tints   45
Which Autumn lays upon the varying leaf.
I like them not; for all their boasted hues
Are kin to Sickliness: mortal Decay
Is drinking up their vital juice; that gone,
They turn to fear and yellow. Should I praise   50
Such false complexions, and for beauty take
A look consumption-bred? As soon, if gray
Were mixt in young Louisa's tresses brown,

I'd call it beautiful variety,
And therefore doat on her. Yet I can spy 55
A beauty in that fruitful change, when comes
The yellow Autumn and the hopes o'the year
Brings on to golden ripeness; nor dispraise
The pure and spotless form of that sharp time,
When January spreads a pall of snow 60
O'er the dead face of th'undistinguish'd earth.
Then stand I in the hollow comb beneath
And bless this friendly mount, that weather-sends
My reed-roof'd cottage, while the wintry blast
From the thick north comes howling: till the Spring 65
Return, who leads my devious steps abroad,
To climb, as now, to LEWESDON's airy top.
    Above the noise and stir of yonder fields
Uplifted, on this height I feel the mind
Expand itself in wider liberty. 70
The distant sounds break gently on my sense,
Soothing to meditation: so methinks,
Even so, sequester'd from the noisy world,
Could I wear out this transitory being
In peaceful contemplation and calm ease. 75
But conscience, which still censures on our acts,
That awful voice within us, and the sense
Of an hereafter, wake and rouse us up
From such unshaped retirement; which were else
A blest condition on this earthy stage. 80
For who would make his life a life of toil
For wealth, o'erbalanced with a thousand cares;
Or power, which base compliance must uphold;
Or honour, lavish'd most on courtly slaves;
Or fame, vain breath of a misjudging world; 85
Who for such perishable gaudes would put
A yoke upon his free unspoken spirit,
And gall himself with trammels and the rubs
Of this world's business; so he might stand clear
Of judgment and the tax of idleness 90
In that dread audit, when his mortal hours
(Which now with soft and silent stealth pace by)
Must all be counted for? But, for this fear,
And to remove, according to our power,
The wants and evils of our brother's state, 95

'Tis meet we justle with the world; content,
If by our sovereign Master we be found
At last not profitless: for worldly meed,
Given or witheld, I deem of it alike.
    From this proud eminence on all sides round   100
Th' unbroken prospect opens to my view;
On all sides large; save only where the head
Of Pillesdon rises, Pillesdon's lofty Pen:
So call (still rendering to his ancient name
Observance due) that rival Height south-west,   105
Which like a rampire bounds the vale beneath.
There woods, there blooming orchards, there are seen
Herds, ranging, or at rest beneath the shade
Of some wide-branching oak; there goodly fields
Of corn, and verdant pasture, whence the kine   110
Returning with their milky treasure home
Store the rich dairy: such fair plenty fills
The pleasant vale of Marshwood; pleasant now,
Since that the Spring has deck'd anew the meads
With flowery vesture, and the warmer sun   115
Their foggy moistness drain'd; in wintry days
Cold, vapourish, miry, wet, and to the flocks
Unfriendly, when autumnal rains begin
To drench the spungy turf: but ere that time
The careful shepherd moves to healthier soil,   120
Rechasing, lest his tender ewes should coath[1]
In the dank pasturage. Yet not the fields
Of Evesham, nor that ample valley named
Of the White Horse, its antique monument
Carved in the chalky bourne, for beauty' and wealth   125
Might equal, though surpassing in extent,

---

[1] To *coath*, Skinner says, is a word common in Lincolnshire; and signifies,
to *faint*. He derives it from the Anglo-Saxon, coðe, a *disease*. In Dorsetshire
it is common use, but is used of sheep only: a *coathed* sheep is a *rotten*
sheep; to *coath* is to *take the rot*. *Rechasing* is also a term in that country
appropriated to flocks: *to chase and rechase* is to drive sheep at certain times
from one sort of ground to another, or from one parish to another.
    The Author having ventured to introduce some provincial and other
terms, takes this occasion to say, that it is a liberty in which he has not
indulged himself, but when he conceived them to be allowable for the sake
of ornament or expression. (Crowe's note)

This fertile vale; in length from LEWESDON's base
Extended to the sea, and water'd well
By many a rill; but chief with thy clear stream,
Thou nameless Rivulet, who from the side   130
Of LEWESDON softly welling forth, dost trip
Adown the valley, wandering sportively.
Alas, how soon thy little course will end!
How soon thy infant stream shall lose itself
In the salt mass of waters, ere it grow   135
To name or greatness! Yet it flows along
Untainted with the commerce of the world,
Nor passing by the noisy haunts of men;
But through sequester'd meads, a little space,
Winds secretly, and in its wanton path   140
May cheer some drooping flower, or minister
Of its cool water to the thirsty lamb:
Then falls into the ravenous sea, as pure
As when it issued from its native hill.

William Gilbert, *The Hurricane: A Theosophical and Western Eclogue* (1796) (extract)

Date of reading: summer 1796

> . . . you I think must assuredly have heard of him: he was a Barrister and had practised in the West Indies, and lived some time in Bristol, between the year –95 and –98, at which time I often conversed with him, and admired his genius though he was in fact insane.
>
> (Wordsworth to John Peace, 19 September 1839)

Wordsworth was probably introduced to William Gilbert by either Joseph Cottle or Coleridge in the spring or summer 1796. An Antiguan by birth, Gilbert's failure as a lawyer led in 1787 to a bout of mental imbalance which according to Southey had by 1796 become permanent: 'he was the most insane person I have ever known at large, and his insanity smothered his genius'. Gilbert was especially preoccupied with the 'Gilberti', an African nation unknown to geographers, but whom he affirmed to exist, and to be related to his family. He contributed an essay, 'The Commercial Academic', to Coleridge's magazine *The Watchman* in April 1796, and the following month an extract from *The Hurricane*, prior to publication of the volume later that year.

The Hurricane is an eccentric book which the *Dictionary of National Biography* describes as 'a poem betokening both the power and the disorder of his faculties'. It is certainly resistant to easy interpretation thanks in large part to its author's so-called theosophical theories. It describes, in allegorical terms, the overthrow of Europe by America, an event symbolised by the hurricane of the poem's title. In a series of notes at the back of the volume Gilbert discusses the various reasons why America was in the ascendant, by contrast with the decadent ways of Europeans. One of the notes inspired a passage in *The Excursion* (1814):

> along the side
> Of Mississippi, or that Northern Stream
> Which spreads into successive seas, he walks;
> Pleased to perceive his own unshackled life,
> And his innate capacities of soul,
> There imaged: or, when having gained the top
> Of some commanding Eminence, which yet

Intruder ne'er beheld, he thence surveys
Regions of wood and wide Savannah, vast
Expanse of unappropriated earth,
With mind that sheds a light on what he sees . . .

(The Excursion iii 939-49)

When he published this, Wordsworth attached to it an extract from
one of Gilbert's notes, commenting: 'The Reader, I am sure, will
thank me for the above Quotation, which, though from a strange
book, is one of the finest passages of modern English Prose'. One
reader was grateful: John Keats, whose concluding sestet of 'On
First Looking into Chapman's Homer' it inspired.

Then I felt like some watcher of the skies
When a new planet swims into his ken;
Or like stout Cortez when with eagle eyes
He stared at the Pacific – and all his men
Looked at each other with a wild surmise –
Silent, upon a peak in Darien.

(ll. 9-14)

My text of Gilbert's note is edited from the printed text of 1796.

A MAN is supposed to improve by going out into the *world*, by
visiting *London*. Artificial man does; he extends with his sphere; but
alas! that sphere is microscopic: It is formed of minutiæ, and he
surrenders his genuine vision to the artist, in order to embrace it in
his ken. His bodily senses grow acute, even to barren and inhuman
pruriency; while his mental become proportionally obtuse. The
reverse is the Man of Mind: He who is placed the sphere of Nature
and of GOD, might be a mock at Tattersall's and Brookes's, and a
sneer at St. James's: He would certainly be swallowed alive by the
first *Pizarro*, that crossed him: – But, when he walks along the River
of Amazons; when he rests his eye on the unrivalled Andes; when
he measures the long and watered Savannah; or contemplates from
a sudden Promontary, the distant, Vast Pacific – and feels himself a
FREEMAN in this vast Theatre, and commanding each ready pro-
duced fruit of this wilderness, and each progeny of this stream – His

exaltation is not less than Imperial. He is as gentle too as he is great: His emotions of tenderness keep pace with his elevation of sentiment; for he says, 'These were made by a good Being, who unsought by me, placed me here to enjoy them.' He becomes at once, a Child and a King. His mind is in himself; from hence he argues and from hence he acts; and he argues unerringly and acts magisterially: His Mind in himself is also in his GOD; and therefore he loves, and therefore he soars.

William Sotheby, *Tour through Parts of Wales* (1794):
Sonnet VIII. A Fancy Sketch

Date of reading: 1797

> I was gratified the other day by meeting in Mr Alaric Watts'
> Souvenir with a very old acquaintance, a Sonnet of yours, which
> I had read with no little pleasure more than 30 years ago. 'I knew
> a gentle Maid'.
>
> (Wordsworth to William Sotheby, 6 February 1827)

Sotheby's sixteen-liner, 'I knew a gentle maid', first appeared in
Poems (1790), and was reprinted in his *Tour through Parts of Wales*
(1794). Wordsworth's letter suggests that he first encountered it
between 1790 and 1797. He had probably seen both of Sotheby's
volumes by the time he met him at Dove Cottage in late June 1802.
At that time Sotheby was best known as a translator from German,
primarily for his rendering of Wieland's *Oberon* (1798). It is not
easy on the basis of his comment in 1827 to know what
Wordsworth really thought of the poem, but that he should have
remembered it over a period of three decades suggests that it made
a strong impression on him.

It is here edited from the text of 1794.

Sonnet VIII.

A Fancy Sketch

I knew a gentle maid: I ne'er shall view
 Her like again: and yet the vulgar eye
 Might pass the charms I traced, regardless by;
For pale her cheek, unmarked with roseate hue;
 Nor beamed from her mild eye a dazzling glance;   5
Nor flashed her nameless graces on the sight;
Yet beauty never woke such pure delight.
 Fine was her form, as DIAN's in the dance;
Her voice was music, in her silence dwelt

Expression, every look instinct with thought: 10
    Though oft her mind by youth to rapture wrought
Struck forth wild wit, and fancies ever new,
The lightest touch of woe her soul would melt:
    And on her lips, when gleamed a lingering smile,
    Pity's warm tear gushed down her cheek the while: 15
Thy like, thou gentle maid! I ne'er shall view.

William Bartram, *Travels Through North and South Carolina* (1791) (extract)

Date of reading: 1797-8

During the intense year of collaboration they spent together in Somerset, from 1797 to 1798, Wordsworth and Coleridge read much poetry and a number of travel books. Coleridge read Bartram's *Travels* before Wordsworth, and its influence registered immediately on *The Ancient Mariner*. While in Somerset he almost certainly lent Wordsworth the copy he was reading, and it shaped some of his poems – notably, 'Complaint of a Forsaken Indian Woman', 'Ruth', and the passage in *The Prelude* in which Wordsworth uses the metaphor of a 'virgin grove / Primeval' for his ideal university:

> Oh, what joy it were
> To see a sanctuary for our country's youth
> With such a spirit in it as might be
> Protection for itself, a virgin grove
> Primeval in its purity and depth,
> Where, though the shades were filled with cheerfulness,
> Nor indigent of songs warbled from crowds
> In under-coverts, yet the countenance
> Of the whole place should wear a stamp of awe –
> A habitation sober and demure
> For ruminating creatures, a domain
> For quiet things to wander in, a haunt
> In which the heron might delight to feed
> By the shy rivers, and the pelican
> Upon the cypress-spire in lonely thought
> Might sit and sun himself. Alas, alas!
> In vain for such solemnity we look.
> Our eyes are crossed by butterflies, our ears
> Hear chattering popinjays; the inner heart
> Is trivial, and the impresses without
> Are of a gaudy region.

> (*The Thirteen-Book Prelude* iii 439-59)

The inspiration for this was Bartram's account of his journey up the Alatamaha river in Part I chapter 5, edited here from the copy of Bartram's *Travels* published in Philadelphia, 1791, presented by

165   *1797-8*

Coleridge to Sara Hutchinson in 1801, now retained at the Wordsworth Library in Grasmere. It was probably the copy Wordsworth and Coleridge read in Somerset, 1797-8, originally owned by their mutual friend James Tobin, who sent it to Wordsworth (via his brother John) in February 1801. Although it remained in Wordsworth's keeping for the rest of his life, Coleridge presented it to Sara Hutchinson, composing a lengthy inscription now pasted onto the inside front cover dated 'Dec. 19. 1801':

> This is not a Book of Travels, properly speaking; but a series of poems, chiefly descriptive, *occasioned* by the objects, which the Traveller observed. – It is a *delicious* Book; and like all *delicious* Things, you must take but a *little* of it at a time. – Was it not about this time of the year, that I read to you parts of the 'Introduction' of this Book, when William and Dorothy had gone out to walk? – I remember the evening well, but not what time of the year it was.

How gently flow thy peaceful floods, O Alatamaha! How sublimely rise to view, on thy elevated shores, yon Magnolian groves, from whose tops the surrounding expanse is perfumed, by clouds of incense, blended with the exhaling balm of the Liquid-amber, and odours continually arising from circumambient aromatic groves of Illicium, Myrica, Laurus and Bignonia.

When wearied, with working my canoe against the impetuous current (which becomes stronger by reason of the mighty floods of the river, with collected force, pressing through the first hilly ascents, where the shores on each side the river present to view rocky cliffs rising above the surface of the water, in nearly flat horizontal masses, washed smooth by the descending floods, and which appear to be a composition, or concrete, of sandy lime-stone) I resigned my bark to the friendly current, reserving to myself the controul of the helm. My progress was rendered delightful by the sylvan elegance of the groves, chearful meadows, and high distant forests, which in grand order presented themselves to view. The winding banks of the river, and the high projecting promontories, unfolded fresh scenes of grandeur and sublimity. The deep forests and distant hills re-echoed the chearing social lowings of domestic herds. The air was filled with the loud and shrill whooping of the wary sharp-sighted crane. Behold, on yon decayed, defoliated Cypress tree, the solitary wood-pelican, dejectedly perched upon its utmost elevated spire; he there, like an ancient venerable sage, sets himself up as a mark of derision, for the safety of his kindred tribes. The crying-bird, another faithful guardian, screaming in the gloomy thickets, warns the feathered tribes of approaching peril; and the plumage of the swift sailing squadrons of Spanish curlews (white as the immaculate robe of innocence) gleam in the cerulean skies.

Thus secure and tranquil, and meditating on the marvellous scenes of primitive nature, as yet unmodified by the hand of man, I gently descended the peaceful stream, on whose polished surface were depicted the mutable shadows from its pensile banks; whilst myriads of finny inhabitants sported in its pellucid floods.

George Wither, *The Shepherd's Hunting* **(extract)**

Date of reading: 1797-8

Coleridge introduced Wordsworth to Wither's poems in 1797, having introduced Lamb to them the year before. Wordsworth immediately took to *The Shepherd's Hunting* (all five eclogues of which Wither composed in prison), and its influence is to be found in 'The Tables Turned', 'To the Daisy' ('In youth from rock to rock'), and the 'Immortality Ode', among others; as late as 1843 his American editor Henry Reed recorded his high opinion of Wither's poetry. Coleridge's copy passed into Wordsworth's possession and was at Rydal Mount after his death.

When compiling a collection of poetry for Lady Mary Lowther in 1819, Wordsworth returned to Wither's poem and extracted a passage from Eclogue 4; it is here edited from his transcription.

On his Muse
(From the Shepherd's hunting)

By George Wither

For though banished from my flocks
And confin'd within these rocks,
Here I waste away the light,
And consume the sullen night,
She doth for my comfort stay   5
And keeps many cares away,
Though I miss the flowery fields,
With these fruits the spring-tide yields,
Though I may not see those groves
Where the Shepherds chaunt their loves,   10
And the Lasses more excel
Than the sweet-voiced Philomel;

Though all these pleasures past
Nothing now remains at last
But remembrance, poor relief   15
That more makes than mends my grief;
She's my minds companion still
Maugre envy's evil will,
Whence she should be driven too
Wer't in mortals power to do.   20
She doth tell me where to borrow
Comfort in the midst of sorrow,
Makest the desolatest place
To her presence be a grace,
And the blackest discontents   25
To be pleasing ornaments.
In my former days of bliss
Her divine skill taught me this,
That from every thing I saw
I could some invention draw,   30
And raise pleasure to her height,
Through the meanest object's sight,
By the murmur of a spring
Or the least boughs *rusteling*;
By a daisy whose leaves spread   35
Shut when Titan goes to bed;
Or a shady bush or tree
She could more infuse in me,
Than all nature's beauties can
In some other wiser man.   40
By her help I also now
Make this churlish place allow
Some things that may sweeten gladness,
In the very gall of sadness.
The dull loneness, the black shade   45
That these hanging vaults have made,
The strange music of the waves,
Beating on these hollow caves;
This black den which rocks emboss
Overgrown with eldest moss   50
The rude portals that give light
More to terror than delight;
This my chamber of neglect,
Walled about with disrespect;

1797-8

From all these and this dull air,   55
A fit object for despair,
She hath taught me by her might
To draw comfort and delight.
Therefore thou best, earthly bliss
I will cherish thee for this, –   60
Poesy! – thou sweetest content
That e'er heaven to mortals lent
Though they as a trifle leave thee
Whose dull thoughts cannot conceive thee;
Though thou be to them a scorn   65
That to nought but earth art born;
Let my Life no longer be
Than I am in love with thee;
Though our wise-ones call thee madness
Let me never taste of gladness   70
If I love not thy maddest fits
More than all their greatest wits.
And though some too, seeming holy,
Do accoūt thy raptures folly,
Thou dost teach me to contemn   75
What makes knaves and fools of them.
Oh high Power! that oft doth carry
Men above . . .

Samuel Daniel, *To the Lady Margaret, Countess of Cumberland*

Date of reading: 1797-8

> Read Daniel – the Civil Wars, or the Triumphs of Hymen. The style and language are just such as a very pure and manly writer of the present day would use; it seems quite modern in comparison with Shakspeare.
>
> (Coleridge, *Table Talk* 15 March 1834)

Such was the advice Coleridge gave Wordsworth in 1797; with the poetry of Wither (see preceding poem), that of Daniel was for Wordsworth a major literary discovery. All Coleridge's friends and acquaintances were introduced to it, including Lamb and Lady Beaumont.

Wordsworth's passion for Daniel's poetry may have been predictable; as Coleridge remarked on another occasion: 'Daniel is a superior man; his diction is preeminently pure – of that sort which I believe has always existed somewhere in society – just such without any alteration as Wordsworth or Sir George Beaumont might have spoken or written in the present day'. It was a perceptive remark, for Daniel occasionally sounds like Wordsworth, especially when discussing the natural world:

> Here have you craggy Rocks to take your Part,
> That never will betray their Faith to you . . .
>
> A Place there is, where proudly rais'd there stands
> A huge aspiring Rock, neighb'ring the skies . . .
>
> (*The Civil Wars* ii stanzas 29, 48)

The idea that the craggy rocks 'never will betray their Faith to you' is echoed in 'Tintern Abbey' where 'Nature never did betray / The heart that loved her' (ll. 123-4). The affinities are so strong that Wordsworth incorporated eight lines of Daniel's 'To the Lady Margaret' verbatim into *The Excursion* Book IV.

Wordsworth's copy of Daniel's *Poems* is now in the Wordsworth Library, Grasmere. The third flyleaf of volume 1 contains a note by Wordsworth's grandson dated March 1858, saying that 'the volumes were among my Grandfathers especial favourites and were frequently in his hands'. That it should be the same edition as that owned by Lamb (1718 – now in the Houghton Library, Harvard) makes me wonder whether both were supplied to their respective owners by Coleridge. At all events, Wordsworth has marked with a cross the title of one of his favourite poems, 'To the Lady Margaret', which he copied into the album he compiled for Lady Mary Lowther in 1819; this text is edited from his transcription. When writing to Lady Beaumont in November 1811 he recommended that she read it, remarking that 'The whole poem is composed in a strain of meditative morality more dignified and affecting than anything of the kind I ever read. It is, besides, strikingly applicable to the revolutions of the present times' (by which he meant the Luddite uprisings of November 1811). Daniel was tutor to Lady Margaret Clifford's daughter Anne in the last years of the sixteenth century.

~♥

To the Lady Margaret,
Countess of Cumberland

He that to such a height hath built his mind,
And reared the dwelling of his thoughts so strong,
As neither fear nor hope can shake the frame
Of his resolved powers; nor all the wind
Of vanity or malice pierce to wrong   5
His settled peace, or to disturb the same:
What a fair seat hath he, from whence he may
The boundless wastes and wields of man survey. –
  And with how free an eye doth he look down
Upon these lower regions of turmoil?   10
Where all the storms of passion mainly beat,
On flesh and blood: where honor, power, renown,
Are only gay afflictions, golden toil;
Where greatness stands upon as feeble feet
As frailty doth; and only great doth seem   15
To little minds who do it so esteem.
  He looks upon the mightiest monarchs wars
But only as an stately robberies;
Where evermore the fortune that prevails
Must be the right: the ill-succeeding mars   20

The fairest and the best-faced enterprize.
Great Pirate Pompey lesser pirates quails:
Justice, he sees (as if seduced) still
Conspires with power whose cause must not be ill.
   He sees the face of Right to appear as manifold   25
As are the passions of uncertain man;
Who puts it in all colours all attires,
To serve his ends, and make his courses hold.
He sees that let deceit do what it can,
Plot and contrive base ways to high desires;   30
That the all-guiding Providence doth yet
All disappoint, and mocks this smoke of wit.
   Nor is he moved with all the thunder-cracks[1]
Of tyrants threats, or with the surly brow
Of power, that proudly sits on others crimes;   35
Charged with more crying sins than those he checks.
The storms of sad confusion that may grow
Up in the present for the coming times,
Appal not him, that hath no side at all,
But of himself and knows the worst can fall.   40
   Although his heart (so near ally'd to earth)
Cannot but pity the perplexed state
Of troublous and distressed mortality,
That thus make way unto the ugly birth
Of their own sorrows, and do still beget   45
Affliction upon imbecillity:
Yet seeing thus the course of things must run
He looks thereon not strange, but as foredone.
   And whilst distraught ambition compasses,
And is encompassed; whilst as craft deceives,   50
And is deceived: Whilst man doth ransack man,
And builds on blood, and rises by distress;
And th' inheritance of Desolation leaves
To great-expecting hopes: He looks thereon,
As from the shore of peace, with unwet eye,   55
And bears no venture in impiety.

---

[1] Lines 33-64 were reprinted entire by Wordsworth in a note to *The Excursion*, with the comment: 'The whole Poem is very beautiful. I will transcribe four stanzas from it, as they contain an admirable picture of the state of a wise Man's mind in a time of public commotion.'

1797-8

Thus, Madam, fares that man, who hath prepared
A rest for his desires; and sees all things
Beneath him; and hath learn'd this book of man,
Full of the notes of frailty; and compared   60
The best of glory with her sufferings:
By whom, I see, you labour all you can
To plant your heart; and set your thoughts as near
His glorious mansion as your powers can bear.

Which, Madam, are so soundly fashionèd   65
By that clear judgment, that hath carried you
Beyond the feeble limits of your kind,
As they can stand against the strongest head
Passion can make; inured to any hue
The world can cast; that cannot cast that mind   70
Out of her form of goodness, that doth see
Both what the best and worst of earth can be.

Which makes, that whatsoever here befals,
You in the region of yourself remain:
Where no vain breath of th' impudent molests,   75
That hath secured within the brazen walls
Of a clear conscience, that (without all stain)
Rises in peace, in innocency rests;
Whilst all what malice from without procures,
Shews her own ugly heart and hurts not your's.   80

And whereas none rejoice more in revenge,
Than women use to do; yet you well know,
That wrong is better checked by being contemned,
Than being pursed; leaving to him to avenge,
To whom it appertains; Wherein you shew,   85
How worthily your clearness hath condemned
Base malediction, living in the dark,
That at the rays of goodness still doth bark.

Knowing the heart of man is set to be
The centre of this world, about the which   90
These revolutions of disturbances
Still roll; where all the aspects of misery
Predominate; whose strong effects are such,
As he must bear, being powerless to redress:
And that unless above himself he can   95
Erect himself, how poor a Thing is man!

And how turmoiled they are that level lie
With earth, and cannot lift themselves from thence;

That never are at peace with their desires
But work beyond their years; and even deny   100
Dotage her rest, and hardly will dispence
With death. That when ability expires,
Desire still lives – So much delight they have,
To carry toil and travel to the grave.
　Whose ends you see; and what can be the best   105
They reach unto, when they have cast the sum
And reck'nings of their glory. And you know,
This floating life hath but this port of rest,
A heart prepared, that fears no ill to come.
And that mans greatness rests but in his show,   110
The best of all whose days consumed are
Either in war or peace-conceiving war.
　This concord, Madam, of a well-tuned mind
Hath been so set by that all-working Hand
Of Heaven, that though the world hath done his worst   115
To put it out by discords most unkind;
Yet doth it still in perfect union stand
With God and man; nor ever will be forced
From that most sweet accord; but still agree,
Equal in fortunes inequality.   120
　And this note, Madam, of your worthiness,
Remains recorded in so many hearts,
As time nor malice cannot wrong your right,
To the inheritance of fame you must possess:
You that have built you by your great deserts   125
(Out of small means) a far more exquisite
And glorious dwelling for your honored name,
Than all the gold that leaden minds can frame.

John Donne, 'Death! be not proud'

Date of reading: 1798

Wordsworth began copying the tenth of Donne's holy sonnets into a notebook in 1798 but stopped in the middle of line 2; perhaps he realised, belatedly, that he had a printed text in his possession. 'Death! be not proud' would always remain a favourite. Advising Alexander Dyce on what to include in an anthology in April 1833, Wordsworth remarked:

> The tenth sonnet of Donne, beginning 'Death, be not proud', is so eminently characteristic of his manner, and at the same time so weighty in thought, and vigorous in the expression, that I would entreat you to insert it, though to modern taste it may be repulsive, quaint, and laboured.

This is a reminder that Wordsworth was ahead of his time in admiring Donne, whose poetry did not come into fashion until the early twentieth century. Wordsworth read him in Anderson's *British Poets* volume 4, from which this text is edited.

Death! be not proud, though some have called thee
Mighty and dreadful, for thou art not so;
For those whom thou think'st thou dost overthrow
Die not, poor Death! nor yet canst thou kill me.
From rest and sleep, which but thy picture be,   5
Much pleasure, then, from thee much more must flow;
And soonest our best men with thee do go,
Rest of their bones, and soul's delivery.
Thou'rt slave to fate, chance, kings, and desperate men,
And dost with poison, war, and sickness, dwell,   10
And poppy or charms can make us sleep as well,
And better than thy stroke. Why swell'st thou, then?
One short sleep past we wake eternally;
And Death shall be no more; Death, thou shalt die.

Christopher Marlowe, *Edward II* (extract)

Date of reading: 1798

Dorothy Wordsworth copied Marlowe's *Edward II*, V v 55-108, with some omissions, into one of her brother's manuscript note-books in use during 1798. Her interest in Edward's death-scene was shared by her brother and Charles Lamb, who included it in his *Specimens of English Dramatic Poets* (1808), with the comment:

> This tragedy is in a very different style from 'mighty Tambur-laine'. The reluctant pangs of abdicating Royalty in Edward furnished hints which Shakspeare scarce improved in his Richard the Second; and the death-scene of Marlowe's king moves pity and terror beyond any scene ancient or modern with which I am acquainted.

Those virtues – pity and terror – are precisely what must have impressed Dorothy and William; the scene is full of insights into Edward's state of mind as he realises that his murderers are closing in. Dorothy's source was Dodsley's *Select Collection of Old Plays* (1744); the text is edited from her transcription.

From C. Marlow's Edward 2nd
Edward in Prison

Edward (to his murderer)

The dungeon, where they keep me, is the sink
Wherein the filth of all the Castle falls;
And there, in mire and puddle have I stood
This ten day's space; and, lest that I should sleep,
One plays continually upon a drum.   5
They give me bread and water, being a King,
So that for want of sleep and sustenance
My mind's distempered, and my body's numbed
And whether I have limbs or no, I know not.
Would my blood drop out from every vein   10
As does this water from my tattered robes.
– Tell Isabel the queen I looked not thus

When, for her sake, I ran at tilt in France
And there unhorsed the Duke of Clairmont.

Murderer
You're overwatched, my Lord, lie down and rest.   15

Edward
But that grief keeps me waking I should sleep
For not these ten days have these eyelids closed
Now while I speak they fall and yet with fear
Open again. Oh! wherefore sitt'st thou here?

Murderer
If you mistrust me I'll be gone, my Lord.   20

Edward
No, no, for if thou mean'st to murder me
Thou wilt return again, and therefore stay.

Murderer
He sleeps.

Edward
Let me not die yet, stay. Oh! stay a while!

Murderer
How now, my Lord?   25

Edward
Something still buzzeth in mine ears
And tells me if I sleep I never wake
This fear is that which makes me tremble thus,
And therefore tell me wherefore art thou come?

Murderer
To rid thee of thy life. Matrevis come!   30

Edward
I am too weak and feeble to resist;
Assist me sweet God! and receive my soul!

Sir Thomas Malory, *The Morte Arthur*
(first published by Caxton, 1485) (extract)

Date of reading: spring 1800

> The Morte Arthur was a favourite book among our ancestors. It continued to be printed till the middle of the 17th century, with much alteration of orthography, but very little change of language; and were it again modernized in the same manner, and published as a book for boys, it could hardly fail of regaining its popularity. When I was a schoolboy I possessed a wretchedly imperfect copy, and there was no book, except the Faery Queen, which I perused so often, or with such deep contentment.
>
> (Southey, Preface to
The Byrth, Lyf, and Actes of Kyng Arthur (1817))

Wordsworth's schoolboy experience was probably the same as that of Southey. *The Morte Arthur* was childhood reading for many people, and often remained a firm favourite in later life. The only real surprise about the appearance of the threnody for Sir Lancelot in Wordsworth's Commonplace Book is that at the time he copied it (1800) the most recent edition of Malory was that produced by William Stansby in 1634. Given Southey's scholarly interest, however, that could be explained by the fact that a copy was probably in his library at Greta Hall, and that Wordsworth consulted it there. What is not surprising is that Wordsworth chose to copy the emotional and narrative climax of *The Morte Arthur*, at the conclusion to Book 21.

The text is edited from Wordsworth's transcription. Although he attributes the speech to Sir Bors (spelt 'Sir Boys' in the transcription), it is actually delivered by Sir Ector. Wordsworth copies the speech entire; it is followed in Southey's text by the following sentences:

> Thenne there was wepyng and dolour oute of mesure. Thus they kepte syr Launcelots corps on lofte .xv. dayes, and thenne they buryed it wyth grete devocyon.

෴

And now I daresay (said Sir Bors), that, Sir Lancelot, there thou liest, thou were never matched of none earthly Knight's hands. And thou were the curtiest Knight that ever beare shield. And thou were the truest Friend to thy lover that ever bestrood horse, and thou were the truest lover, of a sinful man, that ever loved woman. And thou were the kindest man that ever strooke with sword. And thou were the goodliest person that ever came among presse of Knights. And thou were the meekest man and the gentlest, that ever eate in hall among Ladies. And thou were the sternest Knight to thy mortal foe that ever put speare in the rest . . .

**Robert Burns, *Works* (1800): 'Go fetch to me a pint o' wine',
'O that my Father had ne'er on me smil'd'**

Date of reading: by September 1800

Wordsworth was quick to borrow a copy of the new edition of
Burns' *Works* (4 vols., Liverpool, 1800), which contained many
hitherto unpublished letters, as well as a biography of the poet by
James Currie. He had read it by 29 September 1800, for by then he
had copied into his Commonplace Book poems quoted in Burns'
letters, including the two that follow. In later years he acquired his
own copy of the *Works*, which was in his library at Rydal Mount.

'Go fetch to me a pint o' wine' turns up in a letter from Burns to
Mrs Dunlop, 7 December 1788, and is introduced with the remark,
'Now I am on my hobby-horse, I cannot help inserting two other
old stanzas which please me mightily'. Scholars now recognise it as
being by Burns.

'O that my Father had ne'er on me smil'd' was also sent to Mrs
Dunlop, 25 January 1790, and is introduced by a brief preamble:

> Old Scottish songs are, you know, a favourite study and pursuit
> of mine; and now I am on that subject, allow me to give you two
> stanzas of another old simple ballad, which I am sure will please
> you. The catastrophe of the piece is a poor ruined female,
> lamenting her fate. She concludes with this pathetic wish . . .

Modern scholars have failed to find a source for the two stanzas
copied by Burns, which could also be by him. Texts are edited from
Wordsworth's Commonplace Book.

Fragments

Go fetch to me a pint o' wine
An' fill it in a silver tassie;
That I may drink, before I go
A service to my bonnie lassie:
The boat rocks at the pier o' Leith   5
Fu' loud the wind blaws frae the ferry

The ship rides by the Berwick-law
And I maun lea'e my bonnie Mary.

O that my Father had ne'er on me smil'd;
O that my Mother had ne'er to me sung!
O that my cradle had never been rock'd;
But that I had died when I was young!

O that the grave it were my bed   5
My blankets were my winding sheet;
The clocks and the worms my bedfellows a';
And O sae sound as I should sleep![1]

---

[1] In his letter to Mrs Dunlop, Burns comments on the last line: 'I do not
remember in all my reading to have met with any thing more truly the
language of misery, than the exclamation in the last line. Misery is like
love; to speak its language truly, the author must have felt it.'

Anna Seward, *Original Sonnets on Various Subjects*
(1799): *Invitation to a Friend*

Date of reading: 10-14 December 1800

Coleridge gave the proof-sheets of Seward's *Original Sonnets* to
Sara Hutchinson, probably as a Christmas present, when she visited
Greta Hall in Keswick with the Wordsworths, 10-14 December
1800. They bear the affectionate if slightly whimsical inscription:
'The Editor to Asahara, the Moorish Maid, Dec. 1800 Greta Hall
Keswick'.[1] Wordsworth read the sonnets immediately and remem-
bered one, 'Invitation to a Friend', when suggesting some thirty
years later that Alexander Dyce include it in an anthology: 'At the
close of a sonnet of Miss Seward's are two fine verses – "Come, that
I may not hear the winds of night, Nor count the heavy eave-drops
as they fall".' He went on to say that 'her verses please me with all
their faults better than those of Mrs Barbauld'.
 'Invitation to a Friend' is here edited from the 1799 volume.

Invitation to a Friend

Since dark December shrouds the transient day,
    And stormy Winds are howling in their ire,
    Why com'st not THOU, who always can'st inspire
    The soul of cheerfulness, and best array
A sullen hour in smiles? – O haste to pay   5
    The cordial visit sullen hours require! –
    Around the circling walls a glowing fire
    Shines; – but it vainly shines in this delay

---

[1] This was reported by George Whalley in 1955, who saw the sheets at the
Wordsworth Library, Grasmere; they have since disappeared and are not
now to be found.

To blend thy spirit's warm Promethean light.
    Come then, at Science, and at Friendship's call,   10
      Their vow'd Disciple; – come, for they invite!
The social Powers without thee languish all.
    Come, that I may not hear the winds of Night,
    Nor count the heavy eave-drops as they fall.

December 21st, 1782

Thomas Wilkinson, *I love to be alone, Lines written on a Paper wrapt round a Moss-Rose pulled on New Years Day, and sent to M. Wilson*

Date of reading: c. January 1801

Writing to Sir George Beaumont in October 1805, Wordsworth described his friend Thomas Wilkinson as

> an amiable inoffensive man; and a little of a Poet too; who has amused himself upon his own small estate upon the Emont in twining pathways along the banks of the River, making little Cells and bowers with inscriptions of his own writing, all very pretty as not spreading far.

Wilkinson had inherited the Grotto, a forty-acre farm at Yanwath near Penrith, on the River Eamont, where he built his own house. He was known also to Dorothy and Coleridge, and held in high regard by them not least because he petitioned against the slave trade in Penrith marketplace in the early 1790s. A determined Quaker, he remained a pacifist even when in late 1803 Wordsworth joined the Grasmere Volunteers in preparation for Napoleon's threatened invasion.

Wordsworth first stayed with Wilkinson at Yanwath in January 1801, having (as Wilkinson told a correspondent):

> left the College, turned his back on all Preferment, and settled down contentedly among our Lakes with his sister and his Muse. He is very sober and very amiable, and writes in what he conceives to be the language of Nature in opposition to the finery of our present poetry. He has published 2 vols. of Poems mostly of the same character. His name is William Wordsworth.

The '2 vols. of Poems' was *Lyrical Ballads* (1800), published in two volumes in London in January 1801, at the time of Wordsworth's stay. Wordsworth would have shown Wilkinson manuscript copies of some of the new poems, and his host would have reciprocated – perhaps giving his new friend one of his manuscripts. Despite having little in the way of a formal education besides attendance at a dame school, Wilkinson was a keen poet. In a sense, he was the archetypal Wordsworthian primitive – someone who lived off the land and composed poetry in his spare time – 'Whose life combines the best of high and low'. That line is from Wordsworth's moving but oft-ridiculed poem 'To the Spade of a Friend', composed October 1806, which commemorated the afternoon when (as he reminded Wilkinson) 'you and I were labouring together in your pleasure-ground, an afternoon I often think of with pleasure'.

Wordsworth later said that Wilkinson wrote many verses including 'some worthy of preservation', and it is fitting that the two poems presented here are edited from the manuscript in Wilkinson's hand pasted into Wordsworth's Commonplace Book, on which I have put a date of c. January 1801. They are presented with Wilkinson's occasionally wayward spelling and punctuation intact. If they betray occasional hints of his amateur status, and an eighteenth-century diction that seems at first glance un-Wordsworthian, they are striking for directness and strength of feeling – qualities of which Wordsworth would have approved. See also pages 9-11.

I love to be alone

1

While busy Mortals crowd around
    The City, Court, and Throne,
Intent to see, and to be seen,
    To know and to be known,
I turn away, content I turn   5
    To sweet, domestic Bow'rs,
And ponder how I best may spend
    My Life's few fleeting Hours:
The evening Twilight oft I trace,
    Sometimes the dusky Dawn,   10
My steps unseen by Human Race –
    I love to be alone.

2

Yet sure my thoughtful, musing Mind
    The social Transport knows,
Round many a Friend these opening Arms   15
    With Ecstacy would close:

Sure I would leave my couch by Night
    To serve my greatest Foe,
Would quit the brightest Hour of Joy
    To wipe the Tear of Woe: 20
'Tis giddy, trifling, vain Perade
    My Heart and Mind disown,
The *endless Buzz* by Folly made –
    I love to be alone.

3

Yet not averse when Duty calls   25
    I leave my quiate Sphere,
And mingle in the Walks of men
    The Walks of Men are dear!
I love the intelectual Feast
    Shar'd with the Good and Wise,   30
Nor less the little, temperate Meal
    Simplicity supplies:
I freely join the rustic Throng
    (Licentiousness unknown)
With children play: but e'er it's long   35
    I love to be alone.

4

But ah! while sorrow's mingl'd cries
    Through Earth's fair Vales resound,
The *Ear* of pensive Fancy tries
    To catch the piercing sound,   40
Her wistful *Eye* surveys the shores
    Where sable *Lovers* part,
His trembling Limbs, fall Iron tears,
    And anguish breaks *Her* Heart;
Oh! could I aid this injur'd race   45
    I'd seek their flaming Zone,
The White and sable Tyrants face
    Nor wish to be alone –

And Oh! (for sweet sincerity
 The pensive Muse shall guide)   50
I feel the lonely Lot of Man
 Has happiness denied,
Unbless'd is he that wanders o'er
 The vary'd Plains of Time
Without a kind and faithful Maid   55
 Companion of his Prime:
Good natur'd, faithful, kind and fair,
 Was such a Maid my own!
Better with her my Lot to share
 Than live and die alone.   60

Lines written on a Paper wrapt round a Moss-Rose pulled on New Years Day, and sent to M. Wilson

While cold o'er the Hills spread the mid Winter snows,
I pull in my Garden the Moss-cover'd Rose;
Tho' the last and the least, I will send it to Thee,
Of the rest in my Absence they've plunder'd the Tree,
Yet I cannot in Anger their Pillage deplore,   5
'Twas for *one*, who may gather my Roses no more –
Sure Friendship's a Rose-bush, that fragrant and fair
Can shed its sweet Odors all over the Year,
Can shield from the Heat, and can save from the rage,
In the summer of Youth, and the Winter of Age,   10
Between us dear Margaret, we've nurs'd up the Tree,
It grew in my Heart, and was shone on by Thee.

Anon., *The Cruel Mother*

Date of reading: after 28 January 1801

Wordsworth copied these stanzas into his Commonplace Book after 28 January 1801; they were probably known to him at the time he composed 'The Thorn' (spring 1798), with which they share a number of preoccupations. His source was David Herd's *Ancient and Modern Scottish Songs* (1776), from which this text is edited.

The Cruel Mother

And there she's lean'd her back to a thorn,
   Oh, and alas-a-day! Oh, and alas-a-day!
And there she has her baby born,
   Ten thousand times good night, and be wi' thee.

She has houked a grave ayont the sun,   5
   Oh, and alas-a-day! Oh, and alas-a-day!
And there she has buried the sweet babe in,
   Ten thousand times good night, and be wi' thee.

And she's gane back to her father's ha',
   Oh, and alas-a-day! Oh, and alas-a-day!   10
She's counted the leelest maid o' them a',
   Ten thousand times good night, and be wi' thee.

.   .   .   .

O look not sae sweet, my bonny babe,
   Oh, and alas-a-day! Oh, and alas-a-day!
Gin ze smyle sae ze'll smyle me dead;   15
   Ten thousand times good night, and be wi' thee.

John Milton, *Paradise Lost* Book XI (extract)

Date of reading: 2 February 1802

'After tea I read aloud the 11th Book of Paradise Lost we were much impressed and also melted into tears', recorded Dorothy in her Grasmere Journal, 2 February 1802. Book XI deals with the aftermath of the Fall and its immediate consequences, in particular such ominous signs as the appearance of predation in the animal kingdom – the subject of Wordsworth's 'The Redbreast and the Butterfly', written not long after on 18 April:

> Could Father Adam open his eyes,
> And see this sight beneath the skies,
> He'd wish to close them again.

(ll. 12-14)

The extract is here edited from Anderson's *British Poets* volume 5, from which the Wordsworths read *Paradise Lost* in February 1802. It begins with a penitent speech by Eve, who has just been hailed 'Mother of all Mankind' by Adam.

Ill worthy I such title should belong
To me transgressor, who for thee ordain'd
A help, became thy snare; to me reproach   165
Rather belongs, distrust and all dispraise:
But infinite in pardon was my Judge,
That I who first brought death on all, am grac'd
The source of life; next favourable thou,
Who highly thus t' entitle me vouchsaf'st,   170
Far other name deserving. But the field
To labour calls us now with sweat impos'd,
Tho' after sleepless night; for see the morn,
All unconcern'd with our unrest, begins
Her rosy progress smiling; let us forth,   175
I never from thy side henceforth to stray,
Where'er our day's work lies, though now injoin'd

Laborious, till day droop; while here we dwell,
What can be toilsome in these pleasant walks?
Here let us live, tho' in fall'n state, content.   180
    So spake, so wish'd much humbled Eve, but Fate
Subscrib'd not; Nature first gave signs, impress'd
On bird, beast, air, air suddenly eclips'd
After short blush of Morn; nigh in her sight
The bird of Jove stoop'd from his airy tour,   185
Two birds of gayest plume before him drove;
Down from a hill the beast that reigns in woods,
First hunter then, pursu'd a gentle brace,
Goodliest of all the forest, hart and hind;
Direct to th' eastern gate was bent their flight.   190
Adam observ'd, and with his eyes the chace
Pursuing, not unmov'd, to Eve thus spake:
O Eve, some further change awaits us nigh,
Which Heav'n by these mute signs in Nature shews,
Forerunners of his purpose, or to warn   195
Us haply too secure of our discharge
From penalty because from death releas'd
Some days; how long, and what till then our life,
Who knows, or more than this, that we are dust,
And thither must return, and be no more?   200
Why else this double object in our sight
Of flight pursu'd in th' air, and o'er the ground,
One way the self-same hour? why in the east
Darkness e'er day's mid-course, and morning-light
More orient in yon western cloud that draws   205
O'er the blue firmament a radiant white,
And slow descends, with something heav'nly fraught?
    He err'd not; for by this the heav'nly bands
Down from a sky of jasper lighted now
In Paradise, and on a hill made halt,   210
A glorious apparition, had not doubt
And carnal fear that day dimm'd Adam's eye.

Ben Jonson, *On my First Daughter*, *To Penshurst*

Date of reading: 11 February 1802

> William still poorly – we made up a good fire after dinner, and
> William brought his Mattrass out, and lay down on the floor I
> read to him the life of Ben Johnson and some short Poems of his
> which were too *interesting* for him, and would not let him go to
> sleep . . . There is one affecting line in Jonson's Epitaph on his
> first Daughter
>> Here lies to each her Parents ruth,
>> *Mary the Daughter of their youth*
>> At six months end she parted hence
>> In safety of her Innocence . . .
> I continued to read to him – we were much delighted with the
> Poem of Penshurst.
>> (Dorothy Wordsworth, Grasmere Journal, 11 February 1802)

The Wordsworths were reading Jonson from Anderson's *British
Poets* volume 4, and would continue to do so over the following
months: her journal reveals that Dorothy read Jonson on 14 Feb-
ruary, before turning his poems over to William on 9-10 March.
Wordsworth discussed them with Coleridge on 19 March, and was
still reading them several days later on the 23rd. He asked Lamb to
purchase an edition of the poems on his behalf in 1804, but it is not
known whether Lamb obliged, as he protested that 'Ben Jonson is a
guinea Book', and 'I am not plethorically abounding in Cash at this
present'.

One thing is for sure: Jonson had a big impact on Wordsworth.
His work shaped 'The Sailor's Mother' and the 'Immortality Ode',
while Penshurst is the model for Wordsworth's portrayal of
Grasmere in the first book of *The Recluse*:

> Dear Valley, having in thy face a smile
> Though peaceful, full of gladness. Thou art pleased,
> Pleased with thy crags and woody steeps, thy Lake,
> Its one green Island and its winding shores,
> The multitude of little rocky hills,
> Thy Church and Cottages of mountain stone –
> Clustered like stars, some few, but single most,
> And lurking dimly in their shy retreats,
> Or glancing at each other cheerful looks,

Like separated stars with clouds between.
What want we? Have we not perpetual streams,
Warm woods and sunny hills, and fresh green fields,
And mountains not less green, and flocks and herds,
And thickets full of songsters, and the voice
Of lordly birds – an unexpected sound
Heard now and then from morn to latest eve
Admonishing the man who walks below
Of solitude and silence in the sky?
These have we, and a thousand nooks of earth
Have also these; but nowhere else is found –
No where (or is it fancy?) can be found –
The one sensation that is here; 'tis here,
Here as it found its way into my heart
In childhood, here as it abides by day,
By night, here only; or in chosen minds
That take it with them hence, where'er they go.
'Tis (but I cannot name it), 'tis the sense
Of majesty and beauty and repose,
A blended holiness of earth and sky,
Something that makes this individual Spot,
This small abiding-place of many men,
A termination and a last retreat,
A Centre, come from wheresoe'er you will,
A Whole without dependence or defect,
Made for itself and happy in itself,
Perfect Contentment, Unity entire.

('Home at Grasmere' MS B, 135-70)

On my First Daughter

Here lies to each her parents ruth,
Mary, the daughter of their youth:
Yet all heav'n's gifts, being heaven's due,
It makes the father less to rue.
At six months end she parted hence   5
With safety of her innocence;

1802

Whose soul heav'n's queen (whose name she bears),
In comfort of her mother's tears,
Hath plac'd among her virgin-train:
Where, while that fever'd doth remain,   10
This grave partakes the fleshly birth;
Which cover lightly, gentle earth.

To Penshurst

Thou art not, Penshurst, built to envious show
   Of touch or marble; nor canst boast a row
Of polish'd pillars, or a roof of gold:
   Thou hast no lantern, whereof tales are told;
Or stair, or courts; but stand'st an ancient pile,   5
   And these grudg'd at, are reverenc'd the while.
Thou joy'st in better marks, of soil, of air,
   Of wood, of water; therein thou art fair.
Thou hast thy walks for health, as well as sport:
   Thy mount to which thy Dryads do resort,   10
Where Pan and Bacchus their high feasts have made,
   Beneath the broad beech, and the chesnut shade;
That taller tree, which of a nut was set,
   At his great birth, where all the muses met.
There, in the writhed bark, are cut the names   15
   Of many a Sylvan, taken with his flames,
And thence the ruddy Satyrs oft provoke
   The lighter Fawns, to reach thy lady's oak.
Thy copse too, nam'd of Gamage, thou hast there,
   That never fails to serve thee season'd deer,   20
When thou would'st feast, or exercise thy friends.
   The lower land, that to the river bends,
Thy sheep, thy bullocks, kine, and calves do feed;
   The middle grounds thy mares, and horses breed.
Each bank doth yield thee conies; and the tops   25
   Fertile of wood, Ashore and Sydneys copse,
To crown, thy open table doth provide
   The purpled pheasant, with the speckled side:
The painted partridge lies in ev'ry field;

And for thy mess is willing to be kill'd.   30
And if the high-swoll'n Medway fail thy dish,
   Thou hast thy ponds, that pay thee tribute fish,
Fat aged carps, that run into thy net,
   And pikes, now weary their own kind to eat,
As loth the second draught, or cast to stay,   35
   Officiously at first themselves betray.
Bright eels that emulate them, and leap on land,
   Before the fisher, or into his hand.
Then hath thy orchard fruit, thy garden flow'rs,
   Fresh as the air, and new as are the hours.   40
The early cherry, with the later plum,
   Fig, grape, and quince, each in his time doth come:
The blushing apricot, and woolly peach
   Hang on thy walls, that ev'ry child may reach,
And though thy walls be of the country stone,   45
   They're rear'd with no man's ruin, no man's groan;
There's none that dwell about them with them down;
   But all come in, the farmer and the clown;
And no one empty handed, to salute
   Thy lord and lady, though they have no suit.   50
Some bring a capon, some a rural cake,
   Some nuts, some apples; some that think they make
The better cheeses, bring 'em; or else send
   By their ripe daughters, whom they would commend
This way to husbands; and whose baskets bear   55
   An emblem of themselves in plum or pear.
But what can this (more than express their love)
   Add to thy free provisions, far above
The need of such? whose liberal board doth flow,
   With all that hospitality doth know!   60
Where comes no guest, but is allow'd to eat,
   Without his fear, and of thy lord's own meat:
Where the same beer and bread, and self same wine
   That is his lordship's, shall be also mine.
And I not fain to sit (as some this day,   65
   At great mens tables) and yet dine away.
Here no man tells my cups; nor standing by,
   A waiter, doth my gluttony envy:
But gives me what I call, and lets me eat,
   He knows, below, he shall find plenty of meat;   70
Thy tables hoard not up for the next day,

Nor, when I take my lodging, need I pray
For fire, or lights, or livery: all is there;
   As if thou then wert mine, or I reign'd here:
There's nothing I can wish, for which I stay.   75
   That found King James, when hunting late this way
With his brave son the prince, they saw thy fires
   Shine bright on ev'ry hearth, as the desires
Of thy Penates had been set on flame
   To entertain them; or the country came,   80
With all their zeal, to warm their welcome here.
   What (great, I will not say, but) sudden cheer
Didst thou then make 'em! and what praise was heap'd
   On thy good lady, then! who therein reap'd
The just reward of her high huswifry;   85
   To have her linen, plate, and all things nigh,
When she was far: and not a room but drest,
   As if it had expected such a guest!
These, Penshurst, are thy praise, and yet not all;
   Thy lady's noble, fruitful, chaste withal.   90
His children thy great lord may call his own:
   A fortune, in this age, but rarely known.
They are, and have been taught religion: thence
   Their gentler spirits have suck'd innocence.
Each morn, and even, they are taught to pray   95
   With the whole household, and may, ev'ry day,
Read in their virtuous parents noble parts,
   The mysteries of manners, arms, and arts.
Now, Penshurst, they that will proportion thee
   With other edifices, when they see   100
Those proud ambitious heaps, and nothing else,
   May say, their lords have built, but thy lord dwells.

Jonathan Carver, *Travels through the Interior parts of North America* (1768) (extract)

Date of reading: March-June 1802

The water is pure and crystalline; so that, if it were not for the reflections of the incumbent mountains by which it is darkened, a delusion might be felt, by a person resting quietly in a boat on the bosom of Winandermere or Derwent-water, similar to that which Carver so beautifully describes when he was floating alone in the middle of the lake Erie or Ontario, and could almost have imagined that his boat was suspended in an element as pure as air, or rather that the air and water were one.

(Wordsworth, *A Description of the Lakes* (1822))

Wordsworth is actually referring to Carver's description of Lake Superior; though he never went there, Wordsworth seems to have had an interest in America, having read both Carver and Bartram (see p.165). He first saw Carver's *Travels* in 1802, when the passage mentioned in *Description of the Lakes* provided a central image in 'To H.C., Six Years Old':

Thou Faery Voyager! that dost float
In such clear water, that thy Boat
May rather seem
To brood on air than on an earthly stream;
Suspended in a stream as clear as sky,
Where earth and heaven do make one imagery . . .

Lake Superior, formerly termed the Upper Lake, from its northern situation, is so called on account of its being superior in magnitude to any of the Lakes on that vast continent. It might justly be termed the Caspian of America, and is supposed to be the largest body of fresh water on the globe. Its circumference, according to the French charts, is about fifteen hundred miles; but I believe, that if it was coasted round, and the utmost extent of every bay taken, it would exceed sixteen hundred.

After I first entered it from Goddard's River on the west Bay, I coasted near twelve hundred miles of the north and east shores of it, and observed that the greatest part of that extensive tract was bounded by rocks and uneven ground. The water in general appeared to lie on a bed of rocks. When it was calm, and the sun shone bright, I could sit in my canoe, where the depth was upwards of six fathoms, and plainly see huge piles of stone at the bottom, of different shapes, some of which appeared as if they were hewn. The water at this time was as pure and transparent as air; and my canoe seemed as if it hung suspended in that element. It was impossible to look attentively through this limpid medium at the rocks below, without finding, before many minutes were elapsed, my head swim, and my eyes no longer able to behold the dazzling scene.

John Milton, *When the Assault was intended to the City*,
To the Lord General Fairfax, To the Lord General Cromwell,
On the Late Massacre in Piemont, On his blindness,
To Cyriac Skinner

Date of reading: 21 May 1802

> Milton's Sonnets . . . I think manly and dignified compositions,
> distinguished by simplicity and unity of object and aim, and
> undisfigured by false or vicious ornaments. They are in several
> places incorrect, and sometimes uncouth in language, and, per-
> haps, in some, inharmonious; yet, upon the whole, I think the
> music exceedingly well suited to its end, that is, it has an ener-
> getic and varied flow of sound crowding into narrow room more
> of the combined effect of rhyme and blank verse than can be
> done by any other kind of verse I know of. The Sonnets of
> Milton which I like best are that to Cyriack Skinner; on his
> Blindness; Captain or Colonel; Massacre of Piedmont;
> Cromwell except for the last two lines; Fairfax, etc.
>
> (Wordsworth to unknown correspondent, November 1802)

At Dove Cottage on the afternoon of 21 May 1802 Dorothy sat
down with her brother and read to him from Milton: 'Wm wrote
two sonnets on Buonaparte after I had read Milton's sonnets to
him', she later recorded.[1] This was a memorable day, recalled in a
letter Wordsworth wrote two decades later: 'my Sister happened to
read to me the sonnets of Milton, which I could at that time repeat;
but somehow or other I was singularly struck with the style of
harmony, and the gravity, and republican austerity of those com-
positions. In the course of the same afternoon I produced 3
sonnets'. Milton's 'republican austerity' was a strong influence on
Wordsworth. Towards the end of his life, he recalled the occasion
once more (ascribing to it the wrong year):

> In the cottage of Town-End, one afternoon, in 1801, my Sister
> read to me the Sonnets of Milton. I had long been well acquaint-
> ed with them, but I was particularly struck on that occasion with
> the dignified simplicity and majestic harmony that runs through

---

[1] One of the poems Wordsworth wrote that afternoon was 'I griev'd for
Buonaparte' (later published in *Poems in Two Volumes* (1807)).

most of them – in character so totally different from the Italian, and still more so from Shakespeare's fine sonnets.

In 1833 Wordsworth wrote an impassioned letter about sonnets, and Milton's in particular, pointing out that the best of them defy the usual division of octave and sestet:

> In the better half of his sonnets the sense does not close with the rhyme at the eighth line, but overflows into the second portion of the metre. Now it has struck me, that this is not done merely to gratify the ear by variety and freedom of sound, but also to aid in giving that pervading sense of intense Unity in which the excellence of the Sonnet has always seemed to me mainly to consist.

All the sonnets Wordsworth picked out in November 1802 as those 'which I like best' are included here, edited from Anderson's *British Poets* volume 5, from which Dorothy was probably reading on the afternoon of 21 May.

When the Assault was intended to the City

Captain or Colonel, or Knight in arms,
   Whose chance on these defenceless doors may seize,
   If deed of honour did thee ever please,
Guard them, and him within protect from harms.
He can requite thee, for he knows the charms   5
   That call fame on such gentle acts as these;
   And he can spread thy name o'er lands and seas,
Whatever clime the sun's bright circle warms.
   Lift not thy spear against the Muses' bower;
The great Emathion conqueror bid spare   10
   The house of Pindarus, when temple and tow'r
Went to the ground: and the repeated air
   Of sad Electra's poet had the power
To save the Athenian walls from ruin bare.

To the Lord General Fairfax

Fairfax, whose name in arms through Europe rings,
  Filling each mouth with envy or with praise,
  And all her jealous monarchs with amaze
And rumours loud, that daunt remotest kings
Thy firm unshaken virtue ever brings   5
  Victory home, though new rebellions raise
  Their Hydra heads, and the false North displays
Her broken league to imp their serpent wings.
  O yet a nobler task awaits thy hand,
(For what can war, but endless war still breed?)   10
Till truth and right from violence be freed,
  And public faith clear'd from the shameful brand
Of public fraud. In vain doth Valor bleed,
  While Avarice and Rapine share the land.

To the Lord General Cromwell

Cromwell, our chief of men, who through a cloud
  Not of war only, but detractions rude,
  Guided by faith, and matchless fortitude,
To peace and truth thy glorious way hast plough'd,
And on the neck of crowned Fortune proud   5
  Hast rear'd God's trophies, and his work pursued,
  While Darwen stream with blood of Scots imbrued,
  And Dunbar field resounds thy praises loud,
And Worcester's laureat wreath. Yet much remains
  To conquer still; Peace hath her victories   10
  No less renown'd than war: new foes arise
Threat'ning to bind our souls with secular chains:
  Help us to save free conscience from the paw
  Of hireling wolves, whose gospel is their maw.

1802

On the late Massacre in Piedmont

Avenge, O Lord, thy slaughter'd saints, whose bones
  Lie scatter'd on the Alpine mountains cold;
  Ev'n them who kept thy truth so pure of old,
When all our fathers worshipt stocks and stones,
Forget not; in thy book record their groans   5
  Who were thy sheep, and in their ancient fold
  Slain by the bloody Piedmontese that roll'd
Mother with infant down the rocks. Their moans
  The vales redoubled to the hills, and they
To Heav'n. Their martyr'd blood and ashes sow   10
  O'er all th' Italian fields where still doth sway
The triple Tyrant; that from these may grow
  A hundred fold, who having learn'd thy way,
Early may fly the Babylonian woe.

On his blindness

When I consider how my light is spent
  Ere half my days in this dark world and wide,
  And that one talent which is death to hide,
Lodg'd with me useless, though my soul more bent
To serve therewith my Maker, and present   5
  My true account, lest he returning chide;
  Doth God exact day labour, light deny'd,
I fondly ask? but patience to prevent
  That murmur, soon replies, God doth not need
Either man's work or his own gifts; who best   10
    Bear his mild yoke, they serve him best: his state
  Is kingly; thousands at his bidding speed,
And post o'er land and ocean without rest;
    They also serve who only stand and wait.

To Cyriac Skinner

Cyriac, whose grandsire on the royal bench
  Of British Themis, with no mean applause
  Pronounc'd, and in his volumes taught our laws,
Which others at their bar so often wrench;
To day deep thoughts resolve with me to drench   5
  In mirth, that after no repenting draws;
  Let Euclid rest, and Archimedes pause,
And what the Swede intends, and what the French.
  To measure life learn thou betimes, and know
Toward solid good what leads the nearest way;   10
    For other things mild Heav'n a time ordains,
  And disapproves that care, though wise in shew,
That with superfluous burden loads the day,
  And when God sends a cheerful hour refrains.

Henry Kirke White, *To the Herb Rosemary*

Date of reading: February 1804

When in February 1804 Wordsworth copied 'To the Herb Rosemary' into his Commonplace Book its author was nineteen and preparing for an undergraduate career in Cambridge; he would die of tuberculosis in his college rooms in October 1806. Wordsworth was shown the poem by Robert Southey, who was reviewing White's first book, *Clifton Grove*, for the *Annual Review* (1804). In a letter to his brother in January 1804, Southey commented:

> A little volume of poems by Henry Kirke White, of Nottingham, has excited some interest in me for the author, who is very young, and has published them in the hope of obtaining help to pursue his studies and graduate for orders . . . There is a wild little poem there to a Rosemary bush, which affected me. The poor boy is sickly, and will, I suppose, die of consumption . . . In the 'Annual' I have been his friend.

True to his word, Southey described the poems in *Clifton Grove* as 'extraordinary productions of early genius' and published 'To the Herb Rosemary' with the comment: 'This is a most interesting poem. We know no production of so young a poet than can be compared to it, and when we say this, we remember Cowley and Pope and Chatterton'. Here is the poem as it was known to Southey and Wordsworth, edited not from Wordsworth's transcription, which is rushed and unpunctuated, but from the printed text of 1804.

To the Herb Rosemary[1]

1

Sweet scented flower! who art wont to bloom
   On January's front severe:
   And o'er the wintery desert drear
     To waft thy waste perfume!

---

[1] The Rosemary buds in January – It is the flower commonly put in the coffins of the dead. (Kirke White's note)

Come, thou shalt form my nosegay now,   5
And I will bind thee round my brow,
  And as I twine the mournful wreath,
I'll weave a melancholy song,
And sweet the strain shall be, and long,
  The melody of death.   10

2
Come, funeral flow'r! who lov'st to dwell
  With the pale corse in lonely tomb,
  And throw across the desert gloom
    A sweet decaying smell.
Come press my lips, and lie with me   15
Beneath the lowly Alder tree,
  And we will sleep a pleasant sleep,
And not a care shall dare intrude
To break the marble solitude,
    So peaceful, and so deep.   20

3
And hark! the wind-god as he flies,
  Moans hollow in the Forest-trees,
  And sailing on the gusty breeze
    Mysterious music dies.
Sweet flower, that requiem wild is mine,   25
It warns me to the lonely shrine,
    The cold turf altar of the dead;
  My grave shall be in yon lone spot,
  Where as I lie, by all forgot,
A dying fragrance thou wilt o'er my ashes shed.   30

1804

William Cowper, *Yardley-Oak* (1804)

Date of reading: c. September 1804

> – That vast eugh-tree, pride of Lorton Vale,
> Which to this day stands single in the midst
> Of its own darkness as it stood of yore . . .
> (Wordsworth, early draft of *Yew Trees*, 1-3)

In 1804 William Hayley published the third volume of a biography of the recently deceased Cowper, containing some newly published poems including 'Yardley-Oak'. Probably during the third week of September, Lady Beaumont, one of Wordsworth's most fervent admirers, having read it, realised he would be interested and recommended that he look it up. Her letter arrived just as William and Dorothy were about to leave on a five- or six-day tour of the Lake District; fortunately they stopped first at Greta Hall in Keswick, where they would have been sure to find Hayley's latest volume, as both Southey and Coleridge had one.

The following day the Wordsworths passed through the vale of Lorton, as Dorothy told Lady Beaumont after their return to Grasmere: 'We dropped down soon after into the fertile Vale of Lorton, and went to visit a Yew tree which is the Patriarch of Yew trees, green and flourishing, in very old age – the largest tree I ever saw.'

The combined experience of reading Cowper's remarkable, unfinished poem and seeing the 'pride' of Lorton Vale, inspired Wordsworth, after a fallow period, to compose 'Yew Trees'. As Dorothy told Lady Beaumont: 'We have received great pleasure from that poem of Cowper which you mentioned to us. I believe that it did my Brother some good and set him on to writing after a pause sooner than he would otherwise have done.'

A few years later in 1807, as he still did not possess Hayley's biography, he asked his sister-in-law and amanuensis, Sara Hutchinson, to transcribe lines 1-124 of 'Yardley-Oak' into his Commonplace Book, so that he would always have his own copy. Here is the complete text of Cowper's unfinished masterpiece as Wordsworth first read it, in Hayley's text of 1804.

Yardley-Oak

Survivor sole, and hardly such, of all
That once liv'd here thy brethren, at my birth
(Since which I number three-score winters past)
A shatter'd veteran, hollow-trunk'd perhaps
As now, and with excoriate forks deform, 5
Relicts of ages! Could a mind, imbued
With truth from Heaven, created thing adore,
I might with rev'rence kneel, and worship thee!
    It seems idolatry with some excuse,
When our fore-father Druids in their oaks 10
Imagin'd sanctity. The conscience, yet
Unpurified by an authentic act
Of amnesty, the meed of blood divine,
Lov'd not the light, but gloomy, into gloom
Of thickest shades, like Adam after taste 15
Of fruit proscrib'd, as to a refuge, fled!
    Thou wast a bauble once; a cup and ball,
Which babes might play with; and the thievish jay
Seeking her food, with ease might have purloin'd
The auburn nut that held thee, swallowing down 20
Thy yet close-folded latitude of boughs,
And all thine embryo vastness, at a gulp.
But fate thy growth decreed: autumnal rains,
Beneath thy parent-tree, mellow'd the soil
Design'd thy cradle, and a skipping deer, 25
With pointed hoof dibbling the glebe, prepar'd
The soft receptacle, in which secure
Thy rudiments should sleep the winter through.
    So fancy dreams – disprove it if ye can
Ye reas'ners broad awake, whose busy search 30
Of argument, employ'd too oft amiss,
Sifts half the pleasures of short life away!
    Thou fell'st mature, and in the loamy clod
Swelling with vegetative force instinct
Didst burst thine egg, as their's the fabled Twins, 35
Now stars; two lobes protruding pair'd exact:
A leaf succeeded, and another leaf,
And, all the elements thy puny growth
Fost'ring propitious, thou becam'st a twig.
    Who liv'd when thou wast such? Oh! couldst thou speak, 40

      1804

As in Dodona once thy kindred trees
Oracular, I would not curious ask
The future, best unknown, but at thy mouth
Inquisitive, the less ambiguous past!
    By thee I might correct, erroneous oft,   45
The clock of history, facts and events
Timing more punctual, unrecorded facts
Recov'ring, and mistated setting right –
Desp'rate attempt till trees shall speak again!
    Time made thee what thou wast – King of the woods!   50
And time hath made thee what thou art – a cave
For owls to roost in! Once thy spreading boughs
O'erhung the champaign, and the numerous flock,
That graz'd it stood beneath that ample cope
Uncrouded, yet safe-shelter'd from the storm.   55
No flock frequents thee now; thou hast out-liv'd
Thy popularity, and art become
(Unless verse rescue thee awhile) a thing
Forgotten, as the foliage of thy youth!
    While thus through all the stages thou hast push'd   60
Of treeship – first a seedling, hid in grass;
Then twig; then sapling; and, as century roll'd
Slow after century, a giant-bulk
Of girth enormous, with moss-cushion'd root
Upheav'd above the soil, and sides imboss'd   65
With prominent wens globose – till at the last,
The rottenness, which time is charg'd to inflict
On other mighty ones, found also thee.
    What exhibitions various hath the world
Witnessed, of mutability in all,   70
That we account most durable below!
Change is the diet, on which all subsist,
Created changeable, and change at last
Destroys them – skies uncertain, now the heat
Transmitting cloudless, and the solar beam   75
Now quenching, in a boundless sea of clouds –
Calm and alternate storm, moisture and drought,
Invigorate by turns the springs of life
In all that live, plant, animal, and man,
And in conclusion mar them. Nature's threads,   80
Fine, passing thought, e'en in her coarsest works,
Delight in agitation – yet sustain

1804   208

The force that agitates not unimpair'd,
But worn by frequent impulse, to the cause
Of their best tone their dissolution owe.   85
    Thought cannot spend itself comparing still
The great and little of thy lot, thy growth
From almost nullity into a state
Of matchless grandeur, and declension thence
Slow into such magnificent decay.   90
Time was, when settling on thy leaf, a fly
Could shake thee to the root – and time has been
When tempests could not. At thy firmest age
Thou hadst within thy bole solid contents
That might have ribb'd the sides, and plank'd the deck   95
Of some flagg'd admiral, and tortuous arms,
The ship-wright's darling treasure, didst present
To the four quarter'd winds, robust and bold,
Warp'd into tough knee-timber,[1] many a load!
But the axe spar'd thee; in those thriftier days   100
Oaks fell not, hewn by thousands, to supply
The bottomless demands of contest, wag'd
For senatorial honours. Thus to time
The task was left to whittle thee away,
With his sly scythe, whose ever-nibbling edge,   105
Noiseless, an atom, and an atom more,
Disjoining from the rest, has unobserv'd
Achiev'd a labour, which had far and wide,
(By man perform'd) made all the forest ring,
    Embowell'd now, and of thy antient self   110
Possessing nought, but the scoop'd rind, that seems
An huge throat calling to the clouds for drink,
Which it would give in rivulets to thy root;
Thou temptest none, but rather much forbidd'st
The feller's toil, which thou couldst ill requite: 115
Yet is thy root sincere, sound as the rock,
A quarry of stout spurs, and knotted fangs,
Which crook'd into a thousand whimsies, clasp
The stubborn soil, and hold thee still erect.

---

[1] Knee-Timber is found in the crooked arms of oak, which by reason of
their distortion, are easily adjusted to the angle formed where the deck and
the ship-sides meet. (Cowper's note)

So stands a kingdom, whose foundation yet   120
Fails not, in virtue and in wisdom lay'd,
Though all the superstructure, by the tooth
Pulveriz'd of venality, a shell
Stands now – and semblance only of itself!
Thine arms have left thee: winds have rent them off   125
Long since, and rovers of the forest wild,
With bow and shaft, have burnt them. Some have left
A splinter'd stump, bleach'd to a snowy white;
And some, memorial none where once they grew.
Yet life still lingers in thee, and puts forth   130
Proof not contemptible of what she can,
Even where death predominates. The spring
Finds thee not less alive to her sweet force,
Than yonder upstarts of the neighbouring wood,
So much thy juniors, who their birth receiv'd   135
Half a millennium since the date of thine.
But since, although well qualified by age
To teach, no spirit dwells in thee, nor voice
May be expected from thee, seated here,
On thy distorted root, with hearers none,   140
Or prompter, save the scene – I will perform
Myself the oracle, and will discourse
In my own ear, such matter as I may.
One man alone, the father of us all,
Drew not his life from woman; never gaz'd,   145
With mute unconsciousness of what he saw,
On all around him; learn'd not by degrees,
Nor ow'd articulation to his ear;
But moulded by his Maker into man
At once, upstood intelligent, survey'd   150
All creatures, with precision understood
Their purport, uses, properties, assign'd
To each his name significant, and fill'd
With love and wisdom, render'd back to Heaven
In praise harmonious, the first air he drew.   155
He was excus'd the penalties of dull
Minority; no tutor charg'd his hand
With the thought-tracing quill, or task'd his mind
With problems; history, not wanted yet,
Lean'd on her elbow, watching time, whose course   160
Eventful, should supply her with a theme; –

1804   210

Richard Edwardes, *Amantium Irae* (extract)

Date of reading: between 25 March 1804 and 11 February 1805

Edwardes is better known as the author of *Damon and Pithias* (1571), reprinted in Dodsley's *Old Plays*, to which Wordsworth had access during the 1790s. His five-stanza poem 'Amantium Irae' is widely anthologised; Wordsworth chose to transcribe only the first stanza into his Commonplace Book some time between 25 March 1804 and 11 February 1805. It is edited from his transcription.

In going to my naked bed as one that would have slept
I heard a wife sing to her child that long before had wept
She sighed sore and sang full sweet to bring the babe to rest
That would not cease but cried still in sucking at her breast
She was full weary of her watch and grieved with her child   5
She rocked it and rated it until on her it smiled
Then did she say Now have I found this proverb true
The falling out of faithful friends renewing is of love.

John Mayne, 'By Logan's streams that rins sae deep'

Date of reading: between March 1804 and 12 March 1805

Wordsworth's attention was probably drawn to Mayne by Burns, who appropriated two lines from this poem for a 'Logan braes' of his own. Born in 1759 at Dumfries, Mayne used journalism as a means of funding his career as a poet. His most ambitious poem, 'Siller Gun', was issued in twelve stanzas in 1777, and revised over the years until by Mayne's death in 1836 it was five cantos in length, with additional notes.

When Mary Wordsworth copied this poem into Wordsworth's Commonplace Book between March 1804 and 12 March 1805, it was probably at her husband's behest. It is edited from her transcription; the title she gives to it indicates that she was aware of the revised edition of Mayne's *Glasgow*, issued 1803.

By John Mayne Author of the Poem of 'Glasgow'

By Logan's streams that rins sae deep,
Fu' aft, wi' glee, I've herded sheep,
I've herded sheep or gather'd slaes,
Wi' my dear lad on Logan braes:
But waes my heart thae days are gane,   5
And fu' o grief, I herd alane;
While my dear Lad maun face his faes,
Far, far frae me and Logan braes.

Nae mair at Logan Kirk will he,
Atween the preachings meet wi me,   10
Meet wi me, or when it's mirk,
Convoy me hame frae Logan Kirk!
I weil my sing thae days are gane –
Frae Kirk and Fair I come alane,
While my dear Lad maun face his faes,   15
Far, far frae me and Logan braes!

At e'en, when Hope amaist is gane,
I danner dowie and forlane,
Or sit beneath the hawthorne tree,
Where oft he kept his tryste wi' me –   20
Oh! could I see thae days again!
My lover skaithless and my ain!
Belov'd by friends rever'd by faes,
We'd live in bliss on Logan Braes.

Samuel Richardson, *The Correspondence of Samuel Richardson, a selection from the original manuscripts* (1804) (extract)

Suggested date of reading: shortly before 5 January 1805

My Brother chanced to meet with Richardson's letters at a Friend's house, and glancing over them, read those written by Mrs Klopstock, he was exceedingly affected by them and said it was impossible to read them without loving the woman. We have been very desirous to see the Book ever since, and hope to be able to borrow it soon, but any new Book in our neighbourhood passes from house to house, and it is difficult to come at it within any reasonable time.

(Dorothy Wordsworth to Lady Beaumont, 5 January 1805)

Only four letters from Mrs Klopstock to Richardson appear in this six-volume set, all in volume 3. That Wordsworth turned to them immediately suggests that he heard about them from someone else, probably Robert Southey who in November 1804 told his friend Wynn, 'Richardson's correspondence I should think worse than anything of any celebrity that ever was published, if the life prefixed did not happen to be quite as bad. The few letters of Klopstock's Wife must be excepted from this censure: they are very interesting and very affecting; indeed the notice of her death, coming, as it does, after that sweet letter in which she dwells upon her hopes of happiness from that child whose birth destroyed her, came upon me like an electric shock'. Dorothy's remarks indicate that Wordsworth agreed with Southey's assessment. He would have had an interest in the letters having met Klopstock with Coleridge in October 1798, when they conducted a series of interviews with him that failed to improve their opinion of his work.

Of Mrs Klopstock's four letters I present most of the second, and complete texts of the third and fourth.

∾

To Mr Richardson

Hamburg, March 14, 1758

. . . You will know all what concerns me. Love, dear Sir, is all what me concerns! And love shall be all what I will tell you in this letter.

In one happy night, I read my husband's poem, the Messiah. I was extremely touched with it. The next day I asked one of his friends, who was the author of this poem? and this was the first time I heard Klopstock's name. I believe, I fell immediately in love with him. At the least, my thoughts were ever with him filled, especially because his friend told me very much of his character. But I had no hopes ever to see him, when quite unexpectedly I heard that he should pass through Hamburg. I wrote immediately to the same friend, for procuring by his means that I might see the author of the Messiah, when in Hamburg. He told him, that a certain girl at Hamburg wished to see him, and, for all recommendation, showed him some letters, in which I made bold to criticize Klopstock's verses. Klopstock came, and came to me. I must confess, that, though greatly prepossessed of his qualities, I never thought him the amiable youth whom I found him. This made its effect. After having seen him two hours, I was obliged to pass the evening in a company, which never had been so wearisome to me. I could not speak, I could not play; I thought I saw nothing but Klopstock. I saw him the next day, and the following, and we were very seriously friends. But the fourth day he departed. It was an strong hour the hour of his departure! He wrote soon after, and from that time our correspondence began to be a very diligent one. I sincerely believed my love to be friendship. I spoke with my friends of nothing but Klopstock, and showed his letters. They raillied at me, and said I was in love. I raillied them again, and said that they must have a very friendshipless heart, if they had no idea of friendship to a man as well as to a woman. Thus it continued eight months, in which time my friends found as much love in Klopstock's letters as in me. I perceived it likewise, but I would not believe it. At the last Klopstock said plainly, that he loved; and I startled as for a wrong thing. I answered, that it was no love, but friendship, as it was what I felt for him; we had not seen one another to love (as if love must have more time than friendship!). This was sincerely my meaning, and I had this meaning till Klopstock came again to Hamburg. This he did a year after we had seen one another the first time. We saw, we were friends, we loved; and we believed that we loved; and a short time after I could even tell Klopstock that I loved. But we were obliged to part again, and wait two years for our wedding. My mother would not let me marry a stranger. I could marry then without her consentment, as by the death of my father my fortune depended not on her; but this was an horrible idea for me; and thank heaven that I have prevailed by prayers! At this time knowing Klopstock, she loves him as her lifely son, and thanks God that she has not persisted. We married, and I am the happiest wife in the world. In some few months it will be four years that I am so happy, and still I dote upon Klopstock as if he was my bridegroom.

If you knew my husband, you would not wonder. If you knew his poem, I could describe him very briefly, in saying he is in all respects what he is as a poet. This I can say with all wifely modesty . . . But I dare not to speak of my husband; I am all raptures when I do it. And as happy as I am in love, so happy am I in friendship, in my mother, two elder sisters, and five other women. How rich I am!

Sir, you have willed that I should speak of myself, but I fear I have done it too much. Yet you see how it interests me.

I have the best compliments for you of my dear husband. My compliments to all your. Will they increase my treasure of friendship?

I am, Sir,
Your most humble servant,
M. KLOPSTOCK.

TO MR RICHARDSON

Hamburg, May 6, 1758
It is not possible, Sir, to tell you what a joy your letters give me. My heart is very able to esteem the favour that you, my dear Mr Richardson, in your venerable age, are so condescending good, to answer so soon the letters of an unknown young woman, who has no other merit than a heart full of friendship – and of all those sentiments which a reasonable soul must feel for Richardson, though at so many miles of distance. It is a great joyful thought, that friendship can extend herself so far, and that friendship has no need of *seeing*, though this seeing would be coelestial joy to hearts like ours, (shall I be so proud to say as *ours*?) and what will it be, when so many really good souls, knowing or not knowing in this world, will see another in the future, and be *then* friends!

It will be a delightful occupation for me, to make you more acquainted with my husband's poem. Nobody can do it better than

I, being the person who knows the most of that which is not yet published; being always present at the birth of the young verses, which begin always by fragments here and there, of a subject of which his soul is just then filled. He has many great fragments of the whole work ready. You may think that persons who love as we do, have no need of two chambers; we are always in the same. I, with my little work, still, still, only regarding sometimes my husband's sweet face, which is so venerable at that time! with tears of devotion and all the sublimity of the subject. My husband reading me his young verses and suffering my criticisms. Ten books are published, which I think probably the middle of the whole. I will, as soon as I can, translate you the arguments of these ten books, and what besides I think of them. The verses of the poem are without rhymes, and are hexameters, which sort of verses my husband has been the first to introduce in our language; we being still closely attached to rhymes and iambics.

I suspect the gentleman who has made you acquainted with the Messiah, is a certain Mr Kaiser, of Göttingen, who has told me at his return from England what he has done; and he has a sister like her whom you describe in your first letter.

But our dear Dr Young has been so ill? But he is better, I thank God along with you. Oh that his dear instructive life may be extended – if it is not against his own wishes. I read lately in the newspapers, that Dr Young was made Bishop of Bristol; I must think it is another Young. How could the King make him *only* Bishop! and Bishop of *Bristol* while the place of *Canterbury* is vacant! I think the King knows not at all that there is a Young who illustrates his reign.

And you, my dear, dear friend, have not hope of cure of a severe nervous malady? How I trembled as I read it! I pray to God to give you at the least patience and alleviation. I thank you heartily for the cautions you gave me and my dear Klopstock on this occasion. Though I can read very well your handwriting, you shall write no more if it is incommodious to you. Be so good to dictate only to Mrs Patty; it will be very agreeable to me to have so amiable a correspondent. And then I will, still more than now, preserve the two of your own hand-writing as treasures.

I am very glad, Sir, that you will take my English as it is. I knew very well that it may not always be English, but I thought for *you* it was intelligible: my husband asked, as I was writing my first letter, if I would not write French? No, said I, I will not write in this pretty but *false* language to Mr Richardson (though so polite, so cultivated, and no longer *fade* in the mouth of a Bossuet). As far as

I know, neither we, nor you, nor the Italians have the word *fade*. How have the French found this characteristic word for their nation? Our German tongue, which only begins to be cultivated, has much more conformity with the English than the French.

I wish, Sir, I could fulfil your request of bringing you acquainted with so many good people as you think of. Though I love my friends dearly, and though they are good, I have however much to pardon, except in the single Klopstock alone. *He* is good, really good, good at the bottom, in all his actions, in all the foldings of his heart. I know him; and sometimes I think if we knew others in the same manner, the better we should find them. For it may be that an action displeases us which would please us, if we knew its true aim and whole extent. No one of my friends is *so* happy as I am; but no one has had courage to marry as I did. They have married, – as people marry; and they are happy, – as people are happy. Only one as I may say, my dearest friend, is unhappy, though she had as good a purpose as I myself. She has married in my absence: but had I been present, I might, it may be, have been mistaken in her husband, as well as she.

How long a letter this is again! But I can write no short ones to you. Compliments of my husband, and compliments to all yours, always, even though I should not say it.

M. KLOPSTOCK.

To Mr Richardson

Hamburg, August 26, 1758

Why think you, Sir, that I answer so late? I will tell you my reasons . . . But before all, how does Miss Patty and how do yourself? Have you not guessed that I, summing up all my happinesses, and not speaking of children, had none? Yes, Sir, this has been my only wish ungratified for these four years. I have been more than once unhappy with disappointments: but yet, thanks, thanks to God! I am in full hope to be mother in the month of November. The little preparations for my child and child-bed (and they are so dear to me!) have taken so much time, that I could not answer your letter, nor give you the promised scenes of the Messiah. This is likewise the reason wherefore I am still here, for properly we dwell in Copenhagen. Our staying here is only a visit (but a long one) which we pay my family. I not being able to travel yet, my husband has been obliged to make a little voyage alone to Copenhagen. He is yet absent – a cloud over my happiness! He will soon return . . . But what does that help? he is yet equally absent! We write to each other every post . . . But what are letters to presence? – But I will speak no more of this little cloud; I will only tell my happiness! But I cannot tell how I rejoice! A son of my dear Klopstock! Oh, when shall I have him! – It is long since that I have made the remark, that geniuses do not engender geniuses. No children at all, bad sons, or, at the most, lovely daughters, like you and Milton. But a daughter or a son, only with a good heart, without genius, I will nevertheless love dearly.

I think that about this time a nephew of mine will wait on you. His name is *von Winlhem*, a young rich merchant, who has no bad qualities, and several good, which he has still to cultivate. His mother was, I think, twenty years older than I, but we other children loved her dearly like a mother. She had an excellent character, but is long dead.

This is no letter, but only a newspaper of your Hamburg daughter. When I have my husband and my child, I will write you more (if God gives me health and life). You will think that I shall be not a mother only, but nurse also; though the latter (thank God! that the former is not so too) is quite against fashion and good-breeding, and though nobody can think it *possible* to be always with the child at home!

M. KLOPSTOCK

TO MR RICHARDSON

Hanover, December 21, 1758

HONOURED SIR,

As perhaps you do not yet know, that one of your fair correspondents, Mrs Klopstock, died in a very dreadful manner in child-bed, I think myself obliged to acquaint you with this most melancholy accident.

Mr Klopstock in the first motion of his affliction composed an ode to God Almighty, which I have not yet seen, but hope to get by-and-by.

I shall esteem myself highly favoured by a line or two of yours or any of your family, for I presume you sometimes kindly remember
Your most humble servant
and great admirer,
L.L.G. MAJOR

John Milton, *Paradise Lost* Book VI (extract)

Date of reading: between 30 October and 2 November 1806

Wordsworth's patron, Sir George Beaumont, owned a large property, Coleorton Hall, in Leicestershire, close to Ashby-de-la-Zouch, with an attached farm. Wordsworth and his family stayed at Hall Farm from 30 October 1806 to 10 June 1807, and on their first few nights there Wordsworth delivered a series of readings from *Paradise Lost* to an audience which included his hosts. A few days later Beaumont wrote to thank him, mentioning 'that sublime passage in Milton you read the other night (I am not sure of the words) where he describes his, the Messiah's, coming as shining afar off, and this idea was so prevailing that I could almost have imagined I saw movements not to be accounted for, and shapes without a name'.

It was also on one of those evenings that Wordsworth read all of Book I; as Dorothy recalled in a letter to Lady Beaumont of 15 February 1807: 'I often think of the happy evening when, by your fireside, my Brother read to us the first book of the Paradise lost; and not without many hopes that we may again have the same pleasure together.'

The extract to which Sir George referred, from Book VI, is here edited from Anderson's *British Poets* volume 5. It is Raphael's account of the fight between God and Satan, and how on the third day God sent forth the Messiah who was destined to vanquish the fallen angels, his chariot and thunder driving into the midst of the enemy. This was among Wordsworth's favourite episodes, and in his Preface (1815) he used it as an example of the process whereby imagination engages in the task of 'consolidating numbers into unity, and dissolving and separating unity into number':

> Hear again this mighty Poet, – speaking of the Messiah going
> forth to expel from heaven the rebellious angels,
> > Attended by ten thousand thousand Saints
> > He onward came: far off his coming shone, –
> the retinue of Saints, and the Person of the Messiah himself, lost
> almost and merged in the splendour of that indefinite abstraction
> 'His coming!'

In conversation in 1834 Coleridge used the same passage to illustrate much the same argument – that (as he puts it) 'The imagination modifies images and gives unity to variety; it sees all things in one'. In this case it 'gives unity by throwing back into the distance, as after the magnificent approach of the Messiah to battle, the poet by one touch – "far off their coming shone!" – makes the whole one image'.

The extract begins with a brief speech to God by the Messiah.

O Father, O Supreme of heav'nly thrones
First, Highest, Holiest, Best, thou always seek'st
To glorify thy son, I always thee,   725
As is most just; this I my glory account,
My exaltation, and my whole delight,
That thou in me well pleas'd, declar'st thy will
Fulfilled, which to fulfill is all my bliss.
Sceptre and power, thy giving, I assume,   730
And gladlier shall resign, when, in the end,
Thou shalt be all in all, and I in thee
For ever, and in me all whom thou lov'st:
But whom thou hat'st, I hate and can put on
Thy terrors, as I put thy mildness on,   735
Image of thee in all things; and shall soon,
Arm'd with thy might, rid Heav'n of these rebell'd,
To their prepar'd ill mansion driven down,
To chains of darkness, and th' undying worm,
That from thy just obedience could revolt,   740
Whom to obey is happiness entire.
Then shall thy saints unmix'd, and from th' impure
Far separate, circling thy holy Mount
Unfeign'd halleluiahs to thee sing,
Hymns of high praise, and I among them chief.   745
    So said, he o'er his sceptre bowing, rose
From the right hand of Glory where he sat;
And the third sacred morn began to shine,
Dawning through Heav'n: forth rush'd with whirlwind sound
The chariot of paternal Deity,   750
Flashing thick flames, wheel within wheel undrawn,
Itself instinct with spirit, but convey'd
By four cherubic shapes; four faces each
Had wond'rous; as with stars their bodies all

And wings were set with eyes, with eyes the wheels
Of beril, and careering fires between; 755
Over their heads a crystal firmament,
Whereon a saphire throne, inlaid with pure
Amber, and colours of the show'ry arch.
He in celestial panoply all arm'd 760
Of radiant Urim, work divinely wrought,
Ascended; at his right hand Victory
Sat eagle-wing'd; beside him hung his bow
And quiver, with three-bolted thunder stor'd,
And from about him fierce effusion roll'd 765
Of smoke, and bickering flame, and sparkles dire:
Attended with ten thousand thousand saints,
He onward came, far off his coming shone;
And twenty thousand (I their number heard)
Chariots of God, half on each hand were seen: 770
He on the wings of Cherub rode sublime
On the crystalline sky, in saphire thron'd,
Illustrious far and wide, but by his own
First seen; them unexpected joy surpris'd,
When the great ensign of Messiah blaz'd 775
Aloft by angels borne, his sign in Heav'n;
Under whose conduct Michael soon reduc'd
His army, circumfus'd on either wing,
Under their head imbodied all in one.
Before him Power divine his way prepar'd; 780
At his command th' uprooted hills retir'd
Each to his place; they heard his voice, and went
Obsequious; Heav'n his wonted face renew'd,
And with fresh flow'rets hill and valley smil'd.
This saw his hapless foes, but stood obdur'd, 785
And to rebellious fight rallied their powers
Insensate, hope conceiving from despair.
In heav'nly sp'rits could such perverseness dwell?
But to convince the proud what signs avail,
Or wonders move th' obdurate to relent, 790
They harden'd more by what might most reclaim,
Grieving to see his glory, at the sight
Took envy; and aspiring to his height,
Stood reimbattl'd fierce, by force or fraud
Weening to prosper, and at length prevail 795
Against God and Messiah, or to fall

In universal ruin last; and now
To final battle drew, disdaining flight,
Or faint retreat: when the great Son of God
To all his host on either hand thus spake: 800
    Stand still in bright array, ye Saints, here stand
Ye angels arm'd, this day from battle rest;
Faithful hath been your warfare, and of God
Accepted, fearless in his righteous cause;
And as ye have received, so have ye done 805
Invincibly; but of this cursed crew
The punishment to other hand belongs;
Vengeance is his, or whose he sole appoints:
Number to this day's work is not ordain'd,
Nor multitude; stand only and behold 810
God's indignation on these godless pour'd
By me; not you but me they have despis'd,
Yet envied; against me is all their rage,
Because the Father, to whom in Heav'n supreme
Kingdom and power, and glory appertains, 815
Hath honour'd me according to his will.
Therefore to me their doom he hath assign'd;
That they may have their wish, to try with me
In battle which the stronger proves, they all,
Or I alone against them, since by strength 820
They measure all, of other excellence
Not emulous, nor care who them excells;
Nor other strife with them do I vouchsafe.

Fulke Greville, Baron Brooke, *The Life of the Renowned Sir Philip Sidney* (1652) (extract)

Date of reading: November 1806

Although he never owned Fulke Greville's biography of Sir Philip Sidney, Wordsworth had a high regard for it. It was one of the first things he read during his residence at Coleorton Hall Farm, November 1806, when it inspired the last two lines of a sonnet, 'November 1806' ('Another year! – another deadly blow!'). In March 1809, while working on his pamphlet in support of the Spanish freedom fighters, *The Convention of Cintra*, Wordsworth alluded to it in the middle of a particularly important passage about men of 'intellectual courage':

> Neither in general conduct nor in particular emergencies, are his plans subservient to considerations of rewards, estate, or title: these are not to have precedence in his thoughts, to govern his actions, but to follow in the train of his duty. Such men, in ancient times, were Phocion, Epaminondas, and Philopœmen; and such a man was Sir Philip Sidney, of whom it has been said, that he first taught this country *the majesty of honest dealing*. With these may be named, the honour of our own age, Washington, the deliverer of the American Continent; with these, though in many things unlike, Lord Nelson, whom we have lately lost.

Wordsworth does not quote Greville accurately, probably because he was remembering words read over two years before. The relevant passage is edited here from the first edition of 1652, chapter 3, where Greville describes Sidney's virtues.

Indeed he was a true modell of Worth; A man fit for Conquest, Plantation, Reformation, or what Action soever is greatest, and hardest amongst men: Withall, such a lover of Mankind, and Goodnesse, that whosoever had any reall parts, in him found comfort, participation, and protection to the uttermost of his power; like Zephyrus he giving life where he blew. The Universities abroad, and at home, accompted him a generall Mecaenas of Learning;

Dedicated their Books to him; and communicated every Invention, or Improvement of Knowledge with him. Souldiers honoured him, and were so honoured by him, as no man thought he marched under the true Banner of Mars, that had not obtained Sir Philip Sidney's approbation. Men of Affairs in most parts of Christendome, entertained correspondency with him. But what speak I of these, with whom his own waies, and ends did concur? since (to descend) his heart, and capacity were so large, that there was not a cunning Painter, a skilfull Engenier, an excellent Musician, or any other Artificer of extraordinary fame, that made not himself known to this famous Spirit, and found him his true friend without hire; and the common *Rende-vous* of Worth in his time.

Now let Princes vouchsafe to consider, of what importance it is to the honour of themselves, and their Estates, to have one man of such eminence; not onely as a nourisher of vertue in their Courts, or service; but besides for a reformed Standard, by which even the most humorous persons could not but have a reverend ambition to be tried, and approved currant. This I doe the more confidently affirm, because it will be confessed by all men, that this one man's example, and personall respect, did not onely encourage Learning, and Honour in the Schooles, but brought the affection, and true use thereof both into the Court, and Camp. Nay more, even many Gentlemen excellently learned amongst us will not deny, but that they affected to row, and steer their course in his wake. Besides which honour of unequall nature, and education, his very waies in the world, did generally adde reputation to his Prince, and Country, by restoring amongst us the ancient Majestie of noble, and true dealing: As a manly wisdome, that can no more be weighed down, by any effeminate craft, than Hercules could be overcome by that contemptible Army of Dwarfs. This was it which, I profess, I loved dearly in him, and still shall be glad to honour in the great men of this time: I mean, that his heart and tongue went both one way, and so with every one that went with the Truth; as knowing no other kindred, partie, or end.

Lucy Hutchinson, *Memoirs of the Life of Colonel Hutchinson* (1806) (extract)

Date of reading: c. 15 February 1807

During their residence at Coleorton Hall Farm in Leicestershire, the Wordsworths were sent a parcel of books by Sir George and Lady Beaumont, including Hutchinson's *Memoirs*. (They were probably aware that Wordsworth's wife Mary was a descendant of its author.) On 15 February Dorothy reported to Lady Beaumont: 'my Brother and Sister have read the Life of Colonel Hutchinson, which is a most valuable and interesting Book. – My Brother speaks of it with unqualified approbation, and he intends to read it over again'. Later that month Wordsworth recommended it to Walter Scott:

> By the bye speaking of Nottingham have you read Mrs Hutchinson's Life of Colonel Hutchinson, her Husband; he was Governor of Nottingham Town and Castle in the time of the civil Wars; it is a most delightful Book. –

This high opinion was echoed throughout the Wordsworth circle. Coleridge annotated his copy with approving comments, while Southey reviewed it enthusiastically in the *Annual Review*: 'We have seen few histories in which characters are so fairly appreciated, events so candidly related, and causes so naturally developed; it will set her husband's name in the first rank among English patriots, and her own in the first among English writers'. In a letter to his friend John May, Southey asked: 'Have you seen the "Memoirs of Colonel Hutchinson?" Very, very rarely has any book so greatly delighted me. It is in unison with almost every feeling and every principle I have at heart.'

Only in recent years has the *Memoir* been acknowledged as a classic of biographical and historical narrative. Ostensibly written for her children, it describes the career of her husband, Colonel John Hutchinson, a trusted colleague of Cromwell alongside whom he fought in the Civil War, and with whom he signed the death warrant of Charles I. After the Restoration he was imprisoned and died in captivity.

This extract, from the text known to Wordsworth, describes Hutchinson's thwarting of a plot to unseat Cromwell, instigated by John Lambert, who had successfully denounced the proposal to make Cromwell King. Hampered from pursuing a programme of legal reform because of mistrust between him and his colleagues in the Commons, Cromwell had reluctantly dissolved his second Parliament in February 1658. Hutchinson describes how her husband heard about the plot and, in order not to incriminate Lambert, exposed it through Cromwell's son-in-law Charles Fleetwood. In poor health and in need of friends, Cromwell's gratitude to Hutchinson was deeply felt. References to 'the protector' are to Cromwell; 'the colonell' is Hutchinson.

The cavaliers, seeing their victors thus beyond their hopes falling into their hands, had not patience to stay till things ripen'd of themselves, but were every day forming designes, and plotting for the murder of Cromwell, and other insurrections, which being contriv'd in drinke, and manag'd by false and cowardly fellowes, were still reveal'd to Cromwell, who had most excellent intelligence of all things that past, even in the king's closett; and by these unsuccessfull plotts they were the only obstructors of what they sought to advance, while, to speake truth, Cromwell's personall courage and magnanimity upheld him against all enemies and malcontents. His owne armie dislik'd him, and once when sevenscore officers had combin'd to crosse him in something he was persuing, and engag'd one to another, Lambert being the chiefe, with solemne promises and invocations to God, the protector hearing of it, overaw'd them all, and told them, 'it was not they who upheld him, but he them,' and rated them, and made them understand what pittifull fellows they were; whereupon they all, like rated dogs, clapp'd their tayles betweene their leggs, and begg'd his pardon, and left Lambert to fall alone, none daring to owne him publickly, though many in their hearts wisht him the sovereignty. Some of the Lambertonians had at that time a plott to come with a petition to Cromwell, and, while he was reading it, certeine of them had under taken to cast him out of a windore at Whitehall that lookt upon the Thames, where others should be ready to catch him up in a blankett, if he scap'd breaking his neck, and carrie him away in a boate prepar'd for the purpose to kill or keepe him alive, as they saw occasion, and then sett up Lambert. This was so carried on that it was neere the execution before the protector knew aniething of it. Coll. Hutchinson being at that time at London, by chance came to know all the plott;

certeine of the conspirators coming into a place where he was, and not being so cautious of their whispers to each other before him, but that he apprehended something, which making use of to others of the confederates, he at last found out the whole matter, without being committed to him as a matter of trust, but carelessely throwne downe in pieces before him, which he gather'd together, and became perfectly acquainted with the whole designe; and weighing it, and judging that Lambert would be the worse tirant of the two, he determin'd to prevent it, without being the author of any man's punishment. Hereupon having occasion to see Fleetwood (for he had never seene the protector since his usurpation, but publickly declar'd his testimony against it to all the tirant's minions), he bade Fleetwood wish him to have a care of petitioners, by whom he apprehended danger to his life. Fleetwood desir'd a more particular information, but the collonell was resolv'd he would give him no more then to prevent that enterprize which he dislik'd. For indeed those who were deepely engag'd, rather waited to see the cavaliers in arms against him, and then thought it the best time to arme for their owne defence, and either make a new conquest, or fall with swords in their hands. Therefore they all conniv'd at the cavaliers attempts, and although they joyn'd not with them, would not have been sorrie to have seene them up upon equal termes with the protector, that then a third party, which was ready both with arms and men, when there was oppertunity, might have fallen in and capitulated with swords in their hands, for the settlement of the rights and liberties of the good people: but God had otherwise determin'd of things; and now men began so to flatter with this tirant, so to apostatize from all faith, honesty, religion, and English liberty, and there was such a devillish practise of trepanning growne in fashion, that it was not safe to speake to any man in those treacherous dayes.

After Coll. Hutchinson had given Fleetwood that caution, he was going into the country, when the protector sent to search him out with all the earnestnesse and haste that could possibly be, and the collonell went to him: who mett him in one of the galleries, and receiv'd him with open armes and the kindest embraces that could be given, and complain'd that the collonell should be so unkind as never to give him a visitt, professing how wellcome he should have bene, the most wellcome person in the land, and with these smooth insinuations led him allong to a private place, giving him thankes for the advertisement he had receiv'd from Fleetwood, and using all his art to gett out of the collonell the knowledge of the persons engag'd in the conspiracy against him. But none of his cunning, nor promises, nor flatteries, could prevaile with the collonell to informe him more then he thought necessary to prevent the execution of the designe, which when the protector perceiv'd, he gave him most infinite thankes for what he had told him, and acknowledg'd it open'd to him some misteries that had perplext him, and agreed so with other intelligence he had, that he must owe his preservation to him: 'But,' says he, 'deare collonell, why will not you come in and act among us?' The collonell told him plainly, because he liked not any of his wayes since he broke the parliament, as being those which led to certeine and unavoidable destruction, not only of themselves, but of the whole parliament party and cause, and thereupon tooke occasion, with his usuall freedom, to tell him into what a sad hazard all things were put, and how apparent a way was made for the restitution of all former tiranny and bondage. Cromwell seem'd to receive this honest plainnesse with the greatest affection that could be, and acknowledg'd his precipitateness in some things, and with teares complain'd how Lambert had put him upon all those violent actions, for which he now accus'd him and sought his ruine. He expresst an earnest desire to restore the people's liberties, and to take and pursue more safe and sober councells, and wound up all with a very faire courtship of the collonell to engage with him, offering him any thing he would account worthy of him. The collonell told him, he could not be forward to make his owne advantage, by serving to the enslaving of his country. The other told him, he intended nothing more then the restoring and confirming the liberties of the good people, in order to which he would employ such men of honor and interest as the people should rejoyce, and he should not refuse to be one of them. And after, with all his arts, he had endeavour'd to excuse his publique actions, and to draw in the collonell; who againe had taken the opertunity to tell him freely his owne and all good men's discontents and dissatisfactions; he dismist the collonell with such expressions as were publickly taken notice of by all his little courtiers then about him, when he went to the end of the gallery with the collonell, and there, embracing him, sayd allowd to him, 'Well, collonell, satisfied or dissatisfied, you shall be one of us, for wee can no longer exempt a person so able and faithfull from the publique service, and you shall be satisfied in all honest things.' The collonell left him with that respect that became the place he was in; when immediately the same courtiers, who had some of them past him by without knowing him when he came in, although they had bene once of his familiar acquaintance, and the rest who had look'd upon him with such disdainfull neglect as those little people use to those who are not of their faction, now flockt about him, striving who should expresse most respect, and, by an extraordinary officiousnesse, redeeme their late slightings. Some of them desir'd he would command their service in any businesse he had with their lord, and a thousand such frivolous compliments, which the collonell smiled att, and quitting himselfe of them as soone as he could, made hast to returne into the country. There he had not long bene but that he was inform'd, notwithstanding all these faire shewes, the protector finding him too constant to be wrought upon to serve his tirannie, had resolv'd to secure his person, least he should head the people, who now grew very weary of his bondage. But though it was certainly confirm'd to the collonell how much he was afraid of his honesty and freedome, and that he was resolv'd not to let him longer be att liberty, yet, before his guards apprehended the collonell, death imprison'd himselfe, and confin'd all his vast ambition and all his cruell designes into the narrow compasse of a grave. His armie and court substituted his eldest sonne, Richard, in his roome, who was a meeke, temperate, and quiett man, but had not a spirit fit to succeed his father, or to manage such a perplexed government.

William Blake, *Holy Thursday (Innocence)*, *Laughing Song*, *The Tiger*, 'I love the jocund dance'

Date of reading: between mid-March and mid-April 1807, or between mid-May and 10 June 1807

> Many years ago Mr W: read some poems which I had copied And made a remark on them which I would not repeat to every one – 'There is no doubt this man is mad, but there is something in this madness which I enjoy more than the *sense* of W[alter]: Sc[ott]: or Lord B[yron]: – I had lent [Blake] when he died the 8vo Edit in 2 Vols: of WWs poems – They were sent me by his widow with pencil marginalia which I inked over. He admired W:W: 'tho' an atheist' And when I protested against this sentence it was thus supported – 'Whoever worships nature denies God, for nature is the Devils work –' I succumbed, for he always beat me in argument – he almost went into a fit of rapture at the platonic ode –
>
> (Henry Crabb Robinson to Edward Quillinan,
10 August 1848)

In 1807, towards the end of their stay at Coleorton Hall Farm, Wordsworth and his wife copied these Blake lyrics into his Commonplace Book from Benjamin Heath Malkin's *A Father's Memoirs of His Child* (1806), which also contains 'The Divine Image' and 'How sweet I roamed'. Scholars are undecided as to where he found the book; it may have been lent to them by Catherine Clarkson, or may have been in the library at Coleorton Hall. At all events, it was a fortuitous encounter, as Blake's books of poetry, being handmade, were hard to come by.

This was not Wordsworth's sole reading of Blake: on 24 May 1812 Henry Crabb Robinson recorded that 'I read Wordsworth some of Blake's poems; he was pleased with some of them, and considered Blake as having the elements of poetry a thousand times more than either Byron or Scott' – which puts a date on the statements reported by Robinson in his letter to Quillinan. We can only guess what poems Robinson showed Wordsworth – not, presumably – *Jerusalem*, which Robinson regarded as 'a perfectly mad poem'. Hazlitt enjoyed 'The Chimney Sweeper' when Robinson showed it to him on 10 March 1811; in addition, Robinson had transcripts of at least the following: 'To the Muses', 'Night', 'The

Little Black Boy', 'A Dream', 'The Sunflower', 'Introduction (Experience and Innocence)', 'Earth's Answer', 'The Garden of Love', 'A Little Boy Lost', 'The Poison Tree', 'The Sick Rose', 'The Human Abstract', the 'Dedication' of the designs for Blair's *Grave, America* Plate 10, lines 5-10, and *Europe* Plate 1, lines 12-15.

These texts are edited from Wordsworth's Commonplace Book.

∼❧

Holy Thursday

Twas on a Holy Thursday their innocent faces clean
The Children walking two and two in red and blue and green
Grey-headed Beadles walked before, with wands as white as snow
Till into the high dome of Paul's, they, like Thames's waters flow

Oh what a multitude they seem'd, these flowers of London town   5
Seated in companies they sit, with radiance all their own!
The hum of multitudes was there, but multitudes of Lambs
Thousands of little boys and girls raising their innocent hands.

Now like a mighty wind they raise to heavn the voice of song,
Or like harmonious thunderings the seats of heaven among   10
Beneath them sit the aged men, wise guardians of the poor
Then cherish Pity, lest you drive an angel from your door.

Laughing Song

When the green Woods laugh with the voice of joy
And the dimpling stream runs laughing by
When the air does laugh with our merry wit
And the green hill laughs with the noise of it

When the meadows laugh with lively green   5
And the Grasshopper laughs in this merry scene
When Mary and Susan and Emily
With their sweet round mouths sing ha, ha, he!

1807

When the painted Birds laugh in the shade,
Where our table with cherries and nuts is spread   10
Come live and be merry and join with me
To sing the sweet chorus of ha, ha, he!

The Tiger

Tiger, Tiger burning bright
In the forest of the night
What immortal hand or eye
Could frame thy fearful symmetry?

In what distant deeps or skies,   5
Burnt the fire of thine eyes?
On what wings dare he aspire?
What the hand dare seize the fire?

And what shoulder, and what art,
Could twist the sinews of thy heart?   10
When the heart began to beat,
What dread hand and what dread feet?

What the hammer? what the chain?
In what furnace was thy brain?
What the anvil? What dread grasp   15
Dared its deadly terrors clasp?

When the stars threw down their spears,
And watered heaven with their tears,
Did he smile his work to see?
Did he who made the lamb, make thee?   20

Tiger Tiger, burning bright
In the forest of the night;
What immortal hand or eye
Did frame thy fearful symmetry?

1807

'I love the jocund dance'

I love the jocund dance,
The softly breathing song,
Where innocent eyes do glance
    And where lisps the maiden's tongue.

I love the laughing gale,   5
I love the echoing hill,
Where mirth does never fail,
    And the jolly swain laughs his fill.

I love the pleasant cot,
I love the innocent bower,   10
Where white and brown is our lot,
    Or fruit in the mid-day hour.

I love the oaken seat,
Beneath the oaken tree,
Where all the old villagers meet,   15
    And laugh our sports to see.

I love our neighbours all,
But, Kitty I better love thee;
And love them I ever shall;
    But thou art all to me.   20

Isaac Walton, *The Complete Angler*
ed. John Sidney Hawkins (6th ed., 1797) (extract)

Date of reading: from the evening of 3 January 1808 onwards

> I hope that Davy will let me have an Angling Rod, and I will take
> care to bring Isaac Walton.
>
> (Wordsworth to Mary Wordsworth, 3-4 June 1812)

Wordsworth had probably caught sight of Walton's classic volume
before 1808, but a copy was not within permanent reach until 3
January when his sister thanked Lady Beaumont for a 'parcel':

> . . . today arrives your note enclosed in the parcel with Walton's
> complete Angler . . . My dear Lady Beaumont, I cannot say how
> much I am gratified by Sir George's kind remembrance of me,
> nor how highly I shall value his gift, for *his* sake as well as that of
> the pure innocent Spirit that breathed out the tender sentiments
> contained in that book, so many years ago. I have read a few
> pages here and there, and have seen enough to be convinced that
> it has not been overpraised. I was greatly delighted with one
> passage, where Walton speaks familiarly of Sir Henry Wotton,
> Milton's Friend, as his frequent companion in his favourite plea-
> sure, and he repeats some of the expressions of Sir Henry, which
> are very beautiful. My Brother has seized upon the Book for his
> own reading this night, as he fancies that the imagery and senti-
> ments accord with his own train of thought at present, in
> connection with his poem, which he is just upon the point of
> finishing.

Wordsworth's 'poem' of the moment was *The White Doe of Rylstone*
which despite being nearly finished was not published until 1815.
The copy of Walton which Sir George sent as a gift to Dorothy
survives today in the Wordsworth family, and bears an inscription
in ink:

From Sir George Beaumont to
   Dorothy Wordsworth
      Grasmere January 10th
       1808

On page 40 either Wordsworth or Dorothy has marked the passage in which Walton discusses Sir Henry Wotton, commended in her letter to Beaumont. Dorothy would certainly have directed her brother to read it, and they would have shared a high opinion of it. Her reference to 'the pure innocent Spirit' is not clear, but I suspect a recollection of her brother John, drowned in a shipwreck three years before. He and Wordsworth were keen anglers.

Walton's tribute to Wotton is edited here from the text of 1797, Part I, chapter 1. Walton is in the midst of a digression in which he provides character sketches of 'two memorable men, that lived near to our own time, whom I also take to have been ornaments to the art of Angling'. The first is Alexander Nowell, Dean of St Paul's; the second is Wotton.

My next and last example shall be that undervaluer of money, the late provost of Eton College, Sir Henry Wotton, a man with whom I have often fished and conversed; a man whose foreign employments in the service of this nation, and whose experience, learning, wit, and chearfulness, made his company to be esteemed one of the delights of mankind; this man, whose very approbation of Angling were sufficient to convince any modest censurer of it, this man was also a most dear lover, and a frequent practiser of the art of Angling; of which he would say, 'It was an employment for his idle time, which was then not idly spent:' for Angling was, after tedious study, 'a rest to his mind, a chearer of his spirits, a diverter of sadness, a calmer of unquiet thoughts, a moderator of passions, a procurer of contentedness:' and 'that it begat habits of peace and patience in those that professed and practised it.' Indeed, my friend, you will find Angling to be like the virtue of humility, which has a calmness of spirit, and a world of other blessings attending upon it.

Thomas Wilkinson, *To My Thrushes, Blackbirds, etc.*

Suggested date of reading: 13 June 1809

> Among his verses, (he wrote many) are some worthy of preser-
> vation – one little poem in particular upon disturbing by prying
> curiosity a bird while hatching her young in his garden.
>
> (Wordsworth, Fenwick Notes, 1843)

Wordsworth was remembering 'To My Thrushes, Blackbirds, etc.',
which he read over thirty years before, shortly after Coleridge
arrived at Allan Bank after staying with Wilkinson, 13 June 1809.
Nearly a month later he told Wilkinson that 'Mr Coleridge showed
me a little poem of yours upon your Birds which gave us all very
great pleasure'. Wordsworth seems not to have possessed a copy of
this poem (though he had others – see p. 185), which makes his
recollection of this one so many years later all the more notable.

To My Thrushes, Blackbirds, etc.

By Thos. Wilkinson
*(Some friends having found nine of their nests in my garden
and looked into the same, to the annoyance of the inhabitants.)*

Ye finches and linnets, ye blackbirds and thrushes,
Who dwell in my garden among the green bushes,
Your company's sweet, and I'm happy to see
You visit about from the juniper tree
To the gooseberry bush; but a recent intrusion   5
Has thrown all your harmony into confusion!
I pity you greatly. 'Twas very provoking
That while you sang sweetly to strangers a-walking,
They should rush on your privacy, little regarding
Your slumbering babes, and not caring a farthing   10
For your poor loving wives, who required kind attention,
A proceeding so rough is – unpleasant to mention!

Ye blackbirds and linnets, and finches and all,
No longer sit piping aloof when I call:
You know, my sweet birds, and it's known to your spouses,   15
I go not about, peeping into your houses;
Your green sheltered houses as safe are from me
As if they were locked with a lock and a key;
How could I annoy you, when seeing your care
In collecting your mortar, your moss, and your hair!   20
How you tugged at your timbers, and toiled on the wing
While the winds were against you, your rafters to bring!
I once was a builder, nor have I forgot
How I laboured, like you, in erecting my cot;
I thought, peradventure, like you, as I wrought,   25
Of a house of my own, and it might cross my thought
That a mate might sit by me and comfort my nest,
And there, in due time, that my chirpers might rest.
I have lived with you all without scolding or strife,
From the cushat and owl, to the wren and his wife;   30
Round your mansions of moss you may warble all day,
From the apple-tree bough or the juniper spray,
Unmolested by me; I partake of your joy,
Nor went about robbing your nests when a boy.
You've often amused a poor head full of care   35
With a bounce to the clouds or your tumbles in air.
If you sing from the cedar I hear with delight,
And am ready to laugh when you bustle and fight;
I scarce would forbid you the use of my trees
When you go with my cherries and pilfer my peas;   40
With pleasure I see you display your light pinions,
And flutter and fly round your little dominions.
The whole of my garden is open and free,
Each tree shall be yours, and the boughs of each tree.

James Graham, 1st Marquis of Montrose, 'Great, good, and just'

Date of reading: by February 1810

Wordsworth encountered 'Great, good, and just' in William Winstanley's *England's Worthies* (1684), and quoted it in the second of his *Essays upon Epitaphs* (1810). Having done so, he provided a brief commentary that ranks as one of the most inspired pieces of prose he was ever to write:

> These funereal verses would certainly be wholly out of their place upon a tombstone; but who can doubt that the Writer was transported to the height of the occasion? – that he was moved as it became an heroic Soldier, holding those Principles and opinions, to be moved? His soul labours; – the most tremendous event in the history of the Planet, namely, the Deluge, is brought before his imagination by the physical image of tears, – a connection awful from its very remoteness and from the slender bond that unites its ideas: – it passes into the region of Fable likewise; for all modes of existence that forward his purpose are to be pressed into the service. The whole is instinct with spirit, and every word has its separate life; like the Chariot of the Messiah, and the wheels of that Chariot, as they appeared to the imagination of Milton aided by that of the Prophet Ezekiel.

The terminal date for Wordsworth's reading must be February 1810, though I suspect he obtained his copy of Winstanley before then. Introducing it, Winstanley remarks of Montrose that 'he was so zealous of the Fame of his great Master Charles the first, that with the point of his Sword he wrote these following lines'. This text is edited from Winstanley.

❧

Great, good, and just, could I but rate
My griefs, and thy so ridgid fate;
I'de weep the world to such a strain,
As it should deluge once again.
But since thy loud-tongu'd Bloud demands supplies,   5
More from Briareus hands than Argus eyes,
I'll sing thy Obsequies with Trumpet sounds,
And write thy Epitaph with Bloud and Wounds.

Montross.

John Armstrong, *The Art of Preserving Health* Book 2
(extract)

Date of reading: by 1812

Wordsworth doubtless knew Armstrong's poem from childhood onwards, though his earliest reference to it was not until 1812, when he quoted it from memory in a letter to his wife. He felt kinship with Armstrong because he too was brought up on the borders of England and Scotland.

  The Art of Preserving Health is a long, variable poem, and Wordsworth was specific about what he liked in it, as he makes clear in a note attached to his sonnet sequence, *The River Duddon*: 'The power of waters over the minds of Poets has been acknowledged from the earliest ages; – through the "Flumina amem sylvasque inglorius" of Virgil, down to the sublime apostrophe to the great rivers of the earth, by Armstrong'. He would always find Armstrong's apostrophe an inspiration; it lies behind a passage in *The Excursion*, and was doubtless in his mind as he composed *The River Duddon*. He included it in his manuscript collection of poems for Lady Mary Lowther in 1819, from which the present text is edited.

The Art of Preserving Health

Book 2 *(extract)*

Now come, ye Naiads, to the fountains lead;
Now let me wander through your gelid reign.
I burn to view the enthusiastic wilds
By mortal else untrod. I hear the din   355
Of waters thund'ring o'er the ruin'd cliffs.
With holy reverence I approach the rocks
Whence glide the streams renown'd in ancient song.
Here from the desert down the rumbling steep
First springs the Nile; here bursts the sounding Po   360
In angry waves; Euphrates hence devolves

A mighty flood to water half the east;
And there in Gothic solitude reclined
The cheerless Tanais pours his hoary urn.
What solemn twilight! What stupendous shades   365
Enwrap those infant floods! Through every nerve
A sacred horror thrills, a pleasing fear
Glides o'er my frame. The forest deepens round;
And more gigantic still the impending trees
Stretch their extravagant arms athwart the gloom.   370
Are these the confines of some faery world?
A land of genii? Say beyond these wilds
What unknown nations? If indeed beyond
Aught habitable lies. And whither leads,
To what strange regions, or of bliss or pain,   375
That subterraneous way?. . .

James Hogg, *The Queen's Wake* (1814): *The Witch of Fife*

Date of reading: mid-November 1814

> I thank you for the Queen's Wake; since I saw you in Edinburgh
> I have read it. It does Mr Hogg great credit. Of the tales, I liked
> best, much the best, the Witch of Fife . . .
>   (Wordsworth to R.P. Gillies, 23 November 1814)

Wordsworth and Hogg met in Edinburgh in late August 1814;
Hogg would later recall: 'I listened to him that night as a superior
being, far exalted above the common walks of life. His sentiments
seemed just, and his language, though perhaps a little pompous,
was pure, sentient, and expressive'. Hogg's visit to Cumbria a few
weeks later is the occasion of two of the most memorable anecdotes
about Wordsworth.

When he arrived at Rydal Wordsworth showed him the sights;
seeing Hogg beginning to tire, Wordsworth said, 'I'll just show you
another lake, and then we'll go homewards', to which Hogg replied:
'I dinna want to see onny mair *dubs*. Let's step in to the public and
hev a wee drap o' whusky, and then we'll hame!' When retelling this
story, Wordsworth used to say that though initially offended to hear
his beloved lakes called 'dubs', 'on reflection, [I] could not take
umbrage – the *dubs* was so characteristic of the man'.

Two days later Hogg was at Rydal Mount when an unusually
bright meteor was seen in the sky from the upper terrace. Dorothy
expressed fears that 'the splendid stranger might prove ominous', to
which Hogg replied, 'Hout me'em! it is neither mair nor less than
joost a treeumphal airch, raised in honour of the meeting of the
poets'. At that moment, Wordsworth turned away and said to De
Quincey, with whom he was walking, 'Poets? Poets? – What does
the fellow mean? – Where are they?' De Quincey lost no time in
repeating this to Hogg, to whom it would cause lasting offence. As
late as 1832, Hogg wrote: 'Who could forgive this? For my part, I
never can, and never will! . . . but for that short sentence I have a
lingering ill-will at him which I cannot get rid of . . . I have always
some hopes that De Quincey was *leeing*, for I did not myself hear
Wordsworth utter the words'.

These events occurred two months before R.P. Gillies sent
Wordsworth a copy of *The Queen's Wake* in mid-November – in the
light of which Wordsworth's good opinion of 'The Witch of Fife' is

all the more striking. It is probably Hogg's most successful poem, and is edited from the 1814 text.

The Witch of Fife

'Quhare haif ye been, ye ill womyne,
　　These three lang nightis fra hame?
Quhat garris the sweit drap fra yer brow,
　　Like clotis of the saut sea faem?

It fearis me muckil ye haif seen　　　　　　5
　　Quhat good man never knew;
It fearis me muckil ye haif been
　　Quhare the gray cock never crew.

But the spell may crack, and the brydel breck,
　　Then sherpe yer werde will be;　　　　10
Ye had better sleipe in yer bed at hame,
　　Wi yer deire littil bairnis and me.' –

'Sit dune, sit dune, my leile auld man,
　　Sit dune, and listin to me;
I'll gar the hayre stand on yer crown,　　　15
　　And the cauld sweit blind yer e'e.

But tell nae wordis, my gude auld man,
　　Tell never word again;
Or deire shall be yer courtisye,
　　And driche and sair yer pain.　　　　　20

The first leet-night, quhan the new moon set,
　　Quhan all was douffe and mirk,
We saddled ouir naigis wi the moon-fern leif,
　　And rode fra Kilmerrin kirk.

Some horses ware of the brume-cow framit,　25
　　And some of the greine bay tree;
But mine was made of ane humloke schaw,
　　And a stout stallion was he.

We raide the tod doune on the hill,
    The martin on the law;   30
And we huntyd the hoolet out of brethe,
    And forcit him doune to fa.' –

'Quhat guid was that, ye ill womyn?
    Quhat guid was that to thee?
Ye wald better haif bein in yer bed at hame,   35
    Wi yer deire littil bairnis and me.' –

'And ay we raide, and se merrily we raide,
    Throw the merkist gloffis of the night;
And we swam the floode, and we darnit the woode,
    Till we cam to the Lommond height.   40

And quhen we cam to the Lommond height,
    Se lythlye we lychtid doune;
And we drank fra the hornis that never grew,
    The beer that was never browin.

Than up there rase ane wee wee man,   45
    Franethe the moss-gray stane;
His fece was wan like the collifloure,
    For he nouthir had blude nor bane.

He set ane reid-pipe till his muthe,
    And he playit se bonnilye,   50
Till the grey curlew, and the black-cock, flew
    To listen his melodye.

It rang se sweet through the green Lommond,
    That the nycht-winde lowner blew;
And it soupit alang the Loch Leven,   55
    And wakinit the white sea-mew.

It ran se sweet through the grein Lommond,
    Se sweitly butt and se shill,
That the wezilis laup out of their mouldy holis,
    And dancit on the mydnycht hill.   60

The corby craw cam gledgin near,
    The ern gede veerying bye;
And the troutis laup out of the Leven Louch,
    Charmit with the melodye.

And ay we dancit on the green Lommond,   65
    Till the dawn on the ocean grew:
Ne wonder I was a weary wycht
    Quhan I cam hame to you.' –

'Quhat guid, quhat guid, my weird weird wyfe,
    Quhat guid was that to thee?   70
Ye wald better haif bein in yer bed at hame,
    Wi yer deire littil bairnis and me.' –

'The second nychte, quhan the new moon set,
    O'er the roaryng sea we flew;
The cockle-shell our trusty bark,   75
    Our sailis of the grein sea-rue.

And the bauld windis blew, and the fire flauchtis flew,
    And the sea ran to the skie;
And the thunner it growlit, and the sea dogs howlit,
    As we gaed scouryng bye.   80

And ay we mountit the sea green hillis,
    Quhill we brushit thro' the cludis of the hevin;
Than sousit dounright like the stern-shot light,
    Fra the liftis blue casement driven.

But our taickil stood, and our bark was good,   85
    And se pang was our pearily prowe;
Quhan we culdna speil the brow of the wavis,
    We needilit them throu belowe.

As fast as the hail, as fast as the gale,
    As fast as the midnycht leme,   90
We borit the breiste of the burstyng swale,
    Or fluffit i' the flotyng faem.

And quhan to the Norraway shore we wan,
    We muntyd our steedis of the wynd,
And we splashit the floode, and we darnit the woode,   95
    And we left the shouir behynde.

Fleet is the roe on the green Lommond,
    And swift is the couryng grew;
The rein deir dun can eithly run,
    Quhan the houndis and the hornis pursue.   100

But nowther the roe, nor the rein-deir dun,
    The hinde nor the couryng grew,
Culde fly owr muntaine, muir, and dale,
    As owr braw steedis they flew.

The dales war deep, and the Doffrinis steep,   105
    And we rase to the skyis ee-bree;
Quhite, quhite was ouir rode, that was never trode,
    Owr the snawis of eternity!

And quhan we cam to the Lapland lone
    The fairies war all in array,   110
For all the genii of the north
    War keepyng their holeday.

The warlock men and the weerd wemyng,
    And the fays of the wood and the steep,
And the phantom hunteris all war there,   115
    And the mermaidis of the deep.

And they washit us all with the witch-water,
    Distillit fra the moorland dew,
Quhill our beauty blumit like the Lapland rose,
    That wylde in the foreste grew.' –   120

'Ye lee, ye lee, ye ill womyne,
    Se loud as I heir ye lee!
For the warst-faurd wyfe on the shoris of Fyfe
    Is cumlye comparet wi thee.' –

1814

'Then the mer-maidis sang and the woodlandis rang,   125
  Se sweetly swellit the quire;
On every cliff a herpe they hang,
  On every tree a lyre.

And ay they sang, and the woodlandis rang,
  And we drank, and we drank se deep;   130
Then soft in the armis of the warlock men,
  We laid us dune to sleep.' –

'Away, away, ye ill womyne,
  An ill deide met ye dee!
Quhan ye hae pruvit se false to yer God,   135
  Ye can never pruve trew to me.' –

'And there we lernit fra the fairy foke,
  And fra our master true,
The wordis that can beire us throu the air,
  And lokkis and baris undo.   140

Last nycht we met at Maisry's cot;
  Richt weil the wordis we knew;
And we set a foot on the black cruik-shell,
  And out at the lum we flew.

And we flew owr hill, and we flew owr dale,   145
  And we flew owr firth and sea,
Until we cam to merry Carlisle,
  Quhar we lightit on the lea.

We gaed to the vault beyound the towir,
  Quhar we enterit free as ayr;   150
And we drank, and we drank of the bishopis wine
  Quhill we culde drynk ne mair.' –

'Gin that be trew, my gude auld wyfe,
  Whilk thou hast tauld to me,
Betide my death, betide my lyfe,   155
  I'll beire thee companye.

Neist tyme ye gaung to merry Carlisle
   To drynk of the blude-reid wine,
Beshrew my heart, I'll fly with thee,
   If the diel shulde fly behynde.' –   160

'Ah! little do ye ken, my silly auld man,
   The daingeris we maun dree;
Last nichte we drank of the bishopis wyne,
   Quhill near near taen war we.

Afore we wan to the sandy ford,   165
   The gor-cockis nichering flew;
The lofty crest of Ettrick Pen
   Was wavit about with blew,
And, flichtering throu the air, we fand
   The chill chill mornyng dew.   170

As we flew owr the hillis of Braid,
   The sun rase fair and clear;
There gurly James, and his baronis braw,
   War out to hunt the deere.

Their bowis they drew, their arrowis flew,   175
   And peircit the ayr with speede,
Quhill purpil fell the mornyng dew
   With witch-blude rank and reide.

Littil do ye ken, my silly auld man,
   The dangeris we maun dree;   180
Ne wonder I am a weary wycht
   Quhan I come hame to thee.' –

'But tell me the *word*, my gude auld wyfe,
   Come tell it me speedilye;
For I lang to drink of the gude reide wyne,   185
   And the wyng the ayr with thee.

Yer hellish horse I wilna ryde,
   Nor sail the seas in the wynd;
But I can flee as well as thee,
   And I'll drynk quhill ye be blynd.' –   190

1814

'O fy! O fy! my leil auld man,
    That word I darena tell;
It wald turn this warld all upside down,
    And make it warse than hell.

For all the lasses in the land   195
    Wald munt the wynd and fly;
And the men wald doff their doublets syde,
    And after them wald ply.' –

But the auld gudeman was ane cunnyng auld man,
    And ane cunnyng auld man was he;   200
And he watchit, and he watchit for mony a night,
    The witches' flychte to see.

Ane nychte he darnit in Maisry's cot;
    The fearless haggs came in;
And he heard the word of awsome weird,   205
    And he saw their deedis of synn.

Then ane by ane, they said that word,
    As fast to the fire they drew;
Then set a foot on the black cruik-shell,
    And out at the lum they flew.   210

The auld gude-man cam fra his hole
    With feire and muckil dreide,
But yet he culdna think to rue,
    For the wyne came in his head.

He set his foot in the black cruik-shell,   215
    With ane fixit and ane wawlyng ee;
And he said the word that I darena say,
    And out at the lum flew he.

The witches skalit the moon-beam pale;
    Deep groanit the trembling wynde;   220
But they never wist till our auld gude-man
    Was hoveryng them behynde.

They flew to the vaultis of merry Carlisle,
  Quhair they enterit free as ayr;
And they drank and they drank of the byshopis wyne   225
  Quhill they culde drynk ne mair.

The auld gude-man he grew se crouse,
  He dancit on the mouldy ground,
And he sang the bonniest sangis of Fife,
  And he tuzzlit the kerlyngs round.   230

And ay he percit the tither butt,
  And he suckit, and he suckit se lang,
Quhill his een they closit, and his voice grew low,
  And his tongue wold hardly gang.

The kerlyngs drank of the bishopis wyne   235
  Quhill they scentit the mornyng wynde;
Then clove again the yeilding ayr,
  And left the auld man behynde.

And ay he slepit on the damp damp floor,
  He slepit and he snorit amain;   240
He never dremit he was far fra hame,
  Or that the auld wyvis war gane.

And ay he slepit on the damp damp floor
  Quhill past the mid-day highte,
Quhan wakenit by five rough Englishmen,   245
  That trailit him to the lychte.

'Now quha are ye, ye silly auld man,
  That sleepis se sound and se weil?
Or how gat ye into the bishopis vault
  Throu lokkis and barris of steel?' –   250

The auld gude-man he tryit to speak,
  But ane word he culdna fynde;
He tryit to think, but his head whirlit round,
  And ane thing he culdna mynde: –
'I cam fra Fyfe,' the auld man cryit,   255
  'And I cam on the midnycht wynde.'

         1814

They nickit the auld man, and they prickit the auld man,
   And they yerkit his limbis with twine,
Quhill the reid blude ran in his hose and shoon,
   But some cryit it was wyne.   260

They lickit the auld man, and they prickit the auld man,
   And they tyit him till ane stone;
And they set ane bele-fire him about,
   And they burnit him skin and bone.

Now wae be to the puir auld man   265
   That ever he saw the day!
And wae be to all the ill wemyng,
   That lead puir men astray!

Let never ane auld man after this
   To lawless greide inclyne;   270
Let never an auld man after this
   Rin post to the diel for wyne.

Edmund Waller, *Poems* (5th ed., 1686):
Song ('Go lovely Rose!')

Suggested date of reading: by January 1815

> Turning to my own shelves, I find the folio of Cowley, seventh
> edition, 1681. A book near it is Flatman's Poems, fourth edition,
> 1686; Waller, fifth edition, same date.
> (Wordsworth, 'Essay, Supplementary to the Preface' (1815))

This rare glimpse of Wordsworth's bookshelves indicates that he
owned Waller's *Poems* by January 1815. He referred to the volume
in 1819 when copying poems into the album he compiled for Lady
Mary Lowther, including 'Go lovely Rose!', edited here from his
transcription.

Song

Go lovely Rose!
Tell her that wastes her time and me
  That now she knows,
When I resemble her to thee
  How sweet and fair she seems to be.   5

  Tell her thats young
And shuns to have her graces spied,
  That hadst thou sprung,
In desarts where no men abide,
  Thou must have uncommended died.   10

  Small is the worth
Of beauty from the light retired:
  Bid her come forth,
Suffer herself to be desired
  And not blush so to be admired.   15

1815

        Then die! that she
The common fate of all things rare
        May read in thee,
How small a part of time they share
        That are so wondrous sweet and fair.   20

William Shakespeare, *Sonnets*: 'When I have seen by times fell hand defaced', 'Thy bosom is endeared with all hearts', 'When in disgrace with fortune and men's eyes'

Date of reading: 1819

Wordsworth first read the *Sonnets* at school, returning to them periodically. In 1815 he commended them, saying that 'in no part of the writings of this Poet is found, in an equal compass, a greater number of exquisite feelings felicitously expressed'. He entered these three in the album compiled for Lady Mary Lowther at Christmas 1819, from which they are edited. On occasion his readings deviate from those normally published, probably because he was transcribing from memory.

Sonnet

When I have seen by times fell hand defaced
The rich proud cost of outworn buried age,
When sometime lofty towers I see down-razed
And brass eternal slave to mortal rage;
When I have seen the hungry ocean gain   5
Advantage on the kingdom of the shore,
And the firm soil win of the watry main,
Increasing store with loss, and loss with store;
When I have seen such interchange of state,
Or state itself confounded to decay;   10
Ruin hath taught me thus to ruminate –
That time will come and take my love away.
   This thought is like a death, which cannot chuse
   But weep to have what it so fears to lose.

Sonnet

Thy bosom is endeared with all hearts,
Which I by lacking have supposed dead;
And there reigns love and all love's loving parts,
And all those friends which I thought buried.
How many a holy and obsequious tear   5
Hath dear religious love stolen from mine eye,
As interest of the dead, which now appear
But things removed, that hidden in thee lie!
Thou art the grave where buried love doth live
Hung with the trophies of my lovers gone,   10
Who all their parts of me to thee did give;
That due of many now is thine alone:
    Their images I lov'd I view in thee
    And thou (all they) hast all the all of me.

Sonnet

When in disgrace with fortune and men's eyes,
I all alone beweep my outcast state,
And trouble deaf heaven with my bootless cries,
And look upon myself and curse my fate,
Wishing me like to one more rich in hope,   5
Featur'd like him, like him with friends possesst,
Desiring this man's art, and that man's scope,
With what I most enjoy contented least:
Yet in these thoughts myself almost despising,
Haply I think on thee, – and then my state   10
Like to the lark at break of day arising
From sullen earth sing hymns at heaven's gate;
  For thy sweet love remembered such wealth brings,
  That then I scorn to change my state with kings.

John Webster, *The White Devil* (extract):
'Funeral Dirge for Marcello'

Suggested date of reading: by 1819

Wordsworth was an enthusiastic reader of Renaissance drama, and is known also to have read Heywood, Massinger and Marlowe. In 1830 he applauded Alexander Dyce for having edited Webster's complete dramatic works rather than just one or two plays – which suggests that by then he had read most, if not all, of them. He certainly knew *The White Devil* by 1819, because when he made up a collection of poems for Lady Mary Lowther in that year, he included Cornelia's Dirge for Marcello, V iv 94-103, from which the text below is edited. Also an admirer of the Dirge, Charles Lamb included it in *Specimens of English Dramatic Poets* (1808), an anthology he was originally to have compiled with Wordsworth, attaching the following comment:

> I never saw any thing like this Dirge, except the Ditty which reminds Ferdinand of his drowned Father in the Tempest. As that is of the water, watery; so this is of the earth, earthy. Both have that intenseness of feeling, which seems to resolve itself into the elements which it contemplates.

Funeral Dirge for Marcello

(His Mother sings it)

Call for the Robin-red-breast, and the Wren,
Since o'er shady groves they hover,
And with leaves and flowers do cover
The friendless bodies of unburied men.
Call to his funeral dole   5
The Ant the field-mouse, and the mole,
To raise him hillocks that shall keep him warm,
And when gay tombs are robb'd sustain no harm;
But keep the Wolf far hence that's foe to men
For with his nails he'll dig them up again.   10

Alexander Pope, *Ode on Solitude*

Suggested date of reading: by 1819

In May 1830 Wordsworth discussed Pope's merits with Alexander Dyce:

> Pope, in that production of his boyhood, the ode to Solitude, and in his Essay on Criticism, has furnished proofs that at one period of his life he felt the charm of a sober and subdued style, which he afterwards abandoned for one that is to my taste at least too pointed and ambitious, and for a versification too timidly balanced.

Wordsworth included the 'Ode on Solitude' in his manuscript album for Lady Mary Lowther in 1819, and the present text is edited from his transcription.

Ode on Solitude

Happy the man, whose wish and care,
A few paternal acres bound,
Content to breathe his native air
    In his own ground.

Whose herds with milk, whose fields with bread,   5
Whose flocks supply him with attire;
Whose trees in summer yield him shade,
    In winter fire.

Blest who can unconcern'dly find
Hours, days, and years slide soft away   10
In health of body peace of mind,
    Quiet by day

Sound sleep by night; study and ease,
Together mix'd; sweet recreation,
And innocence which most doth please,   15
        With meditation.

Thus let me live, unseen, unknown;
Thus unlamented, let me die,
Steal from the world, and not a stone
        Tell where I lie.   20

                        Pope, *in his 12th year*

Christopher Smart, *Lines Written, whilst confined in a Madhouse*

Suggested date of reading: by 1819

Smart's 'Lines' was published as a discrete work in Anderson's *British Poets* (Wordsworth's source), though it actually comprises three stanzas (18, 21, 40) of 'A Song to David' (1763), the complete poem running to 86 stanzas (516 lines). In Wordsworth's day the 'Song' was believed to have been written during Smart's confinement (mid-1756 to January 1763) because when John Langhorne reviewed it he claimed 'that it was written when the Author was denied the use of his pen, ink, and paper, and was obliged to indent his lines, with the end of a key, upon the wainscot'. This tale was repeated in Anderson's *British Poets*, but it strains credibility: lunatics were surely not given the keys to their cells, and even if they were it would have been an epic labour for the sanest of individuals to have etched all 516 lines of the 'Song' into the wainscot. Modern scholars debate the time of composition, though it is possible that parts of the poem were composed during Smart's residence in the asylum.

Wordsworth entered it in his album of verse compiled for Lady Mary Lowther in 1819, from which this text is edited.

Lines Written, whilst confined in a Madhouse, with a Key on the Wainscot (the rest of them are lost) by C. Smart

He sung of God, the mighty source
Of all things, the stupendous force
    On which all things depend:
From whose right arm, beneath whose eyes,
All period, power, and enterprize,   5
    Commence, and reign, and end.

The world, – the clus'tring spheres, – he made,
The glorious light, the soothing shade,
    Dale, champaign, grove and hill
The multitudinous abyss   10
Where secrecy remains in bliss!
    And wisdom hides her skill.

Tell them I AM, Jehovah said
To Moses, while Earth heard with dread;
    And smitten to the heart   15
At once above, beneath, around,
All nature without voice or sound
    Replied, O Lord, THOU ART.

Percy Bysshe Shelley, *To a Skylark*

Date of reading: between 1819 and July 1826

In the summer of 1819 Wordsworth briefly encountered Shelley's friend Trelawny on the shores of Lake Geneva. Asked what he thought of Shelley, Wordsworth answered 'Nothing':

> Seeing my surprise, he added, 'A poet who has not produced a good poem before he is twenty-five, we may conclude cannot, and never will do so.'
>
> '*The Cenci!*' I said eagerly.
>
> 'Won't do', he replied, shaking his head, as he got into the carriage: a rough-coated Scotch terrier followed him.
>
> 'This hairy fellow is our flea-trap', he shouted out, as they started off.

That was in 1819. Looking back from the vantage point of 1858, Trelawny went on to remark:

> I did not then know that the full-fledged author never reads the writings of his cotemporaries, except to cut them up in a review, – that being a work of love. In after-years, Shelley being dead, Wordsworth confessed this fact; he was then induced to read some of Shelley's poems, and admitted that Shelley was the greatest master of harmonious verse in our modern literature.

Wordsworth was no better disposed towards Shelley when in April 1822 he reported to Landor that:

> Byron, Shelley, Moore, Leigh Hunt (I do not know if you have heard of all these names) are to lay their heads together in some Town of Italy, for the purpose of conducting a Journal to be directed against everything in religion, in morals and probably in government and literature, which our Forefathers have been accustomed to reverence, – the notion seems very extravagant but perhaps the more likely to be realized on that account.

This snooty reference to the quarterly journal *The Liberal* (1822-3) lumps Shelley with other writers for whom Wordsworth had scant regard, in a context that signals disapprobation.

All the more remarkable, then, that at some point before July 1826 he underwent a change of heart, when John James Tayler recorded a recent Wordsworthian encounter: 'He told us he thought the greatest of modern geniuses, had he given his powers a proper direction, and one decidedly superior to Byron, was Shelley, a young man, author of "Queen Mab", who died lately at Rome' (Shelley had died 8 July 1822 at sea off Livorno, Tuscany). This was one of Wordsworth's most radical shifts of opinion, and in the absence of further evidence Trelawny's suggestion that only after Shelley's death did Wordsworth read his verse with the attention it merited seems the likeliest explanation.

Wordsworth wasted no opportunity of expressing his revised opinion. In 1827 he told Christopher Wordsworth Jr that 'Shelley is one of the best *artists* of us all: I mean in workmanship of style'; in 1832 Henry Crabb Robinson recorded his judgement that *The Cenci* was 'the greatest tragedy of the age' (in stark contrast to the opinion expressed at Lake Geneva) – and four years later Wordsworth commended 'To a Skylark' as 'full of imagination', even though 'it did not show the same observation of nature as his own poem on the same bird did' (a reference to his own 'To a Sky-Lark' – 'Up with me! up with me into the clouds!').

Not surprisingly, given the staunch Anglicanism of his later years, he had reservations about Shelley's professions of atheism, as revealed in conversations recorded by Gladstone in his diary for June 1836:

> He . . . thought Shelley had the greatest native powers in poetry of all the men of this age . . . Wordsworth is vehement against Byron. Saw in Shelley the lowest form of irreligion, but a later progress towards better things. Named the discrepancy between his creed and his imagination as the marring idea of his works, in which description I could not concur. Spoke of the *entire* revolution in his own poetical taste.

Wordsworth may have spoken of the 'revolution' in his poetical taste because he was uneasily aware of his changed opinion concerning Shelley. All the same, it is evident from what he said to Gladstone that he felt little sympathy with Shelley's tendency to abstraction. In 1842 he told Aubrey De Vere that 'Shelley, and almost all others who had endeavoured to out-soar the humanities, had suffered deplorably from the attempt', adding that although he 'greatly admired' 'To a Skylark', 'for the most part he considered that Shelley's works were too remote from the humanities'.

Despite such reservations, Wordsworth remained an admirer, and as late as November 1846 told William Bennett that 'Shelley was gifted with a far higher talent, and more artistic power than Lord Byron'.

This text of 'To a Skylark' is drawn from the Galignani edition of Shelley's poetry (Paris, 1829), a copy of which Wordsworth owned, and which may have come into his possession in the early 1830s.

To a Skylark

Hail to thee, blithe spirit!
  Bird thou never wert,
That from heaven, or near it,
  Pourest thy full heart
In profuse strains of unpremeditated art.   5

Higher still and higher,
  From the earth thou springest
Like a cloud of fire;
  The blue deep thou wingest,
And singing still dost soar, and soaring ever singest.   10

In the golden lightning
  Of the sunken sun,
O'er which clouds are brightening,
  Thou dost float and run;
Like an unbodied joy whose race is just begun.   15

The pale purple even
  Melts around thy flight;
Like a star of heaven,
  In the broad day-light
Thou art unseen, but yet I hear thy shrill delight,   20

Keen as are the arrows
  Of that silver sphere,
Whose intense lamp narrows
  In the white dawn clear,
Until we hardly see, we feel that it is there.   25

All the earth and air
  With thy voice is loud,
As, when night is bare,
  From one lonely cloud
The moon rains out her beams, and heaven is overflow'd.   30

What thou art we know not;
  What is most like thee?
From rainbow clouds there flow not
  Drops so bright to see,
As from thy presence showers a rain of melody.   35

Like a poet hidden
  In the light of thought,
Singing hymns unbidden,
  Till the world is wrought
To sympathy with hopes and fears it heeded not: 40

Like a high-born maiden
  In a palace tower,
Soothing her love-laden
  Soul in secret hour
With music sweet as love, which overflows her bower: 45

Like a glow-worm golden
  In a dell of dew,
Scattering unbeholden
  Its aërial hue
Among the flowers and grass, which screen it from the view: 50

Like a rose embower'd
  In its own green leaves,
By warm winds deflower'd,
  Till the scent it gives
Makes faint with too much sweet these heavy-winged thieves.   55

Sound of vernal showers
  On the twinkling grass,
Rain-awaken'd flowers,
  All that ever was
Joyous, and clear, and fresh, thy music doth surpass.   60

Teach us, sprite or bird,
    What sweet thoughts are thine:
I have never heard
    Praise of love or wine
That panted forth a flood of rapture so divine.   65

Chorus hymeneal,
    Or triumphal chaunt,
Match'd with thine would be all
    But an empty vaunt –
A thing wherein we feel there is some hidden want.   70

What objects are the fountains
    Of thy happy strain?
What fields, or waves, or mountains?
    What shapes of sky or plain?
What love of thine own kind? what ignorance of pain?   75

With thy clear keen joyance
    Langour cannot be:
Shadow of annoyance
    Never came near thee:
Thou lovest; but ne'er knew love's sad satiety.   80

Waking or asleep,
    Thou of death must deem
Things more true and deep
    Than we mortals dream,
Or how could thy notes flow in such a crystal stream?   85

We look before and after,
    And pine for what is not:
Our sincerest laughter
    With some pain is fraught;
Our sweetest songs are those that tell of saddest thought.   90

Yet if we could scorn
    Hate, and pride, and fear;
If we were things born
    Not to shed a tear,
I know not how thy joy we ever should come near.   95

Better than all measures
Of delightful sound,
Better than all treasures
That in books are found,
Thy skill to poet were, thou scorner of the ground!   100

Teach me half the gladness
That thy brain must know,
Such harmonious madness
From my lips would flow,
The world should listen then, as I am listening now.   105

Sir Egerton Brydges, *Sonnets and Other Poems* (1785):
On Echo and Silence

Date of reading: 16 May 1823

I cannot resist an impulse to record my admiration for this Sonnet. In *creative* imagination it is not surpassed by any composition, of the kind, in our Language. The *feelings* of melancholy and joyousness are most happily contrasted; and the intermediate line that describes the evanescence of Silence, is sublime. – William Wordsworth.

> (Marginal note dated 16 May 1823 in Wordsworth's copy of Brydges' *Sonnets* (1785) now at Cornell University Library)

Wordsworth's initial response to Brydges' 'On Echo and Silence' was enthusiastic, perhaps because he was reminded of his own 'To Joanna', with its extravagant conceit on the power of sound. In April 1833, in a discussion about sonnets, he told Alexander Dyce that he was pleased, 'above all, among modern writers, [by] that of Sir Egerton Brydges, upon Echo and Silence'.

Wordsworth's commendation is intriguing given that he did not always write generously of its author. In April 1816 he told R.P. Gillies that:

> I never saw Sir E—— *but once*; it was at dinner but in so large a Party that I had scarcely any conversation with him; and to the best of my recollection, he said little. He seemed a Person of very mild and pleasing manners, but with something of that feebleness in his *tout ensemble* which I cannot but think is diffused through such of his writings as I have seen.

Moreover, Wordsworth took issue with Brydges' views on poetry, as in this letter to Alaric Watts of January 1836:

> You have properly animadverted upon the foolish remark of Sir E.B. – that Sonnets – to become interesting – require the name of some distinguished Author. His own Sonnet, Echo and Silence, would be enough to prove the contrary, though the first 5 lines ought to be rewritten. How absurd for any One to affirm that it is impossible to include within the compass of 14 lines, a noble thought, or affecting sentiment, so noble and affecting as to stand unpropped by any name, in solitary beauty or grandeur.

'On Echo and Silence' is edited here from the text of 1785, of which Wordsworth thought so highly; in later years it was revised.

Sonnet V

ON ECHO AND SILENCE
October 20, 1782

In eddying course when leaves began to fly,
 And Autumn in her lap the treasure strew,
 As mid wild scenes I chanc'd the muse to woo
 Thro' glens untrod, and woods that frown'd on high;
Two sleeping nymphs, with wonder mute I spy: –   5
 And lo! she's gone. – In robe of dark-green hue
 'Twas Echo from her sister Silence flew:
 For quick the hunter's horn resounded to the sky.
In shade affrighted Silence melts away.
 Not so her sister. Hark! For onward still   10
 With far-heard step she takes her hasty way,
Bounding from rock to rock, and hill to hill:
 Ah! mark the merry maid, in mockful play,
 With thousand mimic tones the laughing forest fill!

Margaret Cavendish, Duchess of Newcastle, *Mirth and Melancholy*

Date of reading: between 10 and 19 April 1830

Alexander Dyce included Cavendish's 'Dialogue' in his *Specimens of British Poetesses* (1830), a copy of which he sent Wordsworth on 10 April. This was his first reading of her work, and he was impressed by it, as he told Dyce:

> Has the Duchess of Newcastle written much verse? . . . The Mirth and Melancholy has so many fine strokes of Imagination that I cannot but think there must be merit in many parts of her writings. How beautiful those lines, from 'I dwell in groves', towards the conclusion, 'Yet better loved the more that I am known', excepting the 4 verses after 'Walk up the hills'. And surely the latter verse of the couplet,
>
> > The tolling bell which for the dead rings out,
> > A mill where rushing waters run about,
>
> is very noticeable; no person could have hit upon that union of images without being possessed of true poetic feeling.

The text below is edited from Dyce's *Specimens*, where Wordsworth first saw it.

Mirth and Melancholy

As I was musing by myself alone,
My thoughts brought several things to work upon:
At last came two, which diversely were drest,
One Melancholy, t' other Mirth exprest;
Here Melancholy stood in black array,   5
And Mirth was all in colours fresh and gay.

Mirth
Mirth laughing came, and running to me, flung
Her fat white arms about my neck, there hung,
Embrac'd and kiss'd me oft, and stroak'd my cheek,
Saying, she would no other lover seek;   10

I'll sing you songs, and please you every day,
Invent new sports to pass the time away;
I'll keep your heart, and guard it from that thief,
Dull Melancholy, Care, or sadder Grief,
And make your eyes with Mirth to overflow;   15
With springing blood your cheeks soon fat shall grow;
Your legs shall nimble be, your body light,
And all your spirits, like to birds in flight.
Mirth shall digest your meat, and make you strong,
Shall give you health, and your short days prolong;   20
Refuse me not, but take me to your wife;
For I shall make you happy all your life.
But Melancholy, she will make you lean,
Your cheeks shall hollow grow, your jaws be seen;
Your eyes shall buried be within your head,   25
And look as pale as if you were quite dead;
She'll make you start at every noise you hear,
And visions strange shall to your eyes appear;
Thus would it be, if you to her were wed.
Nay, better far it were that you were dead.   30
Her voice is low, and gives an hollow sound,
She hates the light, and is in darkness found;
Or sits with blinking lamps, or tapers small,
Which various shadows make against the wall.
She loves nought else but noise which discord makes,   35
As croaking frogs, whose dwelling is in lakes;
The ravens hoarse, the mandrakes hollow groan,
And shrieking owls, which fly i' th' night alone;
The tolling bell, which for the dead rings out;
A mill, where rushing waters run about;   40
The roaring winds, which shake the cedars tall,
Plough up the seas, and beat the rocks withal.
She loves to walk in the still moonshine night,
And in a thick dark grove she takes delight;
In hollow caves, thatch'd houses, and low cells,   45
She loves to live, and there alone she dwells,
Then leave her to herself alone to dwell,
Let you and I in Mirth and Pleasure swell,
And drink long lusty draughts from Bacchus' bowl,
Untill our brains on vaporous waves do roll;   50
Lets joy ourselves in amorous delights;
There's none so happy as the carpet knights.

Melancholy
Then Melancholy, with sad and sober face,
Complexion pale, but of a comely grace,
With modest countenance thus softly spake; 55
May I so happy be your love to take?
True, I am dull, yet by me you shall know
More of yourself, and so much wiser grow;
I search the depth and bottom of mankind,
Open the eye of ignorance that's blind; 60
All dangers to avoid I watch with care,
And do 'gainst evils that may come prepare;
I hang not on inconstant fortune's wheel,
Nor yet with unresolving doubts do reel;
I shake not with the terrors of vain fears, 65
Nor is my mind fill'd with unuseful cares;
I do not spend my time like idle Mirth,
Which only happy is just at her birth;
And seldom lives so long as to be old,
But if she doth, can no affections hold; 70
Mirth good for nothing is, like weeds doth grow,
Or such plants as cause madness, reason's foe.
Her face with laughter crumples on a heap,
Which makes great wrinkles, and ploughs furrows deep;
Her eyes do water, and her skin turns red, 75
Her mouth doth gape, teeth bare, like one that's dead;
She fulsome is, and gluts the senses all,
Offers herself, and comes before a call;
Her house is built upon the golden sands,
Yet no foundation has, whereon it stands; 80
A palace 'tis, and of a great resort,
It makes a noise, and gives a loud report,
Yet underneath the roof disasters lie,
Beat down the house, and many kill'd thereby:
I dwell in groves that gilt are with the sun, 85
Sit on the banks by which clear waters run;
In summers hot down in a shade I lie,
My music is the buzzing of a fly;
I walk in meadows, where grows fresh green grass,
In fields, where corn is high, I often pass; 90
Walk up the hills, where round I prospects see,
Some brushy woods, and some all champains be;
Returning back, I in fresh pastures go,

To hear how sheep do bleat, and cows do low;
In winter cold, when nipping frosts come on,   95
Then I do live in a small house alone;
Altho' 'tis plain, yet cleanly 'tis within,
Like to a soul that's pure and clear from sin;
And there I dwell in quiet and still peace,
Not fill'd with cares how riches to increase;   100
I wish nor seek for vain and fruitless pleasures,
No riches are, but what the mind intreasures.
Thus am I solitary, live alone,
Yet better lov'd, the more that I am known;
And tho' my face ill-favour'd at first sight,   105
After acquaintance it will give delight.
Refuse me not, for I shall constant be,
Maintain your credit and your dignity.

Anna Laetitia Barbauld, *Life* (1825)

Suggested date of reading: by May 1830

Wordsworth and Barbauld moved in similar circles; she had known Coleridge in the mid 1790s and addressed one of her most important poems to him.[1] In 1798 Coleridge had referred to her as 'that great and excellent woman' – an opinion which Wordsworth probably (at that time) shared. She was also the recipient of a complimentary copy of *Lyrical Ballads* (1800), sent with a letter by Wordsworth, shortly after publication in early 1801. And yet, within the decade, he had declared that a stanza from her 'Ode to Content' was one of his least favourite verses, as he told Henry Crabb Robinson in March 1808:

> He asserts . . . that Mrs Barbauld has a bad heart; that her writings are absolutely insignificant, her poems are mere trash and specimens of every fault may be selected from them. He quoted, to satirise, a Stanza you and I have certainly admired –
>
> > But thou o Nymph retired and coy!
> > In what brown hamlet dost thou joy
> > To tell thy tender tale?
> > The lowliest children of the ground
> > Moss-rose and Violet, blossom round
> > And lily of the vale –
>
> here, he says, there is no genuine feeling or truth. Why is the hamlet *brown*? Because Collins in a description of exquisite beauty describing the introduction of Evening says 'And hamlets brown and dim discovered Spires'. Mrs B. therefore sets down brown hamlets without either propriety or feeling – And who are the lowliest children of the ground . . . ? Moss-rose – a Shrub!

These criticisms went public when on 27 January 1812 Coleridge repeated them in his final 'Lecture on Literature' at the Great Room of the London Philosophical Society in Fleet Street, saying that they were criticisms 'which Wordsworth made to me at Charles Lamb's two years ago'. Robinson, who was part of Coleridge's packed

---

[1] 'To Mr Coleridge'; see my *Romanticism: An Anthology* (2nd ed., Oxford 1998), pp. 26-7.

house, was outraged on Barbauld's behalf, as he declared in a letter to Mrs Clarkson at Purfleet:

> She is a living writer, a woman, and a person who however discordant from himself in character and taste has still always shewn him civilities and attentions. She had friends in the room, and the ridicule will be repeated by every one who knew the author from whom his citations were taken. It was surely ungenerous and unmanly – My only excuse for him is that he wished to fix a sting on some one and had sharpened no other. All the remarks, namely on the *brown hamlet*, the 'moss rose and violet', etc., were made by Wordsworth to me when in Town; I know not who is the author of them.

By a strange coincidence Wordsworth was in London several months later and ran into Mrs Barbauld, as he told his wife in a letter:

> Did I tell you that Mr Henry Robinson took me to Mrs Charles Aikens, Daughter of Gilbert Wakefield. She is a most natural and pleasing Character but there unluckily I met the whole Gang among the rest the old Snake Letitia Barbauld. I had an altercation with Roscoes son upon Francis Burdett, and was so disgusted with the whole Gang save the Hostess that I was made ill.

I wonder whether Robinson deliberately engineered the meeting.

Wordsworth was too disinterested a reader of poetry to dismiss everything Mrs Barbauld had written just because he disliked her – on the contrary. After her death, her niece Lucy Aikin published a collected edition of her poems which included a number of hitherto unpublished works including 'Life'. Henry Crabb Robinson sent a copy to Dorothy, who thanked him for it on 25 February 1826; Robinson takes up the story:

> It was long after I had given the book to Miss Wordsworth that Wordsworth said: 'Repeat me that stanza by Mrs Barbauld.' I did. He made me repeat it again, and so he learned it by heart. He was at the time walking in his sitting-room at Rydal with his hands behind him, when I heard him mutter these words to himself: 'I am not in the habit of grudging people their good things, but I wish I had written those lines.'

Wordsworth had memorised the last eight lines of 'Life'. This must have happened before May 1830, when he advised Alexander Dyce to include it in an anthology he was then compiling:

> Mrs Barbauld . . . was spoiled as a Poetess by being a Dissenter, and concerned with a dissenting Academy. One of the most pleasing passages in her Poetry is the close of the lines upon life, written, I believe, when she was not less than 80 years of age: 'Life, we have been long together', etc.

The text below is edited from Barbauld's *Works* (1825).

Life
Animula, vagula, blandula.[1]

Life! I know not what thou art,
But know that thou and I must part;
And when, or how, or where we met,
I own to me's a secret yet.
But this I know, when thou art fled,   5
Where'er they lay these limbs, this head,
No clod so valueless shall be,
As all that then remains of me.
O whither, whither dost thou fly,
Where bend unseen thy trackless course,   10
    And in this strange divorce,
Ah tell where I must seek this compound I?

To the vast ocean of empyreal flame,
    From whence thy essence came,
Dost thou thy flight pursue, when freed   15
From matter's base encumbering weed?
    Or dost thou, hid from sight,
    Wait, like some spell-bound knight,

---

[1] From Marcus Aurelius, *On the Soul.*

Through blank oblivious years the appointed hour,
To break thy trance and reassume thy power?   20
Yet canst thou without thought or feeling be?
O say what art thou, when no more thou'rt thee?

Life! we've been long together,
Through pleasant and through cloudy weather;
   'Tis hard to part when friends are dear;   25
   Perhaps 't will cost a sigh, a tear;
   Then steal away, give little warning,
      Choose thine own time;
Say not Good night, but in some brighter clime
      Bid me Good morning.   30

Ebenezer Elliott, *The Ranter* (1833) (extract)

Date of reading: December 1833

> Wordsworth speaks highly of the author of *Corn Law Rhymes*.
> He says: 'None of us have done better than he has in his best,
> though there is a deal of stuff arising from his hatred of subsist-
> ing things. Like Byron, Shelley, etc., he looks on all things with
> an evil eye.' This arises naturally enough in the mind of a very
> poor man who thinks the world has not treated him well. But
> Wordsworth says that though a very poor man he has had the
> means of sending his son to college, who did not succeed there.
> Hence perhaps his hatred of universities. The great merit of
> Elliott, says Wordsworth, is his industry: he has laboured
> intensely and, like the Glastonbury thorn, has flowered in winter;
> his later writings are the best. I asked for the name of some
> poem. Wordsworth says *The Ranter* contains some fine passages.
> 'Elliott has a fine eye for nature; he is a very extraordinary man.'
> (Henry Crabb Robinson, diary entry for 29 January 1836)

Wordsworth first saw Elliott's *The Splendid Village: Corn Law
Rhymes* (1833) in December 1833 when visited by William Pearson
(a farmer friend from Crosthwaite). Inviting Pearson to Rydal early
that month, he said: 'We have also a stall for your mule, or pony;
and be so good, if you can spare the Corn-law Poet's book, as to
bring it along with you'. Pearson apparently left his copy at Rydal
Mount; it was still on Wordsworth's shelves at the time of his death.
Wordsworth had probably heard of *Corn Law Rhymes* from
Southey, who had encouraged Elliott. '[I] happen to know what
extraordinary pains he has been taking for more than twenty years
in studying poetry as an art', Southey confided to his friend C.W.
Williams Wynn.

Shortly after reading *Corn Law Rhymes* Wordsworth urged
Southey to edit a collected edition of Elliott's poetry – a task
Southey would not live to undertake. And when Southey wrote an
appreciative critical essay about Elliott for the *Quarterly Review* it
was cut at the last moment, having to wait until 1850 when Elliott
published it himself.

Given the conservatism of the ageing Lake Poets it says much for
their disinterested support of younger writers that they promoted
Elliott as they did. In a letter to Walter Savage Landor, Henry

Crabb Robinson, an astute Wordsworth-watcher, remarked on that very fact:

> I do not think there is any unworthy vanity or envy in W. towards his contemporaries. His moral and religious feelings added to a spice of John Bullism have utterly blinded him for instance to the marvellous talent of Voltaire . . . But I have heard him praise Elliott quite as warmly as you do. It is at *his* urgent recommendation that S[outhey] is now coming out with a complete edition of his poems . . .

Elliott was a curious figure for Southey and Wordsworth to have championed. Descended from border raiders, 'thieves, neither Scotch nor English, who lived on the cattle they stole from both', his father (known as 'Devil Elliott') worked in the iron trade, and was an extreme radical and hardline Calvinist. One of a family of eleven, Elliott was baptised by Tommy Wright, a tinker of the same Calvinist persuasion as his father. He attended dame school and Hollis school, but by sixteen was employed in the family firm; its subsequent failure was blamed by Elliott on the Corn Law.

Throughout his life his politics were stridently radical. Applied by the government as a means of protecting the interests of farmers who feared the import of cheap grain, the Corn Law tightly restricted availability even in times of want, putting bread beyond reach of the poor, and contributing to the famines that devastated the countryside during the first half of the nineteenth century. It was repealed only after widespread agitation in 1846. Elliott was an enthusiastic agitator in the Chartist movement and was present as the Sheffield delegate at the great public meeting in Palace Yard, Westminster in 1838. 'Whoever does not oppose the Corn Law', Elliott stated in the 'Notes' to *Corn Law Rhymes*, 'is a patron of want, national immorality, bankruptcy, child-murder, incendiary fires, midnight assassination, and anarchy'. Among those patrons was one W. Wordsworth, Esq., who as early as 1815 expressed support for the Corn Law, while conceding that the price of corn was too high. And among the poems in *Corn Law Rhymes* were some to which Tories like Southey and Wordsworth must have taken exception, for instance the brief lyric, 'What is Bad Government?'

> What is bad government, thou slave,
>   Whom robbers represent?
> What is bad government, thou knave,
>   Who lov'st bad government?

It is the deadly *Will*, that takes
What labour ought to keep;
It is the deadly *Power*, that makes
Bread dear, and labour cheap.

'Elliott has a fine eye for nature': Wordsworth might have been thinking either of Elliott's eye for human nature, or his observation of the natural world – both distinguishing features of his work. I have selected for inclusion the first quarter of 'The Ranter', which demonstrates Elliott's eye for both kinds of nature, edited from the text of 1833.

The Ranter (extract)

I

Miles Gordon sleeps; his six days' labour done,
He dreams of Sunday, verdant fields, and prayer:
Oh, rise, blest morn, unclouded! Let thy sun
Shine on the artisan, – thy purest air
Breathe on the bread-tax'd labourer's deep despair!　　　　5
Poor sons of toil! I grudge them not the breeze
That plays with Sabbath flowers, the clouds that play
With Sabbath winds, the hum of Sabbath bees,
The Sabbath walk, the skylark's Sabbath lay,
The silent sunshine of the Sabbath day.　　　　10

II

The stars wax pale, the moon is cold and dim;
Miles Gordon wakes, and grey dawn tints the skies;
The many-childed widow, who to him
Is as a mother, hears her lodger rise,
And listens to his prayer with swimming eyes.　　　　15
For her, and for her orphans poor he prays,
For all who earn the bread they daily eat: –
'Bless them, O God, with useful, happy days,
With hearts that scorn all meanness and deceit;

And round their lowly hearths let freemen meet!' – 20
This morn, betimes, she hastes to leave her bed,
For he must preach beneath th' autumnal tree:
She lights her fire, and soon the board is spread
With Sabbath coffee, toast, and cups for three.
Pale he descends; again she starts to see 25
His hollow cheek, and feels they soon must part;
But they shall meet again – that hope is sure;
And, Oh! she venerates his mind and heart,
For he is pure, if mortal e'er was pure!
His words, his silence, teach her to endure; 30
And then, he helps to feed her orphan'd five.
O God! thy judgments cruel seem to be!
While bad men biggen long, and cursing thrive,
The good, like wintry sun-beams, fade and flee –
That we may follow *them*, and come to Thee. 35

III

In haste she turns, and climbs the narrow stair,
To wake her eldest born, but pausing stands,
Bent o'er his bed; for on his forehead bare,
Like jewels ring'd on sleeping beauty's hands,
Tired labour's gems are set in beaded bands; 40
And none, none, none, like bread-tax'd labour know'th
How more than grateful are his slumbers brief.
Thou dost not know, thou pamper'd son of sloth! –
Thou canst not tell, thou bread-tax-eating thief! –
How sweet is rest to bread-tax'd toil and grief! 45
Like sculpture, or like death, serene he lies.
But no – that tear is not a marble tear;
He names, in sleep, his father's injuries;
And now, in silence, wears a smile severe.
How like his sire he looks, when drawing near 50
His journey's close, and that fair form bent o'er
His dark'ning cheek, still faintly tinged with red,
And fondly gazed – too soon to gaze no more! –
While her long tresses, o'er the seeming dead,
Stream'd, in their black profusion, from the head 55
Of matron loveliness – more touchingly,
More sadly beautiful, and pale, and still –
A shape of half-divine humanity,

1833

Worthy of Chantrey's steel,[1] or Milton's quill,
Or heaven-taught Raphael's soul-expressing skill.   60
And must she wake that poor, o'er-labour'd youth?
O yes, or Edmund will his mother chide;
For he this morn, would hear the words of truth
From lips inspired, on Shirecliffe's lofty side,[2]
Gazing o'er tree and tower on Hallam wide. –   65
Up, sluggards, up! the mountains one by one,
Ascend in light; and slow the mists retire
From vale and plain. The cloud on Stannington
Beholds a rocket – No, 'tis Morthen spire!
The sun is risen! cries Stanedge, tipp'd with fire;   70
On Norwood's flowers the dew-drops shine and shake;
Up, sluggards, up! and drink the morning breeze.
The birds on cloud-left Osgathorpe awake;
And Wincobank[3] is waving all his trees
O'er subject towns, and farms, and villages,   75
And gleaming streams, and woods, and waterfalls.
Up, climb the oak-crown'd summit! Hoober Stand,
And Keppel's Pillar, gaze on Wentworth's halls,[4]
And misty lakes, that brighten and expand,
And distant hills, that watch the western strand.   80
Up! trace God's foot-prints, where they paint the mould
With heav'nly green, and hues that blush and glow
Like angel's wings; while skies of blue and gold
Stoop to Miles Gordon on the mountain's brow.
Behold the Great Unpaid! the prophet, lo!   85
Sublime he stands beneath the Gospel tree,
And Edmund stands on Shirecliffe at his side;
Behind him, sinks, and swells, and spreads a sea
Of hills, and vales, and groves; before him glide
Don, Rivelin, Loxley,[5] wandering in their pride   90

---

[1] **Chantrey's steel** Sir Francis Leggatt Chantrey (1781-1841) was one of the best-known sculptors of the day, famous for his bust of Wordsworth.
[2] **Shirecliffe's lofty side** Elliott has in mind the area to the north-east of Sheffield.
[3] **Wincobank** in Elliott's day a village, now a suburb of Sheffield.
[4] **Hoober Stand** and **Keppel's Pillar** are towers overlooking Wentworth village. Wentworth Woodhouse has the longest frontage of any country house in England and was owned in Elliott's day by Viscount Milton.
[5] **Don, Rivelin, Loxley** rivers flowing through Sheffield.

From heights that mix their azure with the cloud;
Beneath him, spire and dome are glittering;
And round him press his flock, a woe-worn crowd.
To other words, while forest echoes ring,
'Ye banks and braes o' bonny Doon,' they sing;   95
And far below, the drover, with a start
Awaking, listens to the well-known strain,
Which brings Shihallian's shadow to his heart,
And Scotia's loneliest vales; then sleeps again,
And dreams, on Loxley's banks, of Dunsinane.   100
The hymn they sing is to their preacher dear;
It breathes of hopes and glories grand and vast,
While on his face they look, with grief and fear;
Full well they know his sands are ebbing fast;
But, hark! he speaks, and feels he speaks his last! –   105

Emmeline Fisher, *On a sound somewhat resembling thunder*, Secrecy

Date of reading: by November 1837

Emmeline Fisher, born 1825, was Wordsworth's cousin – granddaughter of his Uncle William Cookson and daughter of Canon William Fisher of Salisbury. Her mother, Elizabeth Fisher, sent Emmeline's poems to Wordsworth in 1837, and in November received a reply in which he praised her 'astonishing productions':

> It is impossible to foretell what may come in future time out of these promises but I have met in the language of no age or country, with things so extraordinary from so young a Person . . . It would avail little to enter into particulars, for throughout the Poems, are scattered indications of all that can be desired – an observant eye, feeling, thought, fancy, and above all imagination, as evidenced especially in the Poem of Secrecy, and even still more in the Verses on the strange noise heard in a serene sky – in part of these last there is the very spirit of Milton himself . . . Of the not unfrequent, and inevitable faults in language I forebear to speak – and wish others to do the same – let her yield to the impulse of her feelings unembarrassed about minutiae of style, or even correctness or incorrectness in the use of words.

Wordsworth was enthusiastic and sincere; but at the same time he feared for his cousin, as he explained in his next letter to her mother in December: 'her mind ought to grow up quietly and silently; and her extraordinary powers should be left to develope themselves *naturally*, with as little observation as possible'. Not surprisingly he disapproved when in 1840 Henry Nelson Coleridge wrote an article, 'Modern English Poetesses', for the *Quarterly Review*, which discussed her work alongside that of Caroline Norton, Elizabeth Barrett, Caroline Southey and Sara Coleridge. Although she published a volume of *Poems* (1856) she failed to live up to her early promise.

I have selected the two poems singled out by Wordsworth in his initial response to Elizabeth Fisher of November 1837. They are edited from the transcriptions sent to him, now retained at the Wordsworth Library, Grasmere. After 'Secrecy', Elizabeth Fisher has written:

This poem is rugged in metre, and far from faultless, but it strikes me as bold and original. – In making my selection I have been sadly puzzled – I wished chiefly to give specimens of her powers of Imagination but at the same time was anxious that her own simple and affectionate character and pious feeling should appear, that her kind relations might become acquainted with her *heart* as well as her talents.

On a sound somewhat resembling thunder which was heard on a perfectly cloudless day in the summer of 1835. It appeared to traverse the whole heavens and was indescribably awful. Composed at 10 years of age.

Whence art thou, thou mysterious sound,
With thy low deep murmur gathering round,
Slow rolling o'er the bright summer skies,
As their vault in its tranquil beauty lies?
Thou fliest not on the breeze's wing,   5
No breath doth the rose's perfume bring;
Thou comest not on the thunder-cloud,
The heavens no gloomy vapours shroud;
Thou dost not spring from the tempest's ire,
No deadly flames of forked fire,   10
Herald thee through the firmament –
Whence dost thou come? and wherefore sent?
Would I were skill'd in mystic lore,
Would I through star-lit paths might soar!
O! were I not chained to this parent earth   15
Sound! I know thy wondrous birth!
Say, in some bright revolving star,
Are countless myriads waging war?
Art thou the rush of their armies flying,
Art thou the groan of their millions dying?   20
Or, still more dread, is thy sound O say!
That of world like ours, which pass away?
In thee is heard their heaven's vast roll,
Shrivelling away like a parched scroll?

And even now, whilst I hear thy roaring,   25
Are myriads on myriads of spirits soaring –
Soaring to God! – or doom'd – ah me!
Unknown, and unguess'd may thy secrets be!

Secrecy

Secrecy in the Ocean lies,
And where Earth's woods and mountains rise
O'er her rivers' fruitful maze;
Hides in the clouds which rush along,
Soars mid the stars' mysterious throng,   5
And gains the Sun's rich blaze.

Still doth Secrecy upwards fly,
Past the sea, the earth, the sky –
She spreads her dark veil higher,
Mid regions vast of endless light,   10
Where the least ray is far more bright
Than the Sun's continual fire.

In the billows are there many things,
O'er which she spreads her darksome wings;
And guards with jealous care   15
The contents of the Ocean's womb
At once a treasure house and tomb,
The fearful, and the fair!

On earth, she lies in the burning Mount,
Or sleeps by many a secret fount,   20
In Isles which no man knows,
Wanders o'er central Afric's sands,
Or through ice-fettered Northern lands
Tracks the unbounded snows.

In air, in thunder-cloud she hides,   25
On the blaze of lightening rides,
Comes on the rushing wind.

Still she mounts on her strange career,
The blessed realms of light are near –
She leaves the sun behind.   30

Yet a Power there is whom she doth own,
To whom she bows, and bows alone,
Whom every thing obeys –
He, her mantle could pluck away,
Her secrets give to the eye of day,   35
And to the open gaze.

A day shall come O secrecy!
When the shrinking sea shall backward fly,
His awful secrets told,
Earth's mysteries shall then be known,   40
The laws of upper air be shown,
And Heaven its light unfold!

July 29. 1837.

Alfred Lord Tennyson, *Dora* (1842)

Date of reading: 1842

Alfred Tennyson came in and smoked his pipe. He told us with pleasure of his dinner with Wordsworth – was pleased as well as amused by Wordsworth saying to him, 'Come, brother bard, to dinner,' and taking his arm; said that he was ashamed of paying Mr Wordsworth compliments, but said that he had at last, in the dark, said something about the pleasure he had had from Mr Wordsworth's writings, and that the old poet had taken his hand, and replied with some expressions equally kind and complimentary. Tennyson was evidently much pleased with the old man, and glad of having learned to know him.

(Aubrey De Vere, diary entry for 9 May 1845)

'I have been endeavouring all my life to write a pastoral like your "Dora" and have not succeeded', Wordsworth complained to Tennyson – perhaps on the occasion in May 1845 described by De Vere. Although they had moved in similar circles for years, the two men did not develop a rapport until the spring and summer of 1845, when Wordsworth was in his seventy-fifth year and Tennyson in his thirty-sixth. Wordsworth later told his friend and publisher, Henry Reed:

I saw Tennyson when I was in London, several times. He is decidedly the first of our living Poets, and I hope will live to give the world still better things. You will be pleased to hear that he expressed in the strongest terms his gratitude to my writings. To this I was far from indifferent though persuaded that he is not much in sympathy with what I should myself most value in my attempts, viz the spirituality with which I have endeavored to invest the material Universe, and the moral relation under which I have wished to exhibit its most ordinary appearances.

Perhaps it is not surprising that the poem of Tennyson's that Wordsworth most admired was generically akin to some of his own; indeed, similarities between 'Dora' and 'Michael' were discussed by Arnold in his essay 'On Translating Homer' (1862). 'Dora' was highly regarded on its first publication; John Sterling quoted it entire in his essay on Tennyson's *Poems* (1842) in the *Quarterly*

Review. Wordsworth owned a copy of the 1842 volume, from which the present text is drawn.

~&

Dora

With farmer Allan at the farm abode
William and Dora. William was his son,
And she his niece. He often look'd at them,
And often thought 'I'll make them man and wife.'
Now Dora felt her uncle's will in all,   5
And yearn'd towards William; but the youth, because
He had been always with her in the house,
Thought not of Dora.
                Then there came a day
When Allan call'd his son, and said, 'My son,
I married late; but I would wish to see   10
My grandchild on my knees before I die:
And I have set my heart upon a match.
Now therefore look to Dora; she is well
To look to; thrifty too beyond her age.
She is my brother's daughter: he and I   15
Had once hard words, and parted, and he died
In foreign lands; but for his sake I bred
His daughter Dora: take her for your wife;
For I have wish'd this marriage, night and day,
For many years.' But William answer'd short,   20
'I cannot marry Dora; by my life,
I will not marry Dora.' Then the old man
Was wroth, and doubled up his hands, and said,
'You will not, boy! you dare to answer thus!
But in my time a father's word was law,   25
And so it shall be now for me. Look to't.
Consider: take a month to think, and give
An answer to my wish; or by the Lord
That made me, you shall pack, and nevermore
Darken my doors again.' And William heard,   30
And answer'd something madly; bit his lips,

And broke away. The more he look'd at her
The less he liked her; and his ways were harsh;
But Dora bore them meekly. Then before
The month was out he left his father's house,   35
And hired himself to work within the fields;
And half in love, half spite, he woo'd and wed
A labourer's daughter, Mary Morrison.
     Then, when the bells were ringing, Allan call'd
His niece and said, 'My girl, I love you well;   40
But if you speak with him that was my son,
Or change a word with her he calls his wife,
My home is none of yours. My will is law.'
And Dora promised, being meek. She thought,
'It cannot be: my uncle's mind will change!'   45
     And days went on, and there was born a boy
To William; then distresses came on him;
And day by day he pass'd his father's gate,
Heart-broken, and his father help'd him not.
But Dora stored what little she could save,   50
And sent it them by stealth, nor did they know
Who sent it; till at last a fever seized
On William, and in harvest time he died.
     Then Dora went to Mary. Mary sat
And look'd with tears upon her boy, and thought   55
Hard things of Dora. Dora came and said,
     'I have obey'd my uncle until now,
And I have sinn'd, for it was all thro' me
This evil came on William at the first.
But, Mary, for the sake of him that's gone,   60
And for your sake, the woman that he chose,
And for this orphan, I am come to you:
You know there has not been for these five years
So full a harvest: let me take the boy,
And I will set him in my uncle's eye   65
Among the wheat; that when his heart is glad
Of the full harvest, he may see the boy,
And bless him for the sake of him that's gone.'
     And Dora took the child and went her way
Across the wheat, and sat upon a mound   70
That was unsown, where many poppies grew.
Far off the farmer came into the field
And spied her not; for none of all his men

Dare tell him Dora waited with the child;
And Dora would have risen and gone to him,   75
But her heart fail'd her; and the reapers reap'd,
And the sun fell, and all the land was dark.
    But when the morrow came, she rose and took
The child once more, and sat upon the mound;
And made a little wreath of all the flowers   80
That grew about, and tied it round his hat
To make him pleasing in her uncle's eye.
Then when the farmer pass'd into the field
He spied her, and he left his men at work
And came and said, 'Where were you yesterday?   85
Whose child is that? What are you doing here?'
So Dora cast her eyes upon the ground
And answer'd softly, 'This is William's child!'
'And did I not,' said Allan, 'did I not
Forbid you, Dora?' Dora said again,   90
'Do with me as you will, but take the child
And bless him for the sake of him that's gone!'
And Allan said, 'I see it is a trick
Got up betwixt you and the woman there.
I must be taught my duty, and by you!   95
You knew my word was law, and yet you dared
To slight it. Well – for I will take the boy;
But you go hence, and never see me more.'
    So saying, he took the boy, that cried aloud
And struggled hard. The wreath of flowers fell   100
At Dora's feet. She bow'd upon her hands,
And the boy's cry came to her from the field,
More and more distant. She bow'd down her head,
Remembering the day when first she came,
And all the things that had been. She bow'd down   105
And wept in secret; and the reapers reap'd,
And the sun fell, and all the land was dark.
    Then Dora went to Mary's house, and stood
Upon the threshold. Mary saw the boy
Was not with Dora. She broke out in praise   110
To God, that help'd her in her widowhood.
And Dora said, 'My uncle took the boy;
But, Mary, let me live and work with you:
He says that he will never see me more.'
Then answer'd Mary, 'This shall never be,   115

That thou shouldst take my trouble on thyself:
And, now I think, he shall not have the boy,
For he will teach him hardness, and to slight
His mother; therefore thou and I will go,
And I will have my boy, and bring him home; 120
And I will beg of him to take thee back;
But if he will not take thee back again,
Then thou and I will live within one house,
And work for William's child, until he grows
Of age to help us.' 125
               So the women kiss'd
Each other, and set out, and reach'd the farm.
The door was off the latch; they peep'd, and saw
The boy set up betwixt his grandsire's knees,
Who thrust him in the hollows of his arm,
And clapp'd him on the hands and on the cheeks, 130
Like one that loved him; and the lad stretch'd out
And babbled for the golden seal, that hung
From Allan's watch, and sparkled by the fire.
Then they came in: but when the boy beheld
His mother, he cried out to come to her, 135
And Allan set him down; and Mary said:
  'O Father! – if you let me call you so –
I never came a-begging for myself,
Or William, or this child; but now I come
For Dora: take her back; she loves you well. 140
O Sir, when William died, he died at peace
With all men; for I ask'd him, and he said,
He could not ever rue his marrying me;
I had been a patient wife: but, Sir, he said
That he was wrong to cross his father thus. 145
"God bless him!" he said, "and may he never know
The troubles I have gone thro'!" Then he turn'd
His face and pass'd – unhappy that I am!
But now, Sir, let me have my boy, for you
Will make him hard, and he will learn to slight 150
His father's memory; and take Dora back,
And let all this be as it was before.'
  So Mary said, and Dora hid her face
By Mary. There was silence in the room;
And all at once the old man burst in sobs: – 155
  'I have been to blame – to blame. I have kill'd my son.

I have kill'd him – but I loved him – my dear son.
May God forgive me! – I have been to blame.
Kiss me, my children.'
                      Then they clung about
The old man's neck, and kiss'd him many times.   160
And all the man was broken with remorse;
And all his love came back a hundredfold;
And for three hours he sobb'd o'er William's child,
Thinking of William.
                      So those four abode
Within one house together; and as years   165
Went forward, Mary took another mate;
But Dora lived unmarried till her death.

                                                  1842

Select Bibliography

The Cornell Wordsworth. General Ed. Stephen M. Parrish. Ithaca, NY: Cornell University Press, 1977-
    Early Poems and Fragments, 1785-1797. Ed. Carol Landon and Jared Curtis. 1997
    The Borderers. Ed. Robert Osborn. 1982
    Descriptive Sketches. Ed. Eric Birdsall. 1984
    An Evening Walk. Ed. James Averill. 1984
    The Fourteen-Book Prelude. Ed. W.J.B. Owen. 1985
    Home at Grasmere. Ed. Beth Darlington. 1977
    Lyrical Ballads, and Other Poems, 1797-1800. Ed. James Butler and Karen Green. 1992
    Peter Bell. Ed. John Jordan. 1985
    Poems in Two Volumes, and Other Poems, 1800-1807. Ed. Jared Curtis. 1985
    Translations of Chaucer and Virgil. Ed. Bruce Graver. 1998
    The Prelude, 1798-1799. Ed. Stephen Parrish. 1977
    The Ruined Cottage and The Pedlar. Ed. James Butler. 1979
    Shorter Poems, 1807-1820. Ed. Carl H. Ketcham. 1989
    The Thirteen-Book Prelude. Ed. Mark L. Reed. 2 vols. 1991
    The White Doe of Rylstone. Ed. Kristine Dugas. 1988
    Last Poems, 1821-1850. Ed. Jared Curtis. 1999

Dorothy Wordsworth: The Grasmere and Alfoxden Journals. Ed. Pamela Woof. Oxford: Oxford University Press, 2002
The Letters of John Wordsworth. Ed. Carl H. Ketcham. Ithaca, NY: Cornell University Press, 1969
The Letters of William and Dorothy Wordsworth: The Early Years 1787-1805. Ed. Ernest De Selincourt. Revised by Chester L. Shaver. Oxford: Clarendon Press, 1967
The Letters of William and Dorothy Wordsworth: The Middle Years 1806-1820. Ed. Ernest De Selincourt. Revised by Mary Moorman and Alan G. Hill. 2 vols. Oxford: Clarendon Press, 1969-70
The Letters of William and Dorothy Wordsworth: The Later Years 1821-1853. Ed. Ernest De Selincourt. Revised by Alan G. Hill. 4 vols. Oxford: Clarendon Press, 1978-88
The Letters of William and Dorothy Wordsworth: A Supplement of New Letters. Ed. Alan G. Hill. Oxford: Clarendon Press, 1993
The Love Letters of William and Mary Wordsworth. Ed. Beth Darlington. Ithaca, NY: Cornell University Press, 1981

Poems and Extracts Chosen by William Wordsworth for an Album Presented to Lady Mary Lowther, Christmas, 1819. London: Henry Frowde, 1915

The Prose Works of William Wordsworth. Ed. Revd. Alexander B. Grosart. 3 vols. London: Edward Moxon, Son, and Co., 1876

The Prose Works of William Wordsworth. Ed. W.J.B. Owen and Jane Worthington Smyser. 3 vols. Oxford: Clarendon Press, 1974

The Fenwick Notes of William Wordsworth. Ed. Jared Curtis. London: Bristol Classical Press, 1993

William Wordsworth: The Major Works. Ed. Stephen Gill. Oxford: Oxford University Press, 2000

Wordsworth and Coleridge: Lyrical Ballads 1798. Ed. W.J.B. Owen. 2nd edn. Oxford: Oxford University Press, 1969

Stephen Gill. *William Wordsworth: A Life.* Oxford: Oxford University Press, 1990

Duncan Wu. *Wordsworth's Reading 1770-1815.* 2 vols. Cambridge: Cambridge University Press, 1993-6

Subject Index

WW), 12, 16, 18, 20, 25, 55, 177, 185, 199, 206, 214, 220, 235, 275; reads with WW, 13, 114-15, 190, 192, 199; sets up house in Grasmere with WW, 43; compares WW with Beattie's Edwin, 55; WW obtains copy of Burns for her, 78; Grasmere Journal, 114-15, 190, 192; sets up house at Racedown Lodge, Dorset with WW, 155; copies poems and prose into WW's notebooks, 177

Wordsworth, John (WW's father), 25

Wordsworth, John (WW's brother), 18, 133, 166; death of, 19, 133, 236

Wordsworth Library, 41, 130, 141, 166, 171, 183n1, 284

Wordsworth, Mary (WW's wife), née Hutchinson, 212, 226

Wordsworth, Richard (WW's brother), 18, 141

Wordsworth, Richard of Branthwaite (WW's cousin), 16

Wordsworth, William: aesthetic values, 9-11; 'bear in a tulip garden', 16; bibliographical interests, 12, 17-18, 121; books: attitude to them, 11-22; keeps them in his barn, 16; keeps them in a bookcase at Rydal Mount, 16; butter knife used to cut pages of, 17; book 'monster', 17; sent by friends and acquaintances, 18, 139, 155, 192, 226, 235, 275; subscribes to, 41, see also Rydal Mount; book clubs; character in poetry, 78-9; Coleridge introduces him to authors, 160, 165, 168, 171; dialect, familiarity with, 78; diction, poetic, 9-11, 13-14; feeling, importance of for poetry, 9-11, 41, 52, 61, 79, 96, 179, 186, 255, 268, 270, 284;

hieratic tendencies of, 15; imagination, 9-11, 52, 98, 220-1, 263, 268, 270, 284; journalistic career considered by, 20; language, 43, 55, 171, 182n1; mind, subject of his poetry, 11; nature, copies from, 10; love of, 9, 41, 52, 56, 101, 109; poet, what is a, 15; politics of the poem, 10; primitivism, 185, psychological reality in poetry 9-11, 25-6, 96, 107; reading, 11-22; 'sagacity' of, 12; schoolboy poetry, 52, 96; Southey's library, WW uses, 179; style, 98, 171; taste by which he is to be relished, 10; versification, 55-6, 258; see also under Beattie, James; words, 13-14, 78; *Works*: *Adventures on Salisbury Plain*, 144; Advertisement to *Lyrical Ballads*, 48; Commonplace Book, 16, 179, 181, 186, 189, 204, 211, 212, 232; 'Complaint of a Forsaken Indian Woman', 165; *The Convention of Cintra*, 224; *Description of the Scenery of the Lakes*, 43; *Descriptive Sketches*, 142; *Essay on Morals*, 14; 'Essay, Supplementary to the Preface' (1815), 16, 61, 73, 74; *Essays upon Epitaphs*, 13, 239; *The Excursion*, 10, 55, 171, 173n1, 241; 'Expostulation and Reply', 48; *Fragment of a Gothic Tale*, 144; 'Great men have been among us', 148; 'Home at Grasmere', 43-4, 192-3; 'Iona, Upon Landing', 136; 'Immortality Ode', 168, 192; 'Juvenal Imitated', 148; *Letter to a Friend of Robert Burns*, 79-80; 'Lines Written near Richmond upon the Thames', 74; *Lyrical Ballads*, 185, 274; 'Michael', 288; Note to 'The Thorn', 9;

Index of titles and first lines